A PRIMER OF GREEK GRAMMAR

ACCIDENCE

AND

SYNTAX

A PRIMER OF GREEK GRAMMAR

ACCIDENCE

BY

EVELYN ABBOTT, M.A., LL.D.
LATE FELLOW AND TUTOR OF BALLIOL COLLEGE, OXFORD

AND

E. D. MANSFIELD, M.A.
LATE ASSISTANT MASTER AT CLIFTON COLLEGE

SYNTAX

BY

E. D. MANSFIELD, M.A.

With a Preface by

THE RIGHT REV. JOHN PERCIVAL, D.D
LATE HEAD MASTER OF CLIFTON COLLEGE AND RUGBY SCHOOL

Focus Classical Reprints
Focus Publishing
R. Pullins Company
Newburyport MA

This book is published by:
Focus Publishing/R. Pullins Co., Inc.
PO Box 369
Newburyport, MA 01950

PREFACE.

WHEN the Primer of Greek Accidence was published there was no intention of extending the work so as to include a Syntax. It was, however, soon found that Schools which had adopted the Accidence were anxious to have a Syntax in connection with it, and that other Schools were only deterred from adopting it by the absence of such a Syntax.

Accordingly, MR. MANSFIELD has drawn up the brief outline which now forms the second part of the whole Primer.

Special care has been taken to secure clearness and definiteness in the statement of rules, and the arrangement adopted will be found to harmonise with that to which most boys must have been previously accustomed in learning their Latin Syntax.

Thus it is hoped that the book may be of service in effecting a considerable economy of time on the part of learners, and that it may furnish an additional help towards acquiring at the outset a firm hold on the principles that regulate the usage of the language.

As in the case of the Accidence when first issued, so now I am able to say of the Syntax, that it has been used whilst in proof at Clifton College, and has undergone such modifications and improvements as this preliminary use suggested, besides being subjected to the criticism of experienced masters in other Schools.

J. PERCIVAL.

CONTENTS.

ACCIDENCE.

SYNTAX.

PART I.

SYNTAX.

PART II.

EDITORS' NOTE.

THE Editors wish to point out that the Laws of Sound (pp. 15-20) are placed at the beginning of the book merely for convenience of reference, and are not intended to be mastered at the outset. The more necessary laws are given as occasion arises in a form better adapted for beginners; thus, the notes on Nouns (pp. 45, 46), and the rules for Verbs (p. 80), will suffice to explain what is actually required to understand the formation in each case. There is nothing in the arrangement of the book to prevent a teacher from beginning with the Verb, if this order is thought desirable.

Introduction.

1. GREEK is the language spoken by the ancient Hellenes in Greece proper, and the various Greek colonies in Asia Minor, Magna Graecia, Africa, and elsewhere. There are three principal dialects of Greek :—

(1.) AEOLIC, divided into Asian or Lesbian Aeolic (*Sappho*, 611 B.C., *Alcaeus*, 606 B.C.) and Boeotian Aeolic (*Pindar*, in parts, 490 B.C.)

(2.) DORIC, spoken in parts of Peloponnesus, *e.g.* Lacedaemon, Corinth, and their colonies, as Syracuse (*Epicharmus* of Sicily, 477 B.C., *Pindar*, in parts, 490 B.C., *Theocritus*, 280 B.C.)

(3.) IONIC, divided into (*a.*) Old Ionic, the language of the *Homeric* poems (of uncertain date and place); (*b.*) New Ionic (*Herodotus*, 443 B.C., *Hippocrates*, 430 B.C.)

An offshoot of the Ionic was the ATTIC—the ordinary dialect of Athenian writers (*Aeschylus*, 484 B.C., *Thucydides*, 423 B.C., *Plato*, 399 B.C., etc.) This was the dialect of literary Greece after 400 B.C., and in consequence of Alexander's conquests (336-323 B.C.) became, in a debased form, the Greek of the East (Alexandria, etc.), and of the New Testament (ἡ κοινή, *i.e.* διάλεκτος).

Some peculiarities of dialects.—*Aeolic* is distinguished by the want of the 'rough breathing,' the frequent use of υ, the doubling of letters (*e.g.* φθέρρω, *I destroy*, for φθείρω), the peculiar accent, and want of a dual. *Doric* is marked by the prevalence of the broad a, *e.g.* τᾷ for τῇ, etc. *Old Ionic* possesses many archaic forms, and is rather a literary than a local dialect. *New Ionic* is marked by the absence of contraction, by the use of κ for π (κότερος, etc.), by the want of aspiration (ἀπίκοντο), the use of η for ᾱ (σοφίη), and some peculiar forms. The κοινή has lost the dual, and has incorporated a large number of Latin forms.

The Letters

2.   THE letters in common use among the Greeks were twenty-four in number, as follows :—

A	*a*	Alpha	= *a.*
B	*β*	Beta	= *b.*
Γ	*γ*	Gamma	= *g*, always hard, as in ‘garden.
Δ	*δ*	Delta	= *d.*
E	*ε*	Epsĭlon	= *ĕ.*
Z	*ζ*	Zeta	= *z* (= dz).
H	*η*	Eta	= *ē.*
Θ	*θ*	Theta	= *th.*
I	*ι*	Iota	= *i.*
K	*κ*	Kappa	= *k.*
Λ	*λ*	Lambda	= *l.*
M	*μ*	Mu	= *m.*
N	*ν*	Nu	= *n.*
Ξ	*ξ*	Xi	= *x* (= ks).
O	*o*	Omicron	= *ŏ* (little o).
Π	*π*	Pi	= *p.*
P	*ρ*	Rho	= *rh, r.*
Σ	*σ ς*	Sigma	= *s*, ς only at the end of a word.
T	*τ*	Tau	= *t.*
Υ	*υ*	Upsilon	= *ü.*
Φ	*φ*	Phi	= *ph.*
X	*χ*	Chi	= *kh.*
Ψ	*ψ*	Psi	= *ps.*
Ω	*ω*	Omega	= *ō* (great o).

Γ γ is also used for *ν* before κ, γ, χ, ξ, *e.g.* ἄγγελος, *angelos, a messenger.*

In England, *θ, φ, χ* are usually pronounced as in *thin, Philip, chasm.* υ was a thin *u* as in French.

3. *Vowels.*—The vowels are divided into
 (1.) Hard, *a, ε η, o ω.*
 (2.) Soft, *ι, υ.*

In *ε η,* and *o ω,* the long and short vowels are distinguished by separate letters; in *a, ι, υ* the letters are the same for long and short.

Diphthongs.—When a hard vowel *precedes* a soft vowel the two can combine into a diphthong, as *αι αυ, ει ευ, οι ου.* When the hard vowel is *long,* the diphthong is called *improper,* and if the second vowel is *ι,* it is written *under* the first (*Iota subscriptum*), as *āυ, ηυ ωυ, ᾳ ῃ ῳ.* When a soft vowel precedes a hard vowel no diphthong can be formed, *e.g. σοφία* (trisyllabic); when *υ* precedes *ι* the diphthong *υι* (*wy*) is formed.

4. *Consonants* may be classed (cp. 19).

A. By the organ of pronunciation—
 (1.) Gutturals (throat sounds) *κ γ χ γ=ν.*
 (2.) Dentals (tooth sounds) *τ δ θ ν σ.*
 (3.) Labials (lip sounds) *π β φ μ.*

In *ρ* and *λ* the organ is uncertain; *ζ, ξ,* and *ψ* are double consonants.

B. By the power or force of pronunciation—
 I. *Mutes,* silent consonants, which cannot be pronounced without a vowel.
  (*a.*) Hard mutes *κ τ π.*
  (*b.*) Soft mutes *γ δ β.*
  (*c.*) Aspirated mutes *χ θ φ.*
 II. *Semivowels,* consonants which do not require a vowel.
  (*a.*) Nasals *γ=ν ν μ.*
  (*b.*) Spirants *σ F.*
  (*c.*) Liquids *λ ρ.*

The hard mutes are without any accompanying tone or *voice;* the soft have a moderate amount of voice. The aspirated mutes (which in Greek are *hard,* k-h, etc., not g-h) are really double sounds—a mute and a breathing. In the *nasals* the breath is made to pass through the nose; the *spirants* are breathings in a special sense. *F,* the Digamma, sounded as *w,* is only found in older Greek. The term *liquid* expresses the soft rolling nature of the sounds.

Characters and Signs.

5. *Breathings.*—The rough breathing, which we express by the letter *h*, is expressed in Greek at the beginning of a word by the sign ‘ placed over the initial vowel, as ὥρα (sounded *hōra*).

The soft breathing ’ merely marks the absence of the rough, as ὥρα (sounded *ōra*). Initial υ always has the rough breathing, as ὕπνος. The consonant ρ always has the rough breathing at the beginning of a word, as ῥίπτω ; and when two ρ's come together in a word, the first is some-times written with the soft and the second with the rough, as ἔρριπτον. Breathings are placed over the second vowel in a diphthong, and to the left of a capital, as εἶρπον, Ἀντιγόνη.

6. *Apostrophe* is the sign ’ used to mark the cutting off (elision) of a vowel, as τοῦτ’ ἐκεῖνο for τοῦτο ἐκεῖνο.

7. *Coronis.*—The same sign is called a coronis, when it marks crasis, that is, the *mixing* of two words in one, as τοὔνομα for τὸ ὄνομα.

8. *Diaeresis* (a *taking-apart*) is the mark ¨ placed over the latter of two vowels to show that they are to be sounded separately and not as a diphthong. Thus ἄϋπνος is sounded a-upnos (trisyllabic).

9. *Stops.*—The full stop and comma are the same as in English.

The sign · is used as a colon or semicolon, as αἰτία·

The sign ; is used as a note of interrogation, as τίς ἦν ; *quis erat ?*

There is no note of exclamation in Greek.

10. *Accents.*—Three marks are used to denote accent in Greek :—The acute ΄, as ἄνθρωπος.

The grave ΅, as ἀγαθὸς —.

The circumflex ῀, as Μουσῶν.

The accent is written to the left of a capital, and on the *second* vowel of a diphthong, *e.g.* Ἄντιφος, εἶρπον. Thus παῖς is a monosyllable. but πάϊς is a dissyllable, πάϊς.

Laws of Sound.

A.—VOWELS.

(i.) *Contraction.*

11. (1.) *Contraction proper.*—Hard vowels immediately preceding hard vowels in the same word undergo contraction in the following manner :—

(*a.*) a a become ᾱ, ἄατος ᾶτος.

     a ε   ,,   ᾱ, τίμαε τίμα.

     a η   ,,   ᾱ, τιμάῃτον τιμᾶτον.

     a o   ,,   ω, τιμάομεν τιμῶμεν.

     a ω   ,,   ω, τιμάωμεν τιμῶμεν.

     a ει   ,,   ᾳ, τιμάει τιμᾷ.

     a οι   ,,   ῷ, τιμάοιμι τιμῷμι.

     a ου   ,,   ω, τιμάου τιμῶ.

     a η   ,,   ᾳ, τιμάῃς τιμᾷς.

(*b.*) ε a become η, γένεα γένη.

     ε ε   ,,   ει, φίλεε φίλει.

     ε η   ,,   η, φιλέητον φιλῆτον.

     ε o   ,,   ου, φιλέομεν φιλοῦμεν.

     ε ω   ,,   ω, φιλέω φιλῶ.

     ε αι   ,,   ῃ, τύπτεαι τύπτῃ.

     ε ει   ,,   ει, φιλέει φιλεῖ.

     ε οι   ,,   οι, φιλέοιμι φιλοῖμι.

     ε ου   ,,   ου, φιλέουσι φιλοῦσι.

     ε η   ,,   η, φιλέῃς φιλῆς.

     η αι   ,,   ῃ, λύηαι λύῃ.

(*c.*) o a become ω, αἰδόα αἰδῶ.

     o ε   ,,   ου, δηλόετον δηλοῦτον.

     o η   ,,   ω, δηλόητον δηλῶτον.

     o o   ,,   ου, δηλόομεν δηλοῦμεν.

     o ω   ,,   ω, δηλόωμεν δηλῶμεν.

ο ει become οι, δηλόει δηλοῖ.

ο ου   „   ου, δηλόου δηλοῦ.

ο η   „   οι, δηλόη δηλοῖ.

Obs. 1. ο as the heavier vowel prevails in contraction (except in contracted Adjectives, ἁπλόη ἁπλῆ, ἁπλόαι ἁπλαῖ); if ε precedes α the ε-sound prevails; if α precedes ε the α-sound prevails.

Obs. 2. When the vowels differ in length only, a long hard vowel preceding a short one absorbs it, *e.g.* λᾶας λᾶς.

12.   (2.) *Crasis.*—When two words come together, the first ending and the second beginning with a vowel, the two vowels sometimes coalesce (are mixed, κέκραται), and the two words become one. If the word thus formed begins with a consonant, the *crasis* (mixing) is indicated by a coronis (cp. 7), τὸ ὄνομα, τοὔνομα, but ὁ ἀνήρ, ἁνήρ.

Obs. 1. The rules for crasis are not always the same as those for contraction proper. Thus ου and ῳ of the article, if followed by α, disappear, τοῦ ἀνδρός τἀνδρός, τῷ ἀνδρί τἀνδρί, τοῦ αὐτοῦ ταὐτοῦ, etc.

Obs. 2. When the initial vowel of the second word has the rough breathing, the consonant of the preceding word becomes aspirated, *e.g.* τὰ ἕτερα θἄτερα, τὸ ἱμάτιον θοἰμάτιον, etc.

Obs. 3. If the second word begins with a diphthong containing ι, the ι is preserved as *subscriptum*, *e.g.* καὶ εἶτα κᾆτα, but καὶ ἔπειτα κἄπειτα.

13.   (3.) *Synizesis.*—When a word ending with a long vowel or diphthong is followed by a word beginning with a vowel or diphthong, both vowels are sometimes pronounced as one long vowel or diphthong, though no change is made in the writing of the letters, *e.g.* ἐγὼ οὐ (˘ ‾), ἐπεὶ οὐ.

(ii.) Flexional Lengthening.

14.   Vowels are sometimes lengthened or extended into diphthongs, even where there is no contraction, for the purpose of inflexion, *i.e.* to form tenses and the like. Thus :—

ᾰ becomes	{	η,	Verb St.	τιμα,	Fut.	τιμή-σω.
		ᾱ,	„	δρα,	Fut.	δρᾱ́-σω.
ε	„	η,	„	φιλε,	Fut.	φιλή-σω.
ο	„	ω,	„	δηλο,	Fut.	δηλώ-σω.
ῐ	„	{	ῑ,	„	τῐ,	Fut.	τῑ-σω.
		εἰ,	„	λιπ,	Pres.	λείπω.
		οἰ,	„	„	Perf.	λέ-λοιπ-α.
ῠ	„	{	ῡ,	„	λῠ,	Fut. Perf.	λε-λῡσο-μαι.
		ευ,	„	φυγ,	Pres.	φεύγω.

(iii.) *Compensatory Lengthening.*

15. When consonants have been dropped for the sake of euphony (or ease of pronunciation), the vowels which precede them are sometimes lengthened, thus :—

ᾱ is for αντ in πᾶς (παντ-ς).

ει „ εντ in τιθείς (τιθεντ-ς).

ου „ οντ in διδούς (διδοντ-ς).

ην „ ενς in ποιμήν (ποιμεν-ς).

ης „ εςς in ἀληθής (ἀληθες-ς).

ων „ ονς in δαίμων (δαιμον-ς).

„ „ οντς in τύπτων (τυπτοντ-ς).

(iv.) *Vowels at the end of a word.*

16. (1.) *Elision.*—When the final vowel of a word is short it is often cut off (elided) before a word beginning with a vowel, *e.g.* κατ' ἄλλον (for κατὰ ἄλλον). But υ is hardly ever, and ι rarely elided, except in prepositions (περί is never elided). The elision is indicated by apostrophe (cp. 6).

17. (2.) *Paragogic ν.*—In certain forms ending in ι or ε, ν may be attached to the vowel (ν ἐφελκυστικόν). Such forms are :—

(*a.*) Dative Plural of Nouns, in -σι, *e.g.* θηρσί(ν).

(*b.*) 3d Pers. Sing. and Plur. of Verbs in -σι, *e.g.* λέγουσι(ν).

(*c.*) 3d Pers. Sing. of Verbs, in -ε, *e.g.* ἔσωσε(ν).

(*d.*) Certain Adverbs or numerals, as εἴκοσι(ν) παντά· πασι(ν), etc. Also ἐστί(ν).

(v.) *Quantity of Vowels.*

18. All diphthongs and contracted syllables are long. A long vowel is not shortened by standing immediately before another vowel, *e.g.* θωή.

A short vowel followed by two or more consonants is long by *position* (as in Latin), *e.g.* τάσσω, ἐκ νεῶν. But if the consonants be in the same word, and the second is a liquid or nasal (λ, ρ, μ, or ν), the first being a mute, the vowel is common (long or short), *e.g.* τέκνον. To this rule the combinations βλ, γλ, γμ, γν, δν, must be considered exceptions.

B.—CONSONANTS.

19.   *Table of Consonants.*

	MUTES.			SEMIVOWELS.		
	HARD.	SOFT.	ASPIRATES.	NASALS.	SPIRANTS.	LIQUIDS.
GUTTURAL	κ	γ	χ	γ = *ng*		
DENTAL .	τ	δ	θ	ν	ς	λ ρ
LABIAL .	π	β	φ	μ	[F]	

The lateral division is according to the *organ*, the vertical according to the *force* of pronunciation or *power*. ζ, ξ, and ψ, being double consonants, do not require classification.

20. *Similar* consonants are those of the same class, lateral or vertical, *i.e.* of the same organ or power. *Dissimilar* consonants are those of different organs or powers.

As a general rule, the tendency in pronouncing consonants is either to weaken the power, or bring them forward in the mouth. Hence changes are from κ towards the spirants, from κ towards π. Thus in Greek we have κ where in English we have *h, e.g.*

καρδία, *heart*, κώπη, *haft*, etc., and Latin *quinque*= Greek πέντε, *equus*= ἵππος, etc.

Consonants in contact are changed in order to make the pronunciation easier. The consonants are made more similar (*assimilation*), or more dissimilar (*dissimilation*), or one is dropped (*elision*).

21. I.—*Assimilation.*

(*a.*) Of mute dentals :—

Before τ,

Gutturals become κ, λέγω λεκτός, δέχομαι δεκτός.
Labials become π, βλάβη βλάπτω, γράφω γραπτός.

Before δ,

Gutturals become γ, ὀκτώ ὄγδοος.
Labials become β, ἔπτα ἔβδομος.

Before θ,

Gutturals become χ, πλέκω πλεχθῆναι, λέγω λεχθείς.
Labials become φ, τύπτω τυφθῆναι, τρίβω τριφθείς.

Before μ,

Gutturals become γ, πλέκω πέπλεγμαι, βρέχω βέβρεγμαι.
Dentals become σ, ἀνύτω ἤνυσμαι, πείθω πέπεισμαι.
Labials become μ, τύπτω τέτυμμαι, τρίβω τέτριμμαι.

(*b.*) Of nasals :—

ν before

Labials becomes μ, ἐμβάλλω (ἐν-βάλλω), συμμίγνυμι (συν-μ.).
Gutturals „ γ=ν, συγκαλέω (συν-καλέω), ἐγχειρίδιον (ἐν-χ.).
Liquids is completely assimilated, συλλαμβάνω (συν-λαμβ), συρράπτω (συν-ράπτω).

22. II.—*Dissimilation.*

(*a.*) Of mute dentals :—

Before dentals, dentals become σ, ανυτ ἠνύσθην, πιθ ἐπείσθην.

(*b.*) Of aspirates :—

Aspirates are rarely retained at the beginning or end of two consecutive syllables. The first aspirate is usually changed to the corresponding hard letter, as ἐτέθην for ἐ-θε-θην, ἐτύθην for ἐ-θυ-θην. This change always takes place in reduplication, as τίθημι for θι-θη-μι.

23.   III.—*Elision.*

(*a.*) Before s,

(1.) Dental mutes and ν are dropped, λαμπάς (λαμπαδ-s), ἀνύσω (ἀνυτ-σω), ποσί (ποδ-σι), δαίμοσι (δαιμον-σι).

(2.) ντ is dropped with compensatory lengthening, ὀδούς (ὀδοντ-s), τιθείς (τιθεντ-s). Sometimes τs are dropped and ν retained with a long vowel (not a diphthong), τύπτων (τυπτοντ-s).

(*b.*) s is dropped,

(1.) In inflexion between two vowels, γένους (γενεσ-ος, γένε-ος), τύπτου (τυπτεσο, τύπτεο).

(2.) After ν, ρ, σ, with compensatory lengthening, ἔμεινα (ἐ-μεν-σα), ποιμήν (ποιμεν-s), etc.

24.   IV.—*Consonants at the end of a word.*

(*a.*) Only the three consonants ν, ρ, and s (ξ ψ) can stand at the end of a word in Greek, with the exception of οὐκ (οὐχ) and ἐκ. Any other consonant is either changed into s or ν, or dropped altogether. Thus πρᾶγμα is for πραγματ, καλῶς for καλωτ (cp. Lat. *certōd*), γύναι for γυναικ, ἔφερον for ἐ-φερο-μ (cp. *ferebam*), etc.

(*b.*) When elision has taken place, a final consonant is aspirated before a word beginning with rough breathing, *e.g.* ἀφ' ἑστίας (not ἀπ' ἑστίας) for ἀπὸ ἑστίας, ἀνθ' ὧν for ἀντὶ ὧν. So οὐχ οὗτος, but οὐκ αὐτός; ἐκ however becomes ἐξ before a following vowel, ἐξ ὧν, ἐξ αὐτοῦ.

---

25.   (1.) *Auxiliary consonants* are sometimes employed, *e.g.* β between μ and λ (μέμβλωκα) ; between μ and ρ (μεσημβρία) ; and δ between ν and ρ (ἀνδρός).

26.   (2.) *Aspirates.*—When owing to inflexion there is a danger that the aspirate may be lost, it is sometimes changed from one letter to another, *e.g.* from the stem τριχ comes the nom. θρίξ, where the aspirate is lost by the addition of s (χ-s becoming κ-s forms ξ), and reappears in the θ. So fut. θρέψω from τρεφ, and pres. θάπτω from ταφ.

27.   (3.) *Metathesis (transposition)* takes place when a vowel changes places with a following liquid or nasal, *e.g.* θάρσος, θράσος. The vowel is generally lengthened, as in θνή-σκ-ω, from the stem θαν.

Accents.

28. For the marks of accent see **10**.

The position of the accent in Greek depends in part upon the quantity of the final syllable. If this is *short,* the acute *can* go back to the third syllable from the end of the word, and the circumflex to the last but one; if, on the other hand, it is *long,* the acute must be placed on the last, or last but one,—the circumflex on the last only. Thus ἄνθρωπυς but ἀνθρώπου, οὗτος but τούτου. In accentuation, the diphthongs αι and οι are considered *short,* except in the optative mood of verbs, *e.g.* ἄνθρωποι nom. plur. of ἄνθρωπος, παιδεῦσαι aor. inf. act. of παιδεύω, but παιδεύσαι third sing. opt.

Words which have the acute on the last syllable are called *oxytone* (sharp-toned); on the last but one *paroxytone,* on the last but two *proparoxytone.* Words which have the circumflex on the last syllable are called *perispomena ;* on the last but one *properispomena.* All words not accented on the last syllable are called *barytone.*

Oxytone words are written with a grave accent except when followed by a enclitic (**29**) or a stop; and τίς τί interrogative is always acute.

Unless there be some special reason or usage to the contrary, the accent is thrown as far back as the quantity of the final syllable will allow. But the exceptions to this rule are very numerous. For instance, dissyllabic nouns in -αρα, -ευρα, -ουρα, and all nouns in -ορα, are oxytone, ἀρά, *a prayer,* χαρά, *joy,* etc.; all nouns in -ευς are oxytone, and so are adjectives in -ικος, -υς, and, with exceptions, in -νος, -ρος. Nouns in -εια from verbs in -ευω are paroxytone, *e.g.* βασιλεία, *kingdom.* In the Attic declension (**37**) the long vowel does not influence the accentuation. Observe the accent of ποταμός, *river,* οὐρανός, *heaven,* ἀγαθός, *good,* ὀλίγος, *little.*

For exceptions arising from declension, see **35, 37, 51, 67**, and for those arising from conjugation, see **146**. See also Appendix I.

29. Some words are *enclitics, i.e.* they throw their accent, which is always acute, on the last syllable of the preceding word, if it can receive it.

Proparoxytone and properispomenon words receive it, as τράπεζά τις, σῶμά τι.

But the accent of monosyllabic enclitics is lost after paroxytone and perispomenon words, as λόγος τις, γραῦς τις,

While the accent of dissyllables is kept on the *second* syllable after paroxytone words, as ἀνθρώπου τινός; (but φωνῆς τινος).

Oxytone words retain the acute accent before an enclitic, as φωνή τις.

Enclitics are the indefinite pronoun τις in all forms, and the indefinite adverbs που, ποι, πως, etc.; the particles γε, τοι, νυν, τε, etc.; the indic. pres. of φημί, *I say,* and εἰμί, *I am,* except the second pers. sing.; and the personal pronouns in the forms με μου μοι, σε σου σοι, ἐ οὑ οἱ, σφισί(ν). (**91,** *Obs.* 1.)

30. Some words have no accent (ἄτονα): these are ὁ, ἡ, οἱ, αἱ, nom. masc. and fem. sing. and plur. of the article or definite pronoun; the prepositions ἐν, ἐκ, εἰς; the conjunctions εἰ, ὡς; the negative οὐ.

---

31. Accentuation in *contraction:*—

(1.) If the accentuated vowel is not affected by the contraction, the marks remain as in the original word, *e.g.* γένεος, γένους, τίμαε, τίμᾱ.

(2.) If the acute falls upon the *first* of the two contracted vowels, it is changed into a circumflex, *e.g.* ἐτιμάετο, ἐτιμᾶτο.

(3.) If the acute falls upon the *second* of the two contracted vowels, it is retained, *e.g.* ἑσταώς, ἑστώς.

(4.) A circumflex accent undergoes no change, *e.g.* λάας, λᾶς. When *elision* of an accentuated vowel takes place, the accent is thrown on the preceding syllable, *e.g.* αὐτὸ ἦν becomes αὔτ᾽ ἦν. To this rule indeclinable words are an exception. They lose the accent altogether, *e.g.* οὐδὲ ἦν becomes οὐδ᾽ ἦν, παρὰ αὐτοῦ, παρ᾽ αὐτοῦ.

Declension of Substantives.

32. DECLENSION is the alteration which a Noun undergoes to express the relations of number and case. In this alteration part of the word remains the same, and part is changed, as nom. φίλο-ς, *a friend*, acc. φίλο-ν.

The Stem is the part of the word that remains unchanged, as φιλο.

The Termination is the changeable part which is attached to the stem, as ς, ν.

The Character is the last letter of the stem.

The Greek Declensions have

> Three Numbers. The Singular for one, the Dual for two, or a pair, and the Plural for two or more.

> Five Cases. Nominative, Vocative, Accusative, Genitive, and Dative.*

Declensions are best arranged according to the final letter of the stem :—

> I. FIRST DECLENSION.—Stems ending in *a* (or *η*).

> II. SECOND DECLENSION.—Stems ending in *o* (or *ω*).

> III. THIRD DECLENSION.—(1.) Stems ending in soft vowels, *ι, υ.*

> (2.) Stems ending in consonants.

---

* Greek has lost the Ablative Case, for which the Genitive serves in some senses, and the Dative in others.

33. The GENDER of nouns is known partly by the *form* of the word, and partly by the *meaning*.

A. *Form* (*a*.) Masc. are nouns in -αs, -ηs of the first declension.

     „   „   -os of the second declension unless feminine owing to the meaning.

     „   „   -τηρ, -τωρ, -ων, -ην, -ευs of the third declension.

(*b*.) Fem. are nouns in -α, -η of the first declension.

     „   „   -ω of the third declension.

(*c*.) Neut. are nouns in -ν of the second declension.

     „   „   in -ι, -υ, -α, -os of the third declension.

All neuters have α in nom., acc., voc. plural.

B. *Meaning.*—All names of men, male animals, gods, rivers, and winds (which were regarded as gods) are masculine; all names of women, goddesses, trees, and islands, are feminine.

34. The forms of the First and Second Declension may be learnt conveniently, in part, from the declension of ὁ, ἡ, τό, which is used as a definite article = *the* (cp. **91**).

		MASCULINE.	FEMININE.	NEUTER.
Sing.	*Nom.*	ὁ	ἡ	τό
	Acc.	τόν	τήν	τό
	Gen.	τοῦ	τῆs	τοῦ
	Dat.	τῷ	τῇ	τῷ
Dual	*N.A.*	τώ	τώ	τώ
	G.D.	τοῖν	τοῖν	τοῖν
Plur.	*Nom.*	οἱ	αἱ	τά
	Acc.	τούs	τάs	τά
	Gen.	τῶν	τῶν	τῶν
	Dat.	τοῖs	ταῖs	τοῖs

35. FIRST DECLENSION.—*A* STEMS.

	MASCULINES.		FEMININES.		
STEM. ENGLISH.	νεᾱνια, *youth.*	κριτα, *judge.*	χωρα, *country.*	τῑμα, *honour.*	μουσα, *muse.*
Sing. *Nom.*	ὁ νεᾱνίᾱς	ὁ κριτής	ἡ χώρᾱ	ἡ τιμή	ἡ μοῦσα
Voc.	νεᾱνίᾱ	κριτά	χώρᾱ	τιμή	μοῦσα
Acc.	νεᾱνίᾱν	κριτήν	χώρᾱν	τιμήν	μοῦσαν
Gen.	νεᾱνίου	κριτοῦ	χώρᾱς	τιμῆς	μούσης
Dat.	νεᾱνίᾳ	κριτῇ	χώρᾳ	τιμῇ	μούσῃ
Dual *N.V.A.*	νεᾱνίᾱ	κριτά	χώρᾱ	τιμά	μούσᾱ
G. D.	νεᾱνίαιν	κριταῖν	χώραιν	τιμαῖν	μούσαιν
Plur. *N.V.*	νεᾱνίαι	κριταί	χῶραι	τιμαί	μοῦσαι
Acc.	νεᾱνίᾱς	κριτᾱς	χώρᾱς	τιμάς	μούσᾱς
Gen.	νεᾱνιῶν	κριτῶν	χωρῶν	τιμῶν	μουσῶν
Dat.	νεᾱνίαις	κριταῖς	χώραις	τιμαῖς	μούσαις

EXAMPLES.

Masc. Βορέας, *north wind;* πολίτης, *citizen.*

Fem. ἀρά, *curse;* ψῡχή, *soul;* ἅμαξα, *wagon.*

Obs. 1. All duals and plurals are declined alike.

Obs. 2. The following masculines have ᾰ in voc. sing.

> Words in -της, as κριτής.
> Names of Peoples, as Πέρσης, *a Persian.*
> A few compound words.
> All others in -ης have η, as Κρονίδης, *son of Kronos,*
> voc. ὦ Κρονίδη.

Obs. 3. Nominatives in *a pure* (after ε, ι, or ρ) keep α through singular.

> Nominatives in *a impure* have η in gen. and dat. sing. only.
> Nominatives in η keep η through singular.

Obs. 4. To find the nominative from any given case of a fem. substantive, find the α (or η) of the stem ; then

> i. If ε, ι or ρ precedes, the nom. will end in -α.
> ii. If σ, ξ, ζ, ψ, σσ, ττ, or λλ, precedes, nom. will end in -α.
> iii. If any other letter precedes, nom. will end in -η.

36.   SECOND DECLENSION.—*O* STEMS.

	SIMPLE			CONTRACTED.	
STEM. ENGL.	λογο, *speech.*	νησο, *island.*	ζυγο, *yoke.*	νοο, *mind.*	ὀστεο, *bone.*
Sing.					
Nom.	ὁ λόγος	ἡ νῆσος	τὸ ζυγόν	ὁ νοῦς (νόος)	τὸ ὀστοῦν (ὀστέον)
Voc.	λόγε	νῆσε	ζυγόν	νοῦ (νόε)	ὀστοῦν (ὀστέον)
Acc.	λόγον	νῆσον	ζυγόν	νοῦν (νόον)	ὀστοῦν (ὀστέον)
Gen.	λόγου	νήσου	ζυγοῦ	νοῦ (νόου)	ὀστοῦ (ὀστέου)
Dat.	λόγῳ	νήσῳ	ζυγῷ	νῷ (νόῳ)	ὀστῷ (ὀστέῳ)
Dual					
N.V.A.	λόγω	νήσω	ζυγώ	νώ (νόω)	ὀστώ (ὀστέω)
G. D.	λόγοιν	νήσοιν	ζυγοῖν	νοῖν (νόοιν)	ὀστοῖν (ὀστέοιν)
Plur.					
N. V.	λόγοι	νῆσοι	ζυγά	νοῖ (νόοι)	ὀστᾶ (ὀστέα)
Acc.	λόγους	νήσους	ζυγά	νοῦς (νόους)	ὀστᾶ (ὀστέα)
Gen.	λόγων	νήσων	ζυγῶν	νῶν (νόων)	ὀστῶν (ὀστέων)
Dat.	λόγοις	νήσοις	ζυγοῖς	νοῖς (νόοις)	ὀστοῖς (ὀστέοις)

EXAMPLES.

SIMPLE.—ἄνθρωπος, ὁ, *man* ; οἶκος, ὁ, *house* ; ξύλον, τό, *wood.*
CONTR. —πλοῦς, ὁ, *voyage* ; κανοῦν, τό, *basket.*

Obs. 1. In the neuters, nom., acc., and voc. are always the same; and in the plural these cases always end in *a.* The contraction of ὀστέα into ὀστᾶ is irregular, cp. 11.

Obs. 2. The following words are feminine :—ὁδός, *way* ; νῆσος, *island* ; νόσος, *disease* ; δρόσος, *dew* ; σποδός, *ashes* ; ψῆφος, *pebble* ; ἄμπελος, *vine* ; γνάθος, *jaw* ; ἤπειρος, *continent* ; and some others.

ATTIC DECLENSION.

37. In some stems of the second declension the lengthening of *o* into *ω* absorbs the vowels of the terminations. In all terminations where *ι* occurs it is *subscriptum* (**3**). The consonants of the terminations remain as in λόγος, ζυγόν.

STEM. ENGLISH.	λεω, *people.*	ἀνωγεω, *upper room.*
Sing. *N. V.*	ὁ λεώς	τὸ ἀνώγεων
Acc.	λεών	ἀνώγεων
Gen.	λεώ	ἀνώγεω
Dat.	λεῴ	ἀνώγεῳ
Dual *N. V. A.*	λεώ	ἀνώγεω
G. D.	λεῴν	ἀνώγεῳν
Plur. *N. V.*	λεῴ	ἀνώγεω
Acc.	λεώς	ἀνώγεω
Gen.	λεών	ἀνώγεων
Dat.	λεῴς	ἀνώγεῳς

 EXAMPLES.

γάλως, ἡ, *sister-in-law*; κάλως, ὁ, *cable.*

Accentuation in First and Second Declension.—The genitive plural of all nouns of the first declension is *perispomenon*. Oxytone nouns of first and second declension are *perispomenon* in genitive and dative of all numbers. So far as possible the accent is retained on the same syllable, *e.g.* σοφία, σοφίαι though αι is short; in χώρα χῶραι the short final syllable allows the word to be *properispomenon*.

In the N. V. A. dual the circumflex is avoided even when the word is contracted—νόω, νώ, not νῶ.

In the Attic Declension εω appear to have been pronounced as one syllable, and the word is accented accordingly. So also in the genitives sing. and plur. of stems in -ι and -υ (**40**).

THIRD DECLENSION.

38. The Third Declension contains :—

A. Soft Vowel Stems (i.) *Stems in ι and υ.*
                                  (ii.) *Stems in diphthongs.*

B. Consonant Stems :—

I. Stems in Mutes (i.) *Stems in Gutturals, κ, γ, χ.*
                                  (ii.) *Stems in Dentals, τ, δ, θ, etc.*
                                  (iii.) *Stems in Labials, π, β, φ.*

II. Stems in Semivowels (i.) *Stems in Liquids, λ, ρ.*
                                  (ii.) *Stems in Nasals, ν(μ).*
                                  (iii.) *Stems in Spirants, ϛ, ϝ.*

Obs. The soft vowels ι and υ are nearly allied to consonants, and take almost the same terminations.

39. The Terminations of the Third Declension are the following :—

		Masculine and Feminine.	Neuter.
Sing.	*Nom.*	ϛ or lengthened stem	No ending
	Voc.	No ending, or same as Nom.	No ending
	Acc.	-*a* or -*ν*	No ending
	Gen.	-οϛ	-οϛ
	Dat.	-ι	-ι
Dual	*N.V.A.*	-ε	-ε
	G.D.	-οιν	-οιν
Plur.	*N.V.*	-εϛ	··*a*
	Acc.	-αϛ	-*a*
	Gen.	-ων	-ων
	Dat.	-σι(*ν*)	-σι(*ν*)

A.—SOFT VOWEL STEMS.

40. (i.) *Stems in ι and υ.*

MASCULINES AND FEMININES.

STEM. ENGLISH.	πολι, city.	συ, pig.	πηχυ, fore-arm.
Sing. *Nom.*	ἡ πόλις	ὁ, ἡ σῦς	ὁ πῆχυς
Voc.	πόλι	σῦς	πῆχυ
Acc.	πόλιν	σῦν	πῆχυν
Gen.	πόλεως	σὕός	πήχεως
Dat.	πόλει (ε-ἳ)	σὕΐ	πήχει (ε-ἳ)
Dual *N.V.A.*	πόλει (ε-ε)	σύε	πήχει (ε-ε)
G.D.	πολέοιν	σύοῖν	πηχέοιν
Plur. *N.V.*	πόλεις (ε-ες)	σύες	πήχεις (ε-ες)
Acc.	πόλεις (ε-ας)	σύας, σῦς	πήχεις (ε-ας)
Gen.	πόλεων	σὕῶν	πήχεων
Dat.	πόλεσι(ν)	σὕσί(ν)	πήχεσι(ν)

EXAMPLES.

φρόνησις, ἡ, *wisdom;*   ἰχθύς, ὁ, *fish* (like σῦς).
ὕβρις, ἡ, *insolence;*   πέλεκυς, ὁ, *axe* (like πῆχυς).

NEUTERS.

STEM. ENGLISH.	σιναπι, mustard.	δακρυ, tear.	αστυ, city.
Sing. *N.V.A.*	τὸ σίναπι	τὸ δάκρυ	τὸ ἄστυ
Gen.	σινάπεως	δάκρυος	ἄστεως
Dat.	σινάπει (ε-ἳ)	δάκρυῐ	ἄστει (ε-ἳ)
Dual *N.V.A.*	σινάπει (ε-ε)	δάκρυε	ἄστει (ε-ε)
G.D.	σιναπέοιν	δακρύοιν	ἀστέοιν
Plur. *N.V.A.*	σινάπη (ε-α)	δάκρυα	ἄστη (ε-α)
Gen.	σινάπεων	δακρύων	ἄστεων
Den.	σινάπεσι (ν)	δάκρυσι (ν)	ἄστεσι(ν)

Obs. The soft vowel is weakened into ε in ι stems. In υ stems the forms which keep the υ (as σῦς, δάκρυ) are the more usual. The form of the genitive in -ως is called the Attic. Compare the Attic declension.

Accent.—For the accent of the Attic genitive, see note on 37.

41.   (ii.) *Stems in Diphthongs.*

STEM. ENGLISH.	βασιλευ, king.	βου, ox.	γραυ, old woman.
Sing. Nom.	ὁ βασιλεύς	ὁ βοῦς	ἡ γραῦς
Voc.	βασιλεῦ	βοῦ	γραῦ
Acc.	βασιλέᾱ	βοῦν	γραῦν
Gen.	βασιλέως	βοός	γρᾱός
Dat.	βασιλεῖ (ε-ῐ)	βοΐ	γρᾱΐ
Dual N.V.A.	βασιλεῖ (ε-ε)	βόε	γρᾱε
G. D.	βασιλέοιν	βοοῖν	γρᾱοῖν
Plur. N. V.	βασιλῆς (ε-ες)	βόες	γρᾶες
Acc.	βασιλέᾱς	βοῦς	γραῦς
Gen.	βασιλέων	βοῶν	γρᾱῶν
Dat.	βασιλεῦσι (ν)	βουσί (ν)	γραυσί (ν)

EXAMPLES.

χαλκεύς, ὁ, *smith;* δρομεύς, ὁ, *runner;* χοῦς, ὁ, *mound.*

Obs. A later form of the nom. plur. of -ευ stems ends in -εῖς, as βασιλεῖς.

B.—CONSONANT STEMS.

42.   I.—STEMS IN MUTES.

(i.) *Stems in Gutturals,* κ, γ, χ, φυλακ, μαστιγ, ὀνυχ.

(ii.) *Stems in Dentals* (a.) τ, δ, θ, ἐρωτ, λαμπαδ, κορυθ.

                     (b.) ντ, κτ, γιγαντ, λεοντ, νυκτ.

(iii.) *Stems in Labials,* π, β, φ, γυπ, χαλυβ (κατηλιφ).

43. (i.)—*Stems in Gutturals.*

STEM. ENGLISH.	φυλᾰκ, *guard.*	μαστῑγ, *whip.*	ὀνῠχ, *nail.*
Sing. *N.V.*	ὁ φύλαξ	ἡ μάστιξ	ὁ ὄνυξ
Acc.	φύλακα	μάστιγα	ὄνυχα
Gen.	φύλακος	μάστιγος	ὄνυχος
Dat.	φύλακι	μάστιγι	ὄνυχι
Dual *N.V.A.*	φύλακε	μάστιγε	ὄνυχε
G.D.	φυλάκοιν	μαστίγοιν	ὀνύχοιν
Plur. *N.V.*	φύλακες	μάστιγες	ὄνυχες
Acc.	φύλακας	μάστιγας	ὄνυχας
Gen.	φυλάκων	μαστίγων	ὀνύχων
Dat.	φύλαξι(ν)	μάστιξι(ν)	ὄνυξι(ν)

EXAMPLES.—κῆρυξ (ῡκ), ὁ, *herald;* φόρμιγξ (ιγγ), ἡ, *lyre.*

44. (ii.)—*Stems in Dentals.*
(a.) *Stems in* τ, δ, θ.
MASCULINE AND FEMININE.

STEM. ENGLISH.	ἐρωτ, *love.*	λαμπᾰδ, *torch.*	κορῠθ, *helmet.*	χαρῐτ, *favour.*
Sing. *N.V.*	ὁ ἔρως	ἡ λαμπάς	ἡ κόρυς	ἡ χάρις
Acc.	ἔρωτα	λαμπάδα	κόρυθα	χάριν
Gen.	ἔρωτος	λαμπάδος	κόρυθος	χάριτος
Dat.	ἔρωτι	λαμπάδι	κόρυθι	χάριτι
Dual *N.V.A.*	ἔρωτε	λαμπάδε	κόρυθε	χάριτε
G.D.	ἐρώτοιν	λαμπάδοιν	κορύθοιν	χαρίτοιν
Plur. *N.V.*	ἔρωτες	λαμπάδες	κόρυθες	χάριτες
Acc.	ἔρωτας	λαμπάδας	κόρυθας	χάριτας
Gen.	ἐρώτων	λαμπάδων	κορύθων	χαρίτων
Dat.	ἔρωσι(ν)	λαμπάσι(ν)	κόρυσι(ν)	χάρισι(ν)

EXAMPLES.

δαίς (τ), ἡ, *feast;* φυγάς (δ), ὁ, ἡ, *exile;* ὄρνις (ῐθ), ὁ, ἡ, *bird.*
Like χάρις.—ἔρις (δ), ἡ, *strife.*

Obs. κόρυς also makes κόρυν in acc. sing., and ὄρνις makes also ὄρνιν in acc. sing. and ὄρνεις in acc. plural.

NEUTERS.

STEM. ENGLISH.	σωμᾰτ, *body.*	κερᾰτ, *horn.*
Sing. *N.V.A.* *Gen.* *Dat.*	τὸ σῶμα σώματος σώματι	τὸ κέρας κέρᾱτος, κέρως κέρᾱτι, κέρᾳ
Dual *N.V.A.* *G.D.*	σώματε σωμάτοιν	κέρᾱτε [κέρᾱ] κεράτοιν [κερῷν]
Plur. *N.V.A.* *Gen.* *Dat.*	σώματα σωμάτων σώμασι(ν)	κέρᾱτα, κέρᾱ κεράτων, κερῶν κέρᾰσι(ν)

EXAMPLES—πρᾶγμα, τό, *action;* ὄνομα, τό, *name.*
Words like κέρας are rare ; see p. 159.

45.   (b.) *Stems in* ντ, κτ.

STEM. ENGLISH.	γιγαντ, *giant.*	ὀδοντ, *tooth.*	λεοντ, *lion.*	νυκτ, *night.*
Sing. *Nom.* *Voc.* *Acc.* *Gen.* *Dat.*	ὁ γίγᾱς (γίγαν) γίγαντα γίγαντος γίγαντι	ὁ ὀδούς ὀδούς ὀδόντα ὀδόντος ὀδόντι	ὁ λέων [λέον] λέοντα λέοντος λέοντι	ἡ νύξ νύξ νύκτα νυκτός νυκτί
Dual *N.V.A.* *G. D.*	γίγαντε γιγάντοιν	ὀδόντε ὀδόντοιν	λέοντε λεόντοιν	νύκτε νυκτοῖν
Plur. *N.V.* *Acc.* *Gen.* *Dat.*	γίγαντες γίγαντας γιγάντων γίγᾱσι(ν)	ὀδόντες ὀδόντας ὀδόντων ὀδοῦσι(ν)	λέοντες λέοντας λεόντων λέουσι(ν)	νύκτες νύκτας νυκτῶν νυξί(ν)

EXAMPLES.—ἀνδρίας, ὁ, *statue;* γέρων, ὁ, *old man.*

γάλα, τό, *milk,* is thus declined :—Sing. *N. V. A.,* γάλα, *Gen.*
γάλακτος, *Dat.* γάλακτι. There is no dual or plural. (173.)

46. (iii.)— *Stems in Labials.*

STEM. ENGLISH.	γῠπ, *vulture.*	χαλῠβ, *iron.*
Sing. *N. V.*	ὁ γύψ	ὁ χάλυψ
Acc.	γῦπα	χάλυβα
Gen.	γυπός	χάλυβος
Dat.	γυπί	χάλυβι
Dual *N. V. A.*	γῦπε	χάλυβε
G. D.	γυποῖν	χαλύβοιν
Plur. *N. V.*	γῦπες	χάλυβες
Acc.	γῦπας	χάλυβας
Gen.	γυπῶν	χαλύβων
Dat.	γυψί(ν)	χάλυψι(ν)

EXAMPLES.—ὤψ (π), ἡ, *face;* φλέψ (β), ἡ, *vein.*

II.—STEMS IN SEMIVOWELS.

47. (i.)— *Stems in Liquids,* λ, ρ.

STEM. ENGLISH.	ἁλ, *salt.*	θηρ, *wild beast.*	ῥητορ, *rhetorician.*	πατερ, *father.*
Sing. *Nom.*	ὁ ἅλς	ὁ θήρ	ὁ ῥήτωρ	ὁ πατήρ
Voc.	ἅλς	θήρ	ῥῆτορ	πάτερ
Acc.	ἅλα	θῆρα	ῥήτορα	πατέρα
Gen.	ἁλός	θηρός	ῥήτορος	πατρός
Dat.	ἁλί	θηρί	ῥήτορι	πατρί
Dual *N.V.A.*	ἅλε	θῆρε	ῥήτορε	πατέρε
G.D.	ἁλοῖν	θηροῖν	ῥητόροιν	πατέροιν
Plur. *N.V.*	ἅλες	θῆρες	ῥήτορες	πατέρες
Acc.	ἅλας	θῆρας	ῥήτορας	πατέρας
Gen.	ἁλῶν	θηρῶν	ῥητόρων	πατέρων
Dat.	ἁλσί(ν)	θηρσί(ν)	ῥήτορσι(ν)	πατράσι(ν)

EXAMPLES.— ἀροτήρ, ὁ, *ploughman;* ἡγήτωρ, ὁ, *leader.*

Obs. As πατήρ, *i.e.* with omission (syncope) of ε in gen. and dat. sing., and dat. plur. in ᾰσι(ν), are declined—μήτηρ, *mother;* θυγατήρ, *daughter;* γαστήρ, ἡ, *belly.* ἀνήρ, *man,* omits ε throughout, but inserts δ, ἄνδρα, ἀνδρός. **(25.)**

48.   (ii.)—*Stems in the nasal ν.*

STEM. ENG.	Ἕλλην, *Greek.*	ποιμεν, *shepherd.*	ἀγων, *contest.*	ἡγεμον, *leader.*	δελφῑν *dolphin.*
Sing.					
N.V.	ὁ Ἕλλην	ὁ ποιμήν	ὁ ἀγών	ὁ ἡγεμών	ὁ δελφίς
Acc.	Ἕλληνα	ποιμένα	ἀγῶνα	ἡγεμόνα	δελφῖνα
Gen.	Ἕλληνος	ποιμένος	ἀγῶνος	ἡγεμόνος	δελφῖνος
Dat.	Ἕλληνι	ποιμένι	ἀγῶνι	ἡγεμόνι	δελφῖνι
Dual					
N.V.A.	Ἕλληνε	ποιμένε	ἀγῶνε	ἡγεμόνε	δελφῖνε
G.D.	Ἑλλήνοιν	ποιμένοιν	ἀγώνοιν	ἡγεμόνοιν	δελφίνοιν
Plur.					
N.V.	Ἕλληνες	ποιμένες	ἀγῶνες	ἡγεμόνες	δελφῖνες
Acc.	Ἕλληνας	ποιμένας	ἀγῶνας	ἡγεμόνας	δελφῖνας
Gen.	Ἑλλήνων	ποιμένων	ἀγώνων	ἡγεμόνων	δελφίνων
Dat.	Ἕλλησι(ν)	ποιμέσι(ν)	ἀγῶσι(ν)	ἡγεμόσι(ν)	δελφῖσι(ν)

EXAMPLES.

μήν (ην), ὁ, *month* ; λειμών (ων), ὁ, *meadow* ;   ῥίς (ῑν), ἡ, *nose* ;
φρήν (εν), ἡ, *mind* ; γείτων (ον), ὁ, ἡ, *neighbour* ; ἀκτίς (ῑν), ἡ, *ray.*

49.   (iii.)—*Stems in the spirants* s, F (elided).

In these stems the character is always dropped *between two vowels*, and, except in ἥρως, contraction takes place.

STEM. ENGLISH.	Δημοσθενες, *Demosthenes.*	τριηρες, *trireme.*	γενες, *family.*
Sing. *Nom.*	ὁ Δημοσθένης	ἡ τριήρης	τὸ γένος
Voc.	Δημόσθενες	[τριῆρες]	γένος
Acc.	Δημοσθένη (ε-α)	τριήρη (ε-α)	γένος
Gen.	Δημοσθένους (ε-ος)	τριήρους (ε-ος)	γένους (ε-ος)
Dat.	Δημοσθένει (ε-ϊ)	τριήρει (ε-ϊ)	γένει (ε-ϊ)
Du. *N.V.A.*		τριήρη (ε-ε)	γένη (ε-ε)
G.D.		τριηροῖν (ε-οιν)	γενοῖν (ε-οιν)
Plur. *N.V.*		τριήρεις (ε-ες)	γένη (ε-α)
Acc.		τριήρεις (ε-ας)	γένη (ε-α)
Gen.		τριήρων (ε-ων)	γενῶν (ε-ων)
Dat.		τριήρεσι(ν)	γένεσι(ν)

EXAMPLES.—Σωκράτης, ὁ, *Socrates* ; κράτος, τό, *strength.*

50. The final letter of the stem is uncertain in the following. It may have been *F* (digamma).

STEM. ENGLISH.	αἰδο-? shame.	πειθο-? persuasion.	ἡρω-? hero.
Sing. *Nom.*	ἡ αἰδώς	ἡ πειθώ	ὁ ἥρως
Voc.	αἰδοῖ	πειθοῖ	ἥρως
Acc.	αἰδῶ (o-a)	πειθώ (o-a)	ἥρωα, ἥρω
Gen.	αἰδοῦς (o-os)	πειθοῦς (o-os)	ἥρωος
Dat.	αἰδοῖ (o-ï)	πειθοῖ (o-ï)	ἥρωϊ, ἥρῳ
Dual *N.V.A.*	*none*	*none*	ἥρωε
Dat.			ἡρώοιν
Plur. *N.V.*			ἥρωες, ἥρως
Acc.	*none*	*none*	ἥρωας, ἥρως
Gen.			ἡρώων
Dat.			ἥρωσι(ν)

EXAMPLES.

ἠχώ (o), ἡ, *echo,* like πειθώ ; δμώς (ω), ὁ, *slave,* like ἥρως.

51. *Accentuation in Declension.*

(1.) The accent remains, so far as possible, on the syllable which is accentuated in the nom. case. Thus γένος, gen. γένους, χελιδών, gen. χελιδόνος.

(2.) The genitive and dative of monosyllabic nominatives are generally accented on the last syllable in all numbers, *e.g.* θήρ, gen. θηρός, θηρί, θηροῖν, θηρῶν, θηρσί. Short syllables are oxytone, long are perispomenon. So also γυνή, *woman.* παίδων from παῖς, and ὤτων from οὖς, are exceptions.

(3.) The syncopated genitive and dative singular of words like πατήρ are oxytone, and the vocative throws back the accent as far as possible, as θύγατερ, θυγατρός, θυγατρί. Whenever the ε is not omitted, the accent falls on it, except in vocative singular. The dative plural follows the rule (ρα being for ερ), as ἀνδράσι(ν). The accent of ἀνήρ is peculiar in four cases. ἄνδρα, ἄνδρες, ἄνδρας, ἀνδρῶν.

IRREGULAR FORMS.

52. (1.) υἱός, *son;* γυνή, *woman;* ναῦς, *ship,* are thus declined :—

STEM.	υιο,	υιεν,	γυναικ,	ναυ,
Sing. *Nom.*	ὁ υἱός		ἡ γυνή	ἡ ναῦς
Voc.	υἱέ		γύναι	ναῦ
Acc.	υἱόν		γυναῖκα	ναῦν
Gen.	υἱοῦ	υἱέος	γυναικός	νεώς
Dat.	υἱῷ	υἱεῖ (ε-ἵ)	γυναικί	νηΐ
Dual *N.V.A.*		υἱεῖ (ε-ε)	γυναῖκε	[νῆε]
G.D.		υἱέοιν	γυναικοῖν	νεοῖν
Plur. *N.V.*	υἱοί	υἱεῖς (ε-ες)	γυναῖκες	νῆες
Acc.	υἱούς	υἱεῖς (ε-ας)	γυναῖκας	ναῦς
Gen.	υἱῶν	υἱέων	γυναικῶν	νεῶν
Dat.	υἱοῖς	υἱέσι(ν)	γυναιξί(ν)	ναυσί(ν)

53. (2.) ἕως, ἡ, *morning,* is thus declined—Sing. *Nom. Voc.* ἕως, *Acc.* ἕω, *Gen.* ἕω, *Dat.* ἕῳ.

54. (3.) Ζεύς, *Zeus,* is thus declined—Sing. *Nom.* Ζεύς, *Voc.* Ζεῦ, *Acc.* Δία, *Gen.* Διός, *Dat.* Διΐ.

(4.) Some stems in -ον omit ν in declension; compare μείζων (**71**). ἀηδών, ἡ, *nightingale,* stem ἀηδον, *Voc.* ἀηδών or ἀηδοῖ, *Gen.* ἀηδόν-ος and ἀηδοῦς.

εἰκών, ἡ, *image,* stem εικον, Sing. *Acc.* εἰκόνα or εἰκώ, *Gen.* εἰκόνος or εἰκοῦς. Plur. *Acc.* εἰκόνας or εἰκούς.

For other irregularities in declension see Appendix II.

55. (5.) Stems in ρτ. These, *if neuter*, drop ρ in all cases but N. V. A. Sing., in which cases the *a* of the stem is sometimes lengthened into ω. **(173.)**

STEM. ENGLISH.	δαμαρτ, *wife.*	ὑδαρτ, *water.*	ἡπαρτ, *liver.*
Sing. *N.V.*	ἡ δάμαρ	τὸ ὕδωρ	τὸ ἧπαρ
Acc.	δάμαρτα	ὕδωρ	ἧπαρ
Gen.	δάμαρτος	ὕδᾰτος	ἥπᾰτος
Dat.	δάμαρτι	ὕδᾰτι	ἥπᾰτι
Dual *N.V.A.*	δάμαρτε	ὕδᾰτε	ἥπᾰτε
G.D.	δαμάρτοιν	ὑδάτοιν	ἡπάτοιν
Plur. *N.V.*	δάμαρτες	ὕδᾰτα	ἥπᾰτα
Acc.	δάμαρτας	ὕδᾰτα	ἥπᾰτα
Gen.	δαμάρτων	ὑδάτων	ἡπάτων
Dat.	δάμαρσι(ν)	ὕδᾰσι(ν)	ἥπᾰσι(ν)

56. Certain Particles of Place, some of them old case-endings, are found affixed to the Stems of Nouns. These are :—

-δε or -σε, denoting "motion towards" (an enclitic Particle, affixed also to the accus.), as—

οἴκαδε (or οἴκόνδε), *homewards;* ᾿Αθήναζε (for ᾿Αθήνασδε), *to Athens ;* ἄλλοσε, *elsewhither.*

-θεν, denoting "motion from," as οἴκοθεν, *from home;* ἄλλοθεν, *from another place.*

-θι, denoting "rest at" (an old Locative), as—

οἴκοθι, *at home;* ἄλλοθι, *elsewhere;* αὐτόθι, *there.*

Adjectives.

57. ADJECTIVES are declined like substantives according to number and case; but they are further declined according to gender. They may be classed as follows :—

A. *Adjectives of three terminations*, which distinguish all three genders.

B. *Adjectives of two terminations*, in which one form serves for masculine and feminine, the other for the neuter.

C. *Adjectives of one termination* which in the nominative have only one form for all genders.

> But in the acc. sing. the neuter has a separate form, as also in the nom., voc., and acc. plur., where it always ends in -*a*.

A. ADJECTIVES OF THREE TERMINATIONS.

58. I. Vowel Stems of Declensions II. and I.

(i.) *Stems in -o* (fem. in η for α), σοφός, σοφή, σοφόν, *wise.*

(ii.) *Stems in -o pure* (fem. in α pure), φίλιος, φιλία, φίλιον, *friendly.*

STEM.	MASC. σοφο	FEM. σοφα(η)	NEUT. σοφο	MASC. φιλιο	FEM. φιλια	NEUT. φιλιο
Sing. *Nom.*	σοφός	σοφή	σοφόν	φίλιος	φιλίᾱ	φίλιον
Voc.	σοφέ	σοφή	σοφόν	φίλιε	φιλίᾱ	φίλιον
Acc.	σοφόν	σοφήν	σοφόν	φίλιον	φιλίᾱν	φίλιον
Gen.	σοφοῦ	σοφῆς	σοφοῦ	φιλίου	φιλίᾱς	φιλίου
Dat.	σοφῷ	σοφῇ	σοφῷ	φιλίῳ	φιλίᾳ	φιλίῳ
Dual *N.V.A.*	σοφώ	σοφά	σοφώ	φιλίω	φιλίᾱ	φιλίω
G.D.	σοφοῖν	σοφαῖν	σοφοῖν	φιλίοιν	φιλίαιν	φιλίοιν
Plur. *N.V.*	σοφοί	σοφαί	σοφά	φίλιοι	φίλιαι	φίλια
Acc.	σοφούς	σοφάς	σοφά	φιλίους	φιλίας	φίλια
Gen.	σοφῶν	σοφῶν	σοφῶν	φιλίων	φιλίων	φιλίων
Dat.	σοφοῖς	σοφαῖς	σοφοῖς	φιλίοις	φιλίαις	φιλίοις

(iii.) *Stems in -o pure* (contracted) $\begin{cases}\text{χρύσεος, χρυσέα, χρύσεον,} \\ \text{χρυσοῦς, χρυσῆ, χρυσοῦν,}\end{cases}$ *golden.*

$\begin{cases}\text{ἀργύρεος, ἀργυρέα, ἀργύρεον,} \\ \text{ἀργυροῦς, ἀργυρᾶ, ἀργυροῦν,}\end{cases}$ *of silver.*

STEM.	MASC. χρυσεο	FEM. χρυσεα	NEUT. χρυσεο	MASC. ἀργυρεο	FEM. ἀργυρεα	NEUT. ἀργυρεο
Sing. N.V.	χρύσεος χρυσοῦς	χρυσέᾱ χρυσῆ	χρύσεον χρυσοῦν	ἀργύρεος ἀργυροῦς	ἀργυρέᾱ ἀργυρᾶ	ἀργύρεον ἀργυροῦν
Acc.	χρύσεον χρυσοῦν	χρυσέᾱν χρυσῆν	χρύσεον χρυσοῦν	ἀργύρεον ἀργυροῦν	ἀργυρέᾱν ἀργυρᾶν	ἀργύρεον ἀργυροῦν
Gen.	χρυσέου χρυσοῦ	χρυσέας χρυσῆς	χρυσέου χρυσοῦ	ἀργυρέου ἀργυροῦ	ἀργυρέᾱς ἀργυρᾶς	ἀργυρέου ἀργυροῦ
Dat.	χρυσέῳ χρυσῷ	χρυσέᾳ χρυσῇ	χρυσέῳ χρυσῷ	ἀργυρέῳ ἀργυρῷ	ἀργυρέᾳ ἀργυρᾷ	ἀργυρέῳ ἀργυρῷ
Dual N.V.A.	χρυσέω χρυσώ	χρυσέᾱ χρυσᾶ	χρυσέω χρυσώ	ἀργυρέω ἀργυρώ	ἀργυρέᾱ ἀργυρᾶ	ἀργυρέω ἀργυρώ
G.D.	χρυσέοιν χρυσοῖν	χρυσέαιν χρυσαῖν	χρυσέοιν χρυσοῖν	ἀργυρέοιν ἀργυροῖν	ἀργυρέαιν ἀργυραῖν	ἀργυρέοιν ἀργυροῖν
Plur. N.V.	χρύσεοι χρυσοῖ	χρύσεαι χρυσαῖ	χρύσεᾰ χρυσᾶ	ἀργύρεοι ἀργυροῖ	ἀργύρεαι ἀργυραῖ	ἀργύρεᾰ ἀργυρᾶ
Acc.	χρυσέους χρυσοῦς	χρυσέας χρυσᾶς	χρύσεᾰ χρυσᾶ	ἀργυρέους ἀργυροῦς	ἀργυρέας ἀργυρᾶς	ἀργύρεᾰ ἀργυρᾶ
Gen.	χρυσέων χρυσῶν	χρυσέων χρυσῶν	χρυσέων χρυσῶν	ἀργυρέων ἀργυρῶν	ἀργυρέων ἀργυρῶν	ἀργυρέων ἀργυρῶν
Dat.	χρυσέοις χρυσοῖς	χρυσέαις χρυσαῖς	χρυσέοις χρυσοῖς	ἀργυρέοις ἀργυροῖς	ἀργυρέαις ἀργυραῖς	ἀργυρέοις ἀργυροῖς

$\left.\begin{array}{l}\text{ἀπλόος, ἀπλόη, ἀπλόον} \\ \text{ἀπλοῦς, ἀπλῆ, ἀπλοῦν}\end{array}\right\}$ *simple,* contracts as χρυσοῦς.

59. II. Soft Vowel and Consonant Stems of Declensions III. & I.

(i.) *Stems in -υ,* ἡδύς, ἡδεῖα, ἡδύ, *sweet.*

STEM.	MASC. ἡδῠ	FEM. ἡδεια	NEUT. ἡδῠ
Sing. N.V.	ἡδύς	ἡδεῖα	ἡδύ
Acc.	ἡδύν	ἡδεῖαν	ἡδύ
Gen.	ἡδέος	ἡδείας	ἡδέος
Dat.	ἡδεῖ (ε-ϊ)	ἡδείᾳ	ἡδεῖ (ε-ϊ)
Dual N.V.A.	ἡδέε	ἡδείᾱ	ἡδέε
G.D.	ἡδέοιν	ἡδείαιν	ἡδέοιν
Plur. N.V.	ἡδεῖς (ε-ες)	ἡδεῖαι	ἡδέα
Acc.	ἡδεῖς (ε-ας)	ἡδείας	ἡδέα
Gen.	ἡδέων	ἡδειῶν	ἡδέων
Dat.	ἡδέσι(ν)	ἡδείαις	ἡδέσι(ν)

60. (ii.) *Stems in* -οτ (participles), λελυκώς, λελυκυῖα, λελυκός, *having loosed.*

(iii.) *Stems in* -αντ, πᾶς, πᾶσα, πᾶν, *all, every.*

STEM.	MASC. λελυκοτ	FEM. λελυκυια	NEUT. λελυκοτ	MASC. παντ	FEM. πασα	NEUT. παντ
Sing.						
N.V.	λελυκώς	λελυκυῖα	λελυκός	πᾶς	πᾶσα	πᾶν
Acc.	λελυκότα	λελυκυῖαν	λελυκός	πάντα	πᾶσαν	πᾶν
Gen.	λελυκότος	λελυκυίας	λελυκότος	παντός	πάσης	παντός
Dat.	λελυκότι	λελυκυίᾳ	λελυκότι	παντί	πάσῃ	παντί
Dual						
N.V.A.	λελυκότε	λελυκυίᾱ	λελυκότε	πάντε	πάσᾱ	πάντε
G.D.	λελυκότοιν	λελυκυίαιν	λελυκότοιν	πάντοιν	πάσαιν	πάντοιν
Plur.						
N.V.	λελυκότες	λελυκυῖαι	λελυκότα	πάντες	πᾶσαι	πάντα
Acc.	λελυκότας	λελυκυίας	λελυκότα	πάντας	πάσας	πάντα
Gen.	λελυκότων	λελυκυιῶν	λελυκότων	πάντων	πασῶν	πάντων
Dat.	λελυκόσι(ν)	λελυκυίαις	λελυκόσι(ν)	πᾶσι(ν)	πάσαις	πᾶσι(ν)

As λελυκώς are declined all participles in -ως (οτ), as πεπληγώς, *having struck.*

As πᾶς are declined all participles in -ας (αντ), as πατάξας, *having struck.*

61. (iv.) *Stems in* -εντ { λυθείς, λυθεῖσα, λυθέν, *having been loosed.* / χαρίεις, χαρίεσσα, χαρίεν, *pleasing.*

STEM.	MASC. λυθεντ	FEM. λυθεισα	NEUT. λυθεντ	MASC. χαριεντ	FEM. χαριεσσα	NEUT. χαριεντ
Sing.						
N.V.	λυθείς	λυθεῖσα	λυθέν	χαρίεις	χαρίεσσα	χαρίεν
Acc.	λυθέντα	λυθεῖσαν	λυθέν	χαρίεντα	χαρίεσσαν	χαρίεν
Gen.	λυθέντος	λυθείσης	λυθέντος	χαρίεντος	χαριέσσης	χαρίεντος
Dat.	λυθέντι	λυθείσῃ	λυθέντι	χαρίεντι	χαριέσσῃ	χαρίεντι
Dual						
N.V.A.	λυθέντε	λυθείσᾱ	λυθέντε	χαρίεντε	χαριέσσᾱ	χαρίεντε
G.D.	λυθέντοιν	λυθείσαιν	λυθέντοιν	χαριέντοιν	χαριέσσαιν	χαριέντοιν
Plur.						
N.V.	λυθέντες	λυθεῖσαι	λυθέντα	χαρίεντες	χαρίεσσαι	χαρίεντα
Acc.	λυθέντας	λυθείσας	λυθέντα	χαρίεντας	χαριέσσας	χαρίεντα
Gen.	λυθέντων	λυθεισῶν	λυθέντων	χαριέντων	χαριεσσῶν	χαριέντων
Dat.	λυθεῖσι(ν)	λυθείσαις	λυθεῖσι(ν)	χαρίεσι(ν)	χαριέσσαις	χαρίεσι(ν)

As λυθείς are declined all participles in -εις (εντ), as τιθείς, *placing.*

The declension of χαρίεις is peculiar. Observe the formation of the feminine, and of the dative plural.

62. (v.) *Stems in* -οντ, { ἑκών, ἑκοῦσα, ἑκόν, *willing.*
{ διδούς, διδοῦσα, διδόν, *giving.*

STEM.	MASC. ἑκοντ	FEM. ἑκουσα	NEUT. ἑκοντ	MASC. διδοντ	FEM. διδουσα	NEUT. διδοντ
Sing. N.V.	ἑκών	ἑκοῦσα	ἑκόν	διδούς	διδοῦσα	διδόν
Acc.	ἑκόντα	ἑκοῦσαν	ἑκόν	διδόντα	διδοῦσαν	διδόν
Gen.	ἑκόντος	ἑκούσης	ἑκόντος	διδόντος	διδούσης	διδόντος
Dat.	ἑκόντι	ἑκούσῃ	ἑκόντι	διδόντι	διδούσῃ	διδόντι
Dual N.V.A.	ἑκόντε	ἑκούσᾱ	ἑκόντε	διδόντε	διδούσᾱ	διδόντε
G.D.	ἑκόντοιν	ἑκούσαιν	ἑκόντοιν	διδόντοιν	διδούσαιν	διδόντοιν
Plur. N.V.	ἑκόντες	ἑκοῦσαι	ἑκόντα	διδόντες	διδοῦσαι	διδόντα
Acc.	ἑκόντας	ἑκούσας	ἑκόντα	διδόντας	διδούσας	διδόντα
Gen.	ἑκόντων	ἑκουσῶν	ἑκόντων	διδόντων	διδουσῶν	διδόντων
Dat.	ἑκοῦσι(ν)	ἑκούσαις	ἑκοῦσι(ν)	διδοῦσι(ν)	διδούσαις	διδοῦσι(ν)

As the adjective ἑκών are declined all participles in -ων (uncontracted), as λύων, *loosing.* As διδούς are declined all participles in -ους, as γνούς, *knowing.*

63. (vi.) *Stems in* -αοντ, -εοντ, -οοντ (contracted),
{ τιμῶν, τιμῶσα, τιμῶν, *honouring.*
{ φιλῶν, φιλοῦσα, φιλοῦν, *loving.*

STEM.	MASC. τιμαοντ	FEM. τιμαουσα	NEUT. τιμαοντ	MASC. φιλεοντ	FEM. φιλεουσα	NEUT. φιλεοντ
Sing. N.V.	τιμῶν	τιμῶσα	τιμῶν	φιλῶν	φιλοῦσα	φιλοῦν
Acc.	τιμῶντα	τιμῶσαν	τιμῶν κ.τ.λ	φιλοῦντα	φιλοῦσαν	φιλοῦν κ.τ.λ
Plur. Dat.	τιμῶσι(ν)	τιμώσαις	τιμῶσι(ν)	φιλοῦσι(ν)	φιλούσαις	φιλοῦσι(ν)

Stems in -οοντ, as δηλῶν, δηλοῦσα, δηλοῦν, *showing*, have the same contraction as those in -εοντ.

64. (vii.) *Stems in* -υντ, δεικνύς, δεικνῦσα, δεικνύν, *showing.*

STEM.	MASC. δεικνυντ	FEM. δεικνυσα	NEUT. δεικνυντ
Sing. N.V.	δεικνύς	δεικνῦσα	δεικνύν
Acc.	δεικνύντα	δεικνῦσαν	δεικνύν
Gen.	δεικνύντος	δεικνύσης	δεικνύντος
Dat.	δεικνύντι	δεικνύσῃ	δεικνύντι
Dual N.V.A.	δεικνύντε	δεικνύσᾱ	δεικνύντε
G.D.	δεικνύντοιν	δεικνύσαιν	δεικνύντοιν
Plur. N.V.	δεικνύντες	δεικνῦσαι	δεικνύντα
Acc.	δεικνύντας	δεικνύσας	δεικνύντα
Gen.	δεικνύντων	δεικνυσῶν	δεικνύντων
Dat.	δεικνῦσι(ν)	δεικνύσαις	δεικνῦσι(ν)

65.   (viii.) *Stems in -ν, τάλας, τάλαινα, τάλαν, wretched.*

STEM.	MASC. ταλᾰν	FEM. ταλαινα	NEUT. ταλᾰν
Sing. Nom.	τάλᾱς	τάλαινα	τάλαν
Voc.	τάλαν	τάλαινα	τάλαν
Acc.	τάλανα	τάλαιναν	τάλαν
Gen.	τάλανος	ταλαίνης	τάλανος
Dat.	τάλανι	ταλαίνῃ	τάλανι
Dual N.V.A.	τάλανε	ταλαίνᾱ	τάλανε
G.D.	ταλάνοιν	ταλαίναιν	ταλάνοιν
Plur. N.V.	τάλανες	τάλαιναι	τάλανα
Acc.	τάλανας	ταλαίνας	τάλανα
Gen.	ταλάνων	ταλαινῶν	ταλάνων
Dat.	τάλᾰσι(ν)	ταλαίναις	τάλᾰσι(ν)

EXAMPLE.—*μέλας, black.*

66.   The declension of *μέγας, great,* and *πολύς, much,* is irregular.

STEMS.	MASC. μεγα μεγᾰλο	FEM. μεγᾰλα(η)	NEUT. μεγα μεγᾰλο	MASC. πολυ πολλο	FEM. πολλα(η)	NEUT. πολυ πολλο
Sing. N.V.	μέγας	μεγάλη	μέγα	πολύς	πολλή	πολύ
Acc.	μέγαν	μεγάλην	μέγα	πολύν	πολλήν	πολύ
Gen.	μεγάλου	μεγάλης	μεγάλου	πολλοῦ	πολλῆς	πολλοῦ
Dat.	μεγάλῳ	μεγάλῃ	μεγάλῳ	πολλῷ	πολλῇ	πολλῷ
Dual N.V.A.	μεγάλω	μεγάλᾱ	μεγάλω	No Dual in use.		
G.D.	μεγάλοιν	μεγάλαιν	μεγάλοιν			
Plur. N.V.	μεγάλοι	μεγάλαι	μεγάλα	πολλοί	πολλαί	πολλά
Acc.	μεγάλους	μεγάλας	μεγάλα	πολλούς	πολλάς	πολλά
Gen.	μεγάλων	μεγάλων	μεγάλων	πολλῶν	πολλῶν	πολλῶν
Dat.	μεγάλοις	μεγάλαις	μεγάλοις	πολλοῖς	πολλαῖς	πολλοῖς

Accentuation of Adjectives.

67.   In adjectives the accent is preserved as far as possible on the same syllable in declension. In feminines the quantity of the final syllable must be carefully observed, *e.g.* φίλιος but φιλίᾱ, but we also have φίλιαι, κοῦφαι, because αι of the plural is short in accentuation. The fem. plur. of adjectives from stems in -υ, -τ, -ντ and -ν is always perispomenon, ἡδειῶν, τετυφυιῶν, etc.

B. ADJECTIVES OF TWO TERMINATIONS.

68. I. Vowel Stems of Declension II. :—

i. *Stems in* -o (simple), ἀθάνατος, ἀθάνατον, *deathless.*
ii. *Stems in* -o (contracted), εὔνους, εὔνουν, *well-minded.*
iii. *Stems in* -ω (Attic), ἵλεως, ἵλεων, *propitious.*

STEM.		ἀθανατο		εὔνοο		ἱλεω	
		M. F.	N.	M. F.	N.	M. F.	N.
Sing.	Nom.	ἀθάνατος	-ον	εὔνους	εὔνουν	ἵλεως	ἵλεων
	Voc.	ἀθάνατε	-ον	εὔνους	εὔνουν	ἵλεως	ἵλεων
	Acc.	ἀθάνατον		εὔνουν		ἵλεων	
	Gen.	ἀθανάτου		εὔνου		ἵλεω	
	Dat.	ἀθανάτῳ		εὔνῳ		ἵλεῳ	
Dual	N.V.A.	ἀθανάτω		εὔνω		ἵλεω	
	G.D.	ἀθανάτοιν		εὔνοιν		ἵλεῳν	
Plur.	N.V.	ἀθάνατοι	-α	εὔνοι	εὔνοα	ἵλεῳ	ἵλεα
	Acc.	ἀθανάτους	-α	εὔνους	εὔνοα	ἵλεως	ἵλεα
	Gen.	ἀθανάτων		εὔνων		ἵλεων	
	Dat.	ἀθανάτοις		εὔνοις		ἵλεῳς	

Obs. 1. All compound adjectives in -os, with very few exceptions, are of two terminations only, *e.g.* ὁ ἡ πάγκαλος, ὁ ἡ ἔνδοξος, etc. So also βόρβαρος, λάβρος, ἥμερος, ἥσυχος, though not compounds ; and some adjectives in -ιος.

Obs. 2. Compounds of νοῦς, πλοῦς, and ῥοῦς, and Attic forms like ἵλεως, are not contracted in nom. voc. and acc. plural neuter.

Obs. 3. πλέως, *full* (and its compounds) have a fem. πλέα.

69. II. Soft Vowel and Consonant Stems of Declension III. :—

iv. *Stems in* ι, φιλόπολις, φιλόπολι, *patriotic.*
v. *Stems in* υ, δίπηχυς δίπηχυ, *of two cubits.*

STEM.		φιλοπολι		διπηχυ	
		M. F.	N.	M. F.	N.
Sing.	N.V.	φιλόπολις	φιλόπολι	δίπηχυς	δίπηχυ
	Acc.	φιλόπολιν	φιλόπολι	δίπηχυν	δίπηχυ
	Gen.	φιλοπόλεως		διπήχεος	
	Dat.	φιλοπόλει(ε-ϊ)		διπήχει(ε-ϊ)	
Dual	N.V.A.	φιλοπόλει (ε-ε)		διπήχει (ε-ε)	
	G.D.	φιλοπολέοιν		διπήχεοιν	
Plur.	N.V.	φιλοπόλεις(ε-ες) φιλοπόλη(ε-α)		διπήχεις(ε-ες) διπήχη(ε-α)	
	Acc.	φιλοπόλεις(ε-ας) φιλοπόλη(ε-α)		διπήχεις(ε-ας) διπήχη(ε-α)	
	Gen.	φιλοπόλεων		διπήχεων	
	Dat.	φιλοπόλεσι(ν)		διπήχεσι(ν)	

Obs. 1. The stem ἴδρι, *knowing,* keeps ι throughout, and has no long vowel in gen. sing.

Obs. 2. The compounds of δάκρυ keep υ throughout.

70. vi. *Stems in* τ *and* δ, { ἄχαρις, ἄχαρι, *thankless.*
                                    εὔελπις, εὔελπι, *hopeful.*

vii. *Stems in* ρ, ἀπάτωρ, ἄπατορ, *fatherless.*

STEM.	ἀχαριτ	εὐελπιδ	ἀπατορ
	M. F. N.	M. F. N.	M. F. N.
Sing. *N.V.*	ἄχαρις ἄχαρι	εὔελπις εὔελπι	ἀπάτωρ ἄπατορ
Acc.	ἄχαριν ἄχαρι	εὐέλπιδα εὔελπι	ἀπάτορα ἄπατορ
Gen.	ἀχάριτος	εὐέλπιδος	ἀπάτορος
Dat.	ἀχάριτι	εὐέλπιδι	ἀπάτορι
Plur. *Dat.*	ἀχάρισι(ν)	εὐέλπισι(ν)	ἀπάτορσι(ν)

71. viii. *Stems in* -ν, { εὔφρων, εὔφρον, *kindly.*
                              μείζων, μεῖζον, *greater.*

Comparatives like μείζων may elide ν and contract in acc. sing. (masc. and fem.) and in nom. voc and acc. plural.

STEM.	εὐφρον		μειζον	
	M. F. N.		M. F.	N
Sing. *Nom.*	εὔφρων εὔφρον		} μείζων	μεῖζον
Voc.	εὔφρον			
Acc.	εὔφρονα εὔφρον		μείζονα, μείζω	μεῖζον
Gen.	εὔφρονος		μείζονος	
Dat.	εὔφρονι		μείζονι	
Dual *N.V.A.*	εὔφρονε		μείζονε	
G.D.	εὐφρόνοιν		μειζόνοιν	
Plur. *N.V.*	εὔφρονες εὔφρονα		μείζονες, μείζους μείζονα, μείζω	
Acc.	εὔφρονας εὔφρονα		μείζονας, μείζους μείζονα, μείζω	
Gen.	εὐφρόνων		μειζόνων	
Dat.	εὔφροσι(ν)		μείζοσι(ν)	

EXAMPLES.—εὐδαίμων, *fortunate;* θάσσων, *quicker;* μείων, *less.*

72. ix. *Stems in* s (elided), εὐγενής, εὐγενές, *well-born.*

STEM.	εὐγενες	
	M. F.	N.
Sing. *Nom.*	εὐγενής	εὐγενές
Voc.	εὐγενές	εὐγενές
Acc.	εὐγενῆ (ε-α)	εὐγενές
Gen.	εὐγενοῦς (ε-ος)	
Dat.	εὐγενεῖ (εἰ)	
Dual. *N.V.A.*	εὐγενῆ (ε-ε)	
G.D.	εὐγενοῖν (ε-οιν)	
Plur. *N.V.*	εὐγενεῖς (ε-ες) εὐγενῆ (ε-α)	
Acc.	εὐγενεῖς (ε-ας) εὐγενῆ (ε-α)	
Gen.	εὐγενῶν (ε-ων)	
Dat.	εὐγενέσι(ν)	

73.   C. Adjectives of One Termination.

A large number of Adjectives have only one ending in nom. sing. for all genders, because either their meaning or their form excludes a neuter.   In the acc. sing., however, the neuter, when used, has the same form as the nom., and in the nom. voc. acc. plural ends in -*a*.

i. Stems in Gutturals—
> ἧλιξ (ἡλικ) *of the same age*, like φύλαξ.
> ἅρπαξ (ἁρπαγ) *rapacious*, like μάστιξ.
> μῶνυξ (μωνυχ) *single-hoofed*, like ὄνυξ.

ii. Stems in Dentals—
> πένης (πενητ) *poor*.
> ἄπαις (ἀπαιδ) *childless*.

iii. Stems in Liquids—
> Compounds of χείρ, *hand*, as μακρόχειρ, *long-handed*.

Notes on Consonant Nouns.

74.   The variety in the forms of consonant nouns proceeds mainly from the collision of the consonant character with the sigma which is found in the termination of the nom. sing. (of masc. and fem. nouns) and in the dat. plural. The changes which take place are as follows :—

75.   I.—*Stems in Mutes.*

Before ς (in nom. sing. and dat. plur.)
Gutturals become κ and form ξ, as μάστιξ (κ-ς), μάστιξι(ν).
Labials become π and form ψ, as χάλυψ (π-ς), χάλυψι(ν).
Dentals (*a.*) A single dental is dropped without compensatory
> lengthening, as χάρις (τ-ς), χάρι-σι(ν).
> *Exc.* Monosyllables, as πού-ς (ποδ-ς), *foot*.
> (*b.*) ντ is dropped, but with a lengthening of the stem
> vowel, as γίγᾱ-ς (ντ-ς), πᾶ-ς (ντ-ς), ὀδού-ς (ντ-ς),
> χαρίει-ς (ντ-ς).
> *Exc.* dat. plur. χαρίε-σι.

Obs. 1. Most stems in -οντ reject ς in the nom. sing., and, as τ cannot stand at the end of a word (cp. **24**), form the nom. in -ων with a lengthened vowel, as λέων (οντ-ς), ἑκών (οντ-ς).

Obs. 2. Neuter nouns (dentals only) having no termination in nom. voc. acc. sing. either (1.) reject τ altogether, as σῶμα (σωματ), or (2.) change it into s, as κέρας (κερατ).

76.   II.—*Stems in Semivowels.*

Liquids.—λ is unchanged before s, as ἅλ-s, ἁλ-σί(ν).

       Stems in ρ reject s in the nom. sing., lengthening the vowel, as ῥήτωρ (ῥητορ-s) ; in the dat. plur. ρ stands unchanged ῥήτορ-σι(ν).

Nasals.— Stems in ν usually reject s in nom. sing., lengthening the vowel, as ποιμήν (εν-s).

       A few stems in ν drop ν in nom. sing., lengthening the vowel when short, as δελφίς (ῐν-s), κτείς (εν-s), εἷς (ἑν-s), τάλᾱς (αν-s).

       All stems in ν drop ν in dat. plur. without compensation, as ποιμέ-σι(ν), τάλᾰ-σι(ν), κτε-σί(ν).

Spirants.—Stems in s reject s, lengthening the vowel in the nom. sing., but not in the dat. plural, as τριή-ρης (εσ-s), but τριήρε-σι(ν).

Obs. In neuter nouns (stems in ρ, ν, s) the nom. voc. acc. sing. is the stem.

---

77. *Formation of the Vocative.*—The voc. sing. is the same as the nom., except in the following, where it approaches as nearly to the stem as the laws of sound permit :—

(1.) Substantive stems in οντ (nom. in ων) as λέων, voc. λέον.

(2.) Substantive stems in αντ (nom. in αs) as γίγας, voc. γίγαν.

(3.) Stems in ρ as ῥήτωρ, voc. ῥῆτορ.

(4.) Isolated forms as παῖς (παιδ), voc. παῖ; ἄναξ (ἀνακτ), voc. ἄνα; δαίμων (δαιμον), voc. δαῖμον; κύων (κυον), voc. κύον.

Irregular forms are :—Stems in ο (F?), as αἰδώς, voc. αἰδοῖ; and σωτήρ (σωτηρ), voc. σῶτερ.

---

78.   *Formation of Accusative Singular* (-a, -ν).

The acc. sing. ends in ν (for μ). This letter, like λ, μ, and ρ, was originally vowel or consonant. The *vowel* sound of μ or ν generally appears in Greek as a. So χάριτα or χάρι(τ)ν for χαριτμ. Cf. πάτερα for πατερμ, ἔπαθον for ἔπνθον, ἔπτα for σεπτμ, δέκα for δεκμ.

79. *Formation of Feminine of Adjectives of Third Declension.*

The usual termination for the feminine is -ια. Hence stems in -ν, as ἡδύς, have fem. in -εια, as ἡδε-ῖα (for ἡδεF-ια). Stems in -οτ (for -Fοτ) had in fem. -υς for -Fοτ, and thus λελυκυ-ῖα is for λελυκυσ-ια. So also πᾶσα for παντ-ια, etc.

80. A TABLE OF SUBSTANTIVES AND ADJECTIVES.

First Declension. A Stems.

CHARACTER.	NOM. TERM.	GENDER.	EXAMPLE.		FORMATION.
a stems,	ας, ης	M.	νεᾱνίας, ὁ,	young man	νεανια-ς
			κριτής, ὁ,	judge	κριτα(η)-ς
	α, τ	F.	χώρα, ἡ,	country	χωρα
			τιμή, ἡ,	honour	τιμα(η)
			μοῦσα, ἡ,	muse	μουσα

Second Declension. O Stems.

CHARACTER.	NOM. TERM.	GENDER.	EXAMPLE.		FORMATION.
o simple,	ος	M.F.	λόγος, ὁ,	speech	λογο-ς
	οι	N.	ζυγόν, τό,	yoke	ζυγο-ν
o contracted,	ους	M.F.	νοῦς, ὁ,	mind	νοο-ς
	ου	N.	ὀστοῦν, τό,	bone	ὀστεο-ν
ω Attic,	ως	M.F.	λεώς, ὁ,	people	λεω-ς
	ων	N.	ἀνώγεων, τό,	upper room	ἀνωγεω-ν

Third Declension. Soft Vowel and Consonant Stems.

A. SOFT VOWEL STEMS.					
CHARACTER.	NOM. TERM.	GENDER.	EXAMPLE.		FORMATION.
Soft Vowels,	ις, υς	M.F.	πόλις, ἡ,	city	πολι-ς
ι, υ,			σῦς, ὁ, ἡ,	pig	συ-ς
			πῆχυς, ὁ,	forearm	πηχυ-ς
	ι, υ	N.	σίναπι, τό,	mustard	σιναπι
			δάκρυ, τό,	tear	δακρυ
			ἄστυ, τό,	city	ἀστυ
Diphthongs,	ευς	M.	βασιλεύς, ὁ,	king	βασιλευ-ς
ευ, ου, αυ,	ους	M.F.	βοῦς, ὁ, ἡ,	ox, cow	βου-ς
	αυς	F.	γραῦς, ἡ,	old woman	γραυ-ς

Third Declension—(Continued).

B. CONSONANT STEMS.				
CHARACTER.	NOM. TERM.	GENDER.	EXAMPLE.	FORMATION.
I. *Mutes.* i. Gutturals, κ, γ, χ	ξ	M.F.	φύλαξ, ὁ, guard μάστιξ, ἡ, whip ὄνυξ, ὁ, nail	φυλᾰκ-s μαστῑγ-s ὀνυχ-s
ii. Dentals, τ, δ, θ	s	M.F.	ἔρως, ὁ, love λαμπάς, ἡ, torch κόρυς, ἡ, helmet χάρις, ἡ, favour	ἐρωτ-s λαμπαδ-s κορυθ-s χαριτ-s
	α, s, etc.	N.	σῶμα, τό, body κέρας, τό, horn	σωμα(τ) κερατ
ντ, κτ, etc.	s, ν, ξ, etc.	M.F.N.	γίγᾱς, ὁ, giant λέων, ὁ, lion ὀδούς, ὁ, tooth νύξ, ἡ, night γάλα, τό, milk	γιγαντ-s λεοντ(-s) ὀδοντ-s νυκτ-s γαλα(κτ)
iii. Labials, π, β, φ	ψ	M.F.	γύψ, ὁ, vulture χάλυψ, ὁ, iron κατῆλιψ, ἡ, ladder	γυπ-s χαλῠβ-s κατηλῐφ-s
II. *Semivowels.* i. Liquids, λ, ρ	λs ρ	M.F. M.F.N.	ἅλs, ὁ, salt θήρ, ὁ, wild beast ῥήτωρ, ὁ, rhetorician πατήρ, ὁ, father	ἁλ-s θηρ(-s) ῥητορ(-s) πατερ(-s)
ii. Nasals, ν	ν, s	M.F.	Ἕλλην, ὁ, Greek ποιμήν, ὁ, shepherd ἀγών, ὁ, contest ἡγεμών, ὁ, leader δελφίs, ὁ, dolphin	Ἑλλην(-s) ποιμεν(-s) ἀγων(-s) ἡγεμον(-s) δελφῑν-s
iii. Spirants, s, F	ης os ωs, ω	M.F. N. F. M.	Δημοσθένης, ὁ, Demosthenes τριήρης, ἡ, trireme γένος, τό, family αἰδώς, ἡ, shame πειθώ, ἡ, persuasion ἥρως, ὁ, hero	Δημοσθενεs-s τριηρεs-s γενεs αἰδοF-s πειθοF(-s) ἡρωF-s

81.   A.—*Adjectives of Three Terminations.*

I.—VOWEL STEMS OF DECLENSIONS II. AND I.

CHARACT.	MASC.	FEM.	NEUT.	ENGLISH.	FORMATION FROM STEM.	
O	σοφός	σοφή	σοφόν	wise	σοφο-s	σοφο-ν
O pure	φίλιος	φιλία	φίλιον	friendly	φιλιο-s	φιλιο-ν
O contr.	χρυσοῦς	χρυσῆ	χρυσοῦν	golden	χρυσεο-s	χρυσεο-ν
	ἀργυροῦς	ἀργυρᾶ	ἀργυροῦν	of silver	ἀργυρεο-s	ἀργυρεο-ν
	ἁπλοῦς	ἁπλῆ	ἁπλοῦν	simple	ἁπλοο-s	ἁπλοο-ν

II.—SOFT VOWEL AND CONSONANT STEMS OF DECLENSIONS III. AND I.

	MASC.	FEM.	NEUT.	ENGLISH.	FORMATION FROM STEM.	
(1.) Υ	ἡδύς	ἡδεῖα	ἡδύ	sweet	ἡδυ-s	ἡδυ
(2.) οΤ	λελυκώς	λελυκυῖα	λελυκός	having loosed	λελυκοτ-s	λελυκοτ
ανΤ	πᾶς	πᾶσα	πᾶν	all	παντ-s	παν(τ)
ενΤ	λυθείς	λυθεῖσα	λυθέν	loosed	λυθεντ-s	λυθεν(τ)
	χαρίεις	χαρίεσσα	χαρίεν	pleasing	χαριεντ-s	χαριεν(τ)
	ἑκών	ἑκοῦσα	ἑκόν	willing	ἑκον(-s)	ἑκον(τ)
	διδούς	διδοῦσα	διδόν	giving	διδοντ-s	διδον(τ)
ονΤ	τιμῶν	τιμῶσα	τιμῶν	honouring	τιμαοντ(-s)	τιμαον(τ)
	φιλῶν	φιλοῦσα	φιλοῦν	loving	φιλεοντ(-s)	φιλεον(τ)
	δηλῶν	δηλοῦσα	δηλοῦν	showing	δηλοοντ(-s)	δηλοον(τ)
υνΤ	δεικνύς	δεικνῦσα	δεικνύν	showing	δεικνυντ-s	δεικνυν(τ)
Ν	τάλας	τάλαινα	τάλαν	wretched	ταλαν-s	ταλαν

B.—*Adjectives of Two Terminations.*

I.—VOWEL STEMS OF DECLENSION II.

CHARACT.	MASC. FEM.	NEUT.	ENGLISH.	FORMATION FROM STEM.	
O simp.	ἀθάνατος	ἀθάνατον	deathless	ἀθανατο-s	ἀθανατο-ν
O contr.	εὔνους	εὔνουν	well disposed	εὐνοο-s	εὐνοο-ν
Ω Attic.	ἵλεως	ἵλεων	propitious	ἱλεω-s	ἱλεω-ν

II.—SOFT VOWEL AND CONSONANT STEMS OF DECLENSION III.

	MASC. FEM.	NEUT.	ENGLISH.	FORMATION FROM STEM.	
(1.) I	φιλόπολις	φιλόπολι	patriotic	φιλόπολι-s	φιλόπολι
Υ	δίπηχυς	δίπηχυ	of two cubits	διπηχυ-s	διπηχυ
(2.) Τ	ἄχαρις	ἄχαρι	thankless	ἀχαριτ-s	ἀχαρι(τ)
Δ	εὔελπις	εὔελπι	hopeful	εὐελπιδ-s	εὐελπι(δ)
Ρ	ἀπάτωρ	ἄπατορ	fatherless	ἀπατορ(-s)	ἀπατορ
Ν	εὔφρων	εὔφρον	kindly	εὐφρον(-s)	εὐφρον
	μείζων	μείζον	greater	μειζον(-s)	μειζον
Σ	εὐγενής	εὐγενές	well-born	εὐγενες(-s)	εὐγενες

Comparison of Adjectives.

THERE are two degrees of comparison—the Comparative and Superlative. These are formed in two ways.

First Formation.

82. *Principal Rule.*— -τερος for the comparative, and -τατος for the superlative, are added to the masculine stem. The adjective thus formed is declined with three terminations, -τερος, -τερα, -τερον ; -τατος, -τατη, -τατον.

N.B.—In o stems the character is lengthened into ω, if the preceding syllable is short.

	STEM.	COMPARATIVE.	SUPERLATIVE.
δεινός, *strange,*	δεινο,	δεινό-τερος	δεινό-τατος.
μέλας, *black,*	μελαν,	μελάν-τερος	μελάν-τατος.
λεπτός, *thin,*	λεπτο,	λεπτό-τερος	λεπτό-τατος.
ἀληθής, *true,*	ἀληθεσ,	ἀληθέσ-τερος	ἀληθέσ-τατος.
σοφός, *wise,*	σοφο,	σοφώ-τερος	σοφώ-τατος.
φρόνιμος, *prudent,*	φρονιμο,	φρονιμώ-τερος	φρονιμώ-τατος.
γλυκύς, *sweet,*	γλυκυ,	γλυκύ-τερος	γλυκύ-τατος.

(1.) Stems in -αιο sometimes drop the o, as—

   ἡσυχαῖος, *quiet,* ἡσυχαιο, ἡσυχαί-τερος, ἡσυχαί-τατος.

      But ἀρχαῖος, *ancient,* σπουδαῖος, *earnest,* βέβαιος, *firm,* δίκαιος, *just,* ἀναγκαῖος, *necessary,* follow the principal rule.

(2.) Some stems change o into αι—

     μέσος, *middle,* μεσο,   μεσαίτερος   μεσαίτατος
     ἴσος, *equal,* ἰσο,   ἰσαίτερος   ἰσαίτατος.
     εὔδιος, *calm,* εὐδιο,   εὐδιαίτερος   εὐδιαίτατος.

   φίλος, *friendly,* has two forms—

     o becomes αι,   φιλαίτερος   φιλαίτατος.
     o is dropt,   φίλ-τερος   φίλ-τατος.

(3.) Stems in -ον and some others strengthen -τερος, -τατος, into -εστερος, -εστατος. A final o is dropped.

εὐδαίμων, *fortunate,* εὐδαιμον, εὐδαιμον-έστερος εὐδαιμον-έστατος.
εὔνους, *kindly,* εὔνοο, εὐνούστερος εὐνούστατος.
ἀφῆλιξ, *aged,* ἀφηλικ, ἀφηλικ-έστερος ἀφηλικ-έστατος.
αἴδοιος, *revered,* αἰδοιο, αἰδοι-έστερος αἰδοι-έστατος.
ἄκρᾶτος, *unmixed,* ἄκρατο, ἀκρατ-έστερος ἀκρατ-έστατος.

(4.) A few add -ιστερος, -ιστατος, dropping the vowel—

λάλος, *talkative,* λαλο, λαλ-ίστερος λαλ-ίστατος.
κλέπτης, *thievish,* κλεπτα, [κλεπτ-ίστερος] κλεπτ-ίστατος.

Second Formation.

83. *Principal Rule.*—The final vowel of the stem is dropped, and -ῑων is added for the comparative, -ιστος for the superlative. The comparatives are declined as μείζων (cp. **71**), and the superlatives as σοφός (cp. **58**).

N.B.—Stems in -ρο lose -ρο.

	STEM.	COMPARATIVE.	SUPERLATIVE.
ἡδύς, *sweet,*	ἡδυ,	ἡδ-ίων	ἥδ-ιστος.
μέγας, *great,*	μεγα,	μείζων (for μεγ-ιων)	μέγ-ιστος.
ταχύς, *swift,*	ταχυ,	θάσσων (for ταχ-ιων)	τάχ-ιστος.
αἰσχρός, *shameful,*	αἰσχρο,	αἰσχ-ίων	αἴσχ-ιστος.
ἐχθρος, *hostile,*	ἐχθρο,	ἐχθίων	ἔχθιστος.

84.   *Irregular Comparison.*

ἀγαθός, *good,*	βελτίων	βέλτιστος
	ἀμείνων	ἄριστος
κακός, *bad,*	κακίων	κάκιστος
	χείρων	χείριστος
καλός, *beautiful,*	καλλίων	κάλλιστος
μικρός, *little,*	μικρότερος	μικρότατος
	μείων	
ὀλίγος, *little,*	ἥσσων	ὀλίγιστος
few,	ἐλάσσων	ἐλάχιστος
πολύς, *much,*	πλείων, πλέων	πλεῖστος
πέπων, *ripe,*	πεπαίτερος	πεπαίτατος
πίων, *fat,*	πιότερος	πιότατος
ῥᾴδιος, *easy,*	ῥᾴων	ῥᾷστος

Obs. These irregularities arise partly from changes made in the stem, and partly from the use of distinct words with a similar meaning.

Formation of Adverbs.

85. ADVERBS may be formed from adjectives by changing the last syllable of the genitive case singular into -ως, *e.g.*

φίλος, *friendly,*	gen. φίλου	adv. φίλως.
σώφρων, *sober,*	gen. σώφρονος	adv. σωφρόνως.
εὐμενής, *kindly,*	gen. εὐμενοῦς	adv. εὐμενῶς.
ταχύς, *swift,*	gen. ταχέος	adv. ταχέως.

Comparison of Adverbs.

86. FOR the comparative degree the neuter *singular* of the comparative adjective is taken, and for the superlative the neuter *plural* of the superlative adjective, *e.g.*—

σοφῶς, *wisely*	σοφώτερον	σοφώτατα
ταχέως, *swiftly*	θᾶσσον	τάχιστα

Similarly

ἄγχι, *near*	ἆσσον	ἄγχιστα
μάλα, *much*	μᾶλλον	μάλιστα
εὖ, *well*	ἄμεινον	ἄριστα

Obs. 1. Sometimes the comparative and superlative have the termination -ως.

Obs. 2. Adverbs ending in -ω preserve ω in the comparative and superlative, *e.g.* ἄνω, *up,* ἀνωτέρω, ἀνωτάτω.

87. Numerals.

		CARDINALS.	ORDINALS.	ADVERBS.
1	αʹ	εἶς, μία, ἕν, one	πρῶτος, -η, -ον, first	ἅπαξ, once
2	βʹ	δύο, two	δεύτερος, second	δίς, twice
3	γʹ	τρεῖς, τρία	τρίτος	τρίς
4	δʹ	τέσσαρες, τέσσᾰρα, or τέτταρες -α	τέταρτος	τετράκις
5	εʹ	πέντε	πέμπτος	πεντάκις
6	ςʹ	ἕξ	ἕκτος	ἑξάκις
7	ζʹ	ἑπτά	ἕβδομος	ἑπτάκις
8	ηʹ	ὀκτώ	ὄγδοος	ὀκτάκις
9	θʹ	ἐννέα	ἔνατος (ἔννατος)	ἐνάκις, ἐννάκις
10	ιʹ	δέκα	δέκατος	δεκάκις
11	ιαʹ	ἕνδεκα	ἑνδέκατος	ἑνδεκάκις
12	ιβʹ	δώδεκα	δωδέκατος	δωδεκάκις
13	ιγʹ	τρεῖς (τρία) καὶ δέκα	τρισκαιδέκατος	τρισκαιδεκάκις
14	ιδʹ	τέσσαρες καὶ δέκα τεσσαρακαίδεκα	τεσσαρακαιδέκατος	τεσσαρακαιδεκά·κις
15	ιεʹ	πεντεκαίδεκα	πεντεκαιδέκατος	πεντεκαιδεκάκις
16	ιςʹ	ἑκκαίδεκα	ἑκκαιδέκατος	ἑκκαιδεκάκις
17	ιζʹ	ἑπτακαίδεκα	ἑπτακαιδέκατος	ἑπτακαιδεκάκις
18	ιηʹ	ὀκτωκαίδεκα	ὀκτωκαιδέκατος	ὀκτωκαιδεκάκις
19	ιθʹ	ἐννεακαίδεκα	ἐννεακαιδέκατος	ἐννεακαιδεκάκις
20	κʹ	εἴκοσι(ν)	εἰκοστός	εἰκοσάκις
30	λ	τριάκοιτα	τριᾱκοστός	τριᾱκοντάκις
40	μʹ	τεσσαρᾰκοντα	τεσσαρᾱκοστός	τεσσαρᾰκοντάκις
50	νʹ	πεντήκοντα	πεντηκοστός	πεντηκοντάκις
60	ξʹ	ἑξήκοντα	ἑξηκοστός	ἑξηκοντάκις
70	ό	ἑβδομήκοντα	ἑβδομηκοστός	ἑβδομηκοντάκις
80	πʹ	ὀγδοήκοντα	ὀγδοηκοστός	ὀγδοηκοντάκις
90	φ	ἐνενήκοντα	ἐνενηκοστός	ἐνενηκοντάκις
100	ρʹ	ἑκατόν	ἑκατοστός	ἑκατοντάκις
200	σʹ	διᾱκόσιοι, αι, α	διακοσιοστός	διακοσιάκις
300	τ	τριᾱκόσιοι, αι, α	τριακοσιοστός	τριακοσιάκις
400	υ	τετρᾰκόσιοι, αι α	τετρακοσιοστός	τετρακοσιάκις
500	φʹ	πεντᾰκόσιοι, αι, α	πεντακοσιοστός	πεντακοσιάκις
600	χʹ	ἑξᾰκόσιοι, αι, α	ἑξακοσιοστός	ἑξακοσιάκις
700	ψʹ	ἑπτᾰκόσιοι, αι, α	ἑπτακοσιοστός	ἑπτακοσιάκις
800	ώ	ὀκτᾰκόσιοι, αι, α	ὀκτακοσιοστός	ὀκτακοσιάκις
900	⊅	ἐνᾰκόσιοι, αι, α	ἐνακοσιοστός	ἐνακοσιάκις
1,000	͵α	χῐλιοι, αι, α	χιλιοστός	χιλιάκις
2,000	͵β	δισχῐλιοι, αι, α	δισχιλιοστός	δισχιλιάκις
10,000	͵ι	μῠριοι, αῖ, α	μυριοστός	μυριάκις

Cardinals from 5 to 199 are indeclinable, except where, in compound numbers, εἶς, δύο, τρεῖς, τέσσαρες, occur as distinct words.

88. *Declension of* εἷς, *one;* δύο, *two;* τρεῖς, *three.*

STEM.	M. ἑν	F. μια	N. ἑν	M. F. N. δυο	M. F. N. τρι
N.V.	εἷς	μίᾰ	ἕν	δύο	τρεῖς τρία
Acc.	ἕνα	μίαν	ἕν	δύο	τρεῖς τρία
Gen.	ἑνός	μιᾶς	ἑνός	δυοῖν	τριῶν
Dat.	ἑνί	μιᾷ	ἑνί	δυοῖν	τρισί(ν)

τέσσᾰρες, *four,* stem τεσσαρ, *Nom.* τέσσαρες τέσσαρα, *Acc.* τέσσαρας τέσσαρα, *Gen.* τεσσάρων, *Dat.* τεσσαρσί(ν).

Obs. Like εἷς are its compounds οὐδείς, οὐδεμία, οὐδέν, and μηδείς, μηδεμία, μηδέν, *no one.* ἄμφω, *both,* has gen. and dat. ἀμφοῖν.

89. *Compound Numbers.*

The parts may be arranged in three ways :—

(1.) The larger number precedes the smaller *with* καί, εἴκοσι καὶ δύο (20 and 2).

(2.) The smaller number precedes the larger *with* καί, δύο καὶ εἴκοσι (2 and 20).

(3.) The larger number precedes the smaller *without* καί, εἴκοσι δύο (22).

In compound ordinals the ordinal is generally used in each part—εἰκοστὸς τρίτος (*twenty-third*).

To express compounds with eight and nine the next decimal is often taken, and two or one subtracted from it, *e.g.* ' 18 *ships*'=νῆες εἴκοσι δυοῖν δέουσαι (20 *ships wanting* 2).

Multiples end in -πλους, ἁπλοῦς, *single,* διπλοῦς, *double,* τριπλοῦς, *triple,* etc. 'Half' is ἥμισυς, -εια, -υ. To express a half after a whole number the Greeks used compound substantives with ἡμι-, *e.g.* τρίτον ἡμι-τάλαντον, 2½ *talents,* literally, *the third o half talent.*

Pronouns.

90. MOST Pronouns not only stand instead of Nouns, but also represent or refer to one of the three Persons, namely :—

First Person.—The speaker, *I.*

Second Person.—The person to whom I speak, *You.*

Third Person.—The person of whom we speak, *He.*

Personal, Reflexive, and Reciprocal Pronouns are purely Substantival. All the rest *can* be used as Adjectives.

91. I.—*Personal Pronouns.*

		First Person, *I.*	Second Person, *Thou.*	Third Person, *Himself,* etc.
Sing.	*Nom.*	St. ἐμε* ἐγώ	St. σε σύ (also Voc.)	St. ἑ —
	Acc.	ἐμέ, με	σέ	[ἕ]
	Gen.	ἐμοῦ, μου	σοῦ	[οὗ]
	Dat.	ἐμοί, μοι	σοί	οἷ
Dual	*N.V.A.*	St. νω νώ	St. σφω σφώ	
	G.D.	νῷν	σφῷν	
Plur.	*Nom.*	St. ἡμε ἡμεῖς	St. ὑμε ὑμεῖς (also Voc.)	St. σφε σφεῖς
	Acc.	ἡμᾶς	ὑμᾶς	σφᾶς
	Gen.	ἡμῶν	ὑμῶν	σφῶν
	Dat.	ἡμῖν	ὑμῖν	σφίσι(ν)

Obs. 1. The forms με, μου, μοι, are always enclitic; sometimes also in the Second Person σέ, σοῦ, σοί, and in the Third Person ἑ, οὗ, οἷ, σφίσι(ν) are enclitic, and accentuated accordingly. (29.)

Obs. 2. The Pronoun ἑ, originally a Personal Pronoun of the Third Person, is, in Attic Greek, compounded with αὐτόν, and used as a Reflexive. As a rule, there is no Personal Pronoun of the Third Person in Greek. The nominative is borrowed from the Demonstratives, and the oblique cases, *him, her, them,* etc., are generally taken from the Definitive αὐτός. In a few phrases ὁ, ἡ, τό, is used.

* The Nom. of the First Person requires a different stem from the oblique cases.

92. II.— *Possessive Pronouns* are formed from the stems of the Personal. They are declined as Adjectives in -os, -η, -ον, but only ἐμός and ἡμέτερος have vocatives.

First Person, ἐμός, ἐμή, ἐμόν, *my, mine;* ἡμέτερος, -α, -ον, *our.*
Second Person, σός, σή, σόν, *thy, thine;* ὑμέτερος, -α, -ον, *your.*
Third Person, [ὅς, ἥ, ὅν, *his own;* σφέτερος, α, ον, *their own*].

Obs. In Attic Greek the Genitives of ἑαυτόν take the place of Reflexive Adjectives like the Latin *suus*, while the Genitives of αὐτός correspond to the Possessive Genitives *ejus, eorum*, etc.

93. III.—*Definitive Pronouns.*

αὐτός, *self;* ὁ αὐτός, *the same.*

In ὁ αὐτός crasis takes place wherever two vowels clash.

STEM.	MASC. αὐτο	FEM. αὐτα	NEUT. αὐτο	MASC.	FEM.	NEUT.
Sing.						
Nom.	αὐτός	αὐτή	αὐτό	{ ὁ αὐτός / αὐτός	{ ἡ αὐτή / αὐτή	{ τὸ αὐτό / ταὐτό or / ταὐτόν
Acc.	αὐτόν	αὐτήν	αὐτό	τὸν αὐτόν	τὴν αὐτήν	„
Gen.	αὐτοῦ	αὐτῆς	αὐτοῦ	{ τοῦ αὐτοῦ / ταὐτοῦ	τῆς αὐτῆς	{ τοῦ αὐτοῦ / ταὐτοῦ
Dat.	αὐτῷ	αὐτῇ	αὐτῷ	{ τῷ αὐτῷ / ταὐτῷ	{ τῇ αὐτῇ / ταὐτῇ	{ τῷ αὐτῷ / ταὐτῷ
Dual						
N.A.	αὐτώ	} all genders.		{ τώ αὐτώ / ταὐτώ / τοῖν αὐτοῖν	} all genders.	
G.D.	αὐτοῖν					
Plur.						
Nom.	αὐτοί	αὐταί	αὐτά	{ οἱ αὐτοί / αὐτοί	{ αἱ αὐταί / αὐταί	{ τὰ αὐτά / ταὐτά
Acc.	αὐτούς	αὐτάς	αὐτά	τοὺς αὐτούς	τὰς αὐτάς	„
Gen.	αὐτῶν	αὐτῶν	αὐτῶν	τῶν αὐτῶν	τῶν αὐτῶν	τῶν αὐτῶν
Dat.	αὐτοῖς	αὐταῖς	αὐτοῖς	τοῖς αὐτοῖς	ταῖς αὐταῖς	τοῖς αὐτοῖς

Obs. The oblique cases of αὐτός, when used as substantives, are Pronouns of the Third Person, as ἔπεμψαν αὐτόν, *they sent him* (*miserunt eum*). The nominatives always keep the meaning of *self*, as αὐτὸς ἐποίησα, *I did it myself* (*ipse feci*).

94. IV.—*Reflexive Pronouns* are formed from the stems of the Personal Pronouns with the addition of the Definitive αὐτός, -ή, -ό, (cp. *me ipsum*).

	FIRST PERSON. *Myself.*	SECOND PERSON. *Thyself.*	THIRD PERSON. *Himself, Herself, etc.*
Sing.	Masc. Fem.	Masc. Fem.	Masc. Fem. Neut.
Acc.	ἐμαυτόν -ήν	σεαυτόν -ήν σαυτόν -ήν	ἑαυτόν -ήν -ό αὐτόν -ήν -ό
Gen.	ἐμαυτοῦ -ῆς	σεαυτοῦ -ῆς σαυτοῦ -ῆς	ἑαυτοῦ -ῆς -οῦ αὐτοῦ -ῆς -οῦ
Dat.	ἐμαυτῷ -ῇ	σεαυτῷ -ῇ σαυτῷ -ῇ	ἑαυτῷ -ῇ -ῷ αὐτῷ -ῇ -ῷ
Plur.			
Acc.	ἡμᾶς αὐτούς, -άς	ὑμᾶς αὐτούς, -άς	σφᾶς αὐτούς -άς
Gen.	ἡμῶν αὐτῶν	ὑμῶν αὐτῶν	σφῶν αὐτῶν
Dat.	ἡμῖν αὐτοῖς, -αῖς	ὑμῖν αὐτοῖς, -αῖς	σφίσιν αὐτοῖς -αῖς

The third person has more usually the compound plural :—

Acc. { ἑαυτούς, -άς, -ά.
 αὐτούς, -άς, -ά. *Gen.* { ἑαυτῶν.
 αὐτῶν. *Dat.* { ἑαυτοῖς, -αῖς, -οῖς.
 αὐτοῖς, -αῖς, -οῖς.

95. V.—*Demonstrative Pronouns* are—

ὅδε, ἥδε, τόδε
 οὗτος, αὕτη, τοῦτο, } *this* (near me).
 ἐκεῖνος, -η, -ο, *that* (yonder).

STEM.	MASC. τοδε*	FEM. ταδε	NEUT. τοδε	MASC. τουτο*	FEM. ταυτα	NEUT. τουτο
Sing. *Nom.*	ὅδε	ἥδε	τόδε	οὗτος	αὕτη	τοῦτο
Acc.	τόνδε	τήνδε	τόδε	τοῦτον	ταύτην	τοῦτο
Gen.	τοῦδε	τῆσδε	τοῦδε	τούτου	ταύτης	τούτου
Dat.	τῷδε	τῇδε	τῷδε	τούτῳ	ταύτῃ	τούτῳ
Dual *N.A.*	τώδε } all genders.			τούτω } all genders.		
G.D.	τοῖνδε			τούτοιν		
Plur. *Nom.*	οἵδε	αἵδε	τάδε	οὗτοι	αὗται	ταῦτα
Acc.	τούσδε	τάσδε	τάδε	τούτους	ταύτας	ταῦτα
Gen.	τῶνδε	τῶνδε	τῶνδε	τούτων	τούτων	τούτων
Dat.	τοῖσδε	ταῖσδε	τοῖσδε	τούτοις	ταύταις	τούτοις

ἐκεῖνος, -η, -ο, is declined as the definitive.

τοσοῦτος, τοσαύτη, τοσοῦτο, or τοσοῦτον, *so great,*
 τοιοῦτος, τοιαύτη, τοιοῦτο, or τοιοῦτον, *such,* } are declined as οὗτος, omitting the initial τ.

* The nom. sing. and plur., masc. and fem., like the Article, has a different stem from the neut. and oblique cases.

96.   VI.—*Interrogative Pronoun*—τίς, *who?*

      VII.—*Indefinite Pronoun*—τις, *any* (enclitic).

    (6.) INTERROGATIVE.   (7.) INDEFINITE.

STEM.	M. F. τιν	N. τιν	M. F. τιν	N. τιν
Sing. Nom.	τίς	τί	τις	τι
Acc.	τίνα	τί	τινά	τι
Gen.	τίνος or τοῦ		τινός or του	
Dat.	τίνι or τῷ		τινί or τῳ	
Dual N.A.	τίνε		τινέ	
G.D.	τίνοιν		τινοῖν	
Plur. Nom.	τίνες	τίνα	τινές	τινά or ἄττα
Acc.	τίνας	τίνα	τινάς	τινά or ἄττα
Gen.	τίνων		τινῶν	
Dat.	τίσι(ν)		τισί(ν)	

97.   VIII.—*Relative Pronouns*—ὅς, ἥ, ὅ, *who, which.*

        ὅστις, ἥτις, ὅτι, *whoever, whatever ; or who, which.*

STEM.	M. ὁ	F. ἁ	N. ὁ	MASC. FEM. NEUT. Stems of ὅς and τις combined.			M. N.
S. Nom.	ὅς	ἥ	ὅ	ὅστις	ἥτις	ὅτι	
Acc.	ὅν	ἥν	ὅ	ὅντινα	ἥντινα	ὅτι	
Gen.	οὗ	ἧς	οὗ	[οὗτινος]	ἧστινος	[οὗτινος] or	ὅτου
Dat.	ᾧ	ᾗ	ᾧ	[ᾧτινι]	ᾗτινι	[ᾧτινι] or	ὅτῳ
D. N.A.	ὥ } all			ὥτινε		all genders	
G.D.	οἷν } genders			[οἷντινοιν]			
P. Nom.	οἵ	αἵ	ἅ	οἵτινες	αἵτινες	ἅτινα or ἅττα	
Acc.	οὕς	ἅς	ἅ	οὕστινας	ἅστινας	ἅτινα or ἅττα	
Gen.	ὧν	ὧν	ὧν	[ὧντινων]	ὧντινων	[ὧντινων] or	ὅτων
Dat.	οἷς	αἷς	οἷς	[οἷστισι(ν)]	αἷστισι(ν)	[οἷστισι(ν)] or	ὅτοις

ὅστις is a General or Indefinite Relative, and is also used as an Indirect Interrogative.

98. IX. *The Reciprocal Pronoun*—ἀλλήλω, -α, -ω, *each other*.
The stem ἀλληλο (for ἀλλ-αλλο) results from the doubling of the
stem of ἄλλος, -η, -ο, *other* (Lat. *alius*). It can have no singular.

STEM.	MASC. ἀλληλο	FEM. ἀλληλα	NEUT. ἀλληλο
Dual			
Acc.	ἀλλήλω	ἀλλήλα	ἀλλήλω
G.D.	ἀλλήλοιν	ἀλλήλαιν	ἀλλήλοιν
Plur.			
Acc.	ἀλλήλους	ἀλλήλας	ἀλλήλα
Gen.	ἀλλήλων	ἀλλήλων	ἀλλήλων
Dat.	ἀλλήλοις	ἀλλήλαις	ἀλλήλοις

99. *Pronominal Correlatives.*

INTERROGATIVE. DIRECT.	INDIRECT.	INDEFINITE.	DEMONSTRATIVE.	RELATIVE.
τίς ; quis ? who ?	ὅστις quis who	τις quis any, some	ὅδε hic this	ὅς, ὅστις qui who
πότερος ; uter ? which of two ?	ὁπότερος uter which of two	ποτερός alteruter one of two	ἅτερος (ὁ ἕτερος) alter the one of two	
ποῖος ; qualis ? of what sort ?	ὁποῖος qualis of what sort	ποιός qualis of some sort	τοιόσδε τοιοῦτος talis of that sort	οἷος qualis of which sort, as
πόσος ; quantus ? how large ?	ὁπόσος quantus how large	ποσός aliquantus of any size	τοσόσδε τοσοῦτος tantus, tot. of that size	ὅσος quantus of which size, as

Adverbial Correlatives

που ; ubi ? where ?	ὅπου ubi where	που alicubi anywhere	ἐκεῖ, ibi, there,	ἐνθάδε hic here	οὗ ubi where
ποῖ ; quo ? whither ?	ὅποι quo whither	ποι aliquo to any place	ἐκεῖσε, eo, thither,	δεῦρο huc hither	οἷ quo whither
πόθεν ; unde ? whence ?	ὁπόθεν unde whence	ποθέν alicunde from any place	ἐκεῖθεν, inde, thence,	ἐνθένδε hinc hence	ὅθεν unde whence

100.   *A Table of Greek and Latin Pronouns.*

PERSONAL.

1st Pers.	{ ἐγώ	ego	*I*
	{ ἡμεῖς	nos	*we*
2d Pers.	{ σύ	tu	*thou*
	{ ὑμεῖς	vos	*you*
3d Pers.	(supplied by Demonstratives)		{ *he, she* / *they*

POSSESSIVE.

1st Pers.	{ ἐμός, -ή, -όν	meus, -a, -um	*my, mine*
	{ ἡμέτερος, -α, -ον	noster, -tra, -trum	*our*
2d Pers.	{ σός, -ή, -όν	tuus, -a, -um	*thy, thine*
	{ ὑμέτερος, -α, -ον	vester, -tra, -trum	*your*
3d Pers.	(use gen. of reflexive)	suus, -a, -um	{ *his, her own,* / *their own*

DEFINITIVE.

All Pers.	αὐτός, -ή, -ό	ipse, -a, -um	*self*
	{ ὁ αὐτός, etc.	idem, etc.	*the same*
	{ αὐτός, etc.		

REFLEXIVE.

1st Pers.	ἐμαυτόν, -ήν	me ipsum, -am	*myself*
2d Pers.	{ σεαυτόν, -ήν	te ipsum, -am	*yourself*
	{ σαυτόν, -ήν		
3d Pers.	{ ἑαυτόν, -ήν, -ό		
	{ αὐτόν, -ήν, -ό	se	*himself,* etc.
	(ἕ)		

DEMONSTRATIVE.

	(oblique cases, αὐτός)	is, ea, id	*that*
	{ ὅδε, ἥδε, τόδε	hic, hæc, hoc	*this (near me)*
	{ οὗτος, αὕτη, τοῦτο		
	οὗτος, αὕτη, τοῦτο	iste, ista, istud	*that (near you)*
	ἐκεῖνος, -η, -ο	ille, illa, illud	*that (yonder)*

INTERROGATIVE. τίς; τί ;   quis, quis, quid   *who ? what ?*

INDEFINITE.   τις, τι   quis, qua, quid   *any*

RELATIVE   ὅς, ἥ, ὅ   qui, quae, quod   *who, which*

	{ qui, quae, quod	*who, which*
ὅστις, ἥτις, ὅτι	{ quicunque, etc.	*whoever,* etc.

RECIPROCAL.   ἀλλήλω, -α. ω   (none)   *each other*

Prepositions.

101. Prepositions are used with one, two, or three cases.

I. Prepositions with *one* case only :—

    (*a.*) With Acc., ἀνά, *up;* εἰς, *into;* ὡς, *to* (of persons).

    (*b.*) With Gen., ἀντί, *in place of;* ἀπό, *from;* ἐκ (or ἐξ), *out of;* πρό, *before.*

        Also ἄνευ, ἄτερ, *without;* ἄχρι, μέχρι, *until;* μεταξύ, *between;* ἕνεκα, *on account of;* πλήν, *except.*

    (*c.*) With Dat., ἐν, *in;* σύν, *with.*

II. Prepositions with *two* cases :—

	With Acc.	With Gen.
διά,	*on account of,*	*through.*
κατά,	*down* (along), *according to,*	*down* (upon or *from*).
ὑπέρ,	*beyond,*	*above, on behalf of.*

III. Prepositions with *three* cases :—

	With Acc.	With Gen.	With Dat.
ἀμφί,	*about,*	*about, concerning* (poetic),	*at, near* (poetic).
ἐπί,	*against, to,*	*on, during,*	*on condition of.*
μετά,	*after,*	*with,*	*among* (poetic).
παρά,	*to the side of, alongside of,*	*from the side of,*	*at the side of.*
περί,	*about* (place or time),	*about* (= *concerning*),	*about* (poetic).
πρός,	*towards,*	*from, on the side of, by* (Agent. Poetic).	*at the face of, in addition to.*
ὑπό,	*under, near,*	*by* (Agent.)	*under.*

Prepositions are cases of Nouns which have been preserved in peculiar uses. The original termination of a great part of them seems to have been ι, which is the sign of the Locative case. In the first instance they were attached to Verbs as Adverbs, and afterwards became used with Nouns.

The Verb.

102. In the Greek Verb there are—

(i.) Three Persons—First, Second, and Third.

(ii.) Three Numbers—Singular, Dual, and Plural.

(iii.) Six Tenses—Three Primary and three Historic.

Primary—Present, Future, and Perfect.
Historic—Imperfect, Aorist, and Pluperfect.

A Future Perfect (Primary) also occurs in some verbs.

(iv.) Three Moods of the Verb Finite—Indicative, Imperative, and Conjunctive (Primary and Historic).

(v.) Three Verb-Nouns of the Verb Infinite—Infinitive (Substantive), Participle and Verbal Adjective (Adjectives).

(vi.) Three Voices—Active, Middle, and Passive.

There are Two Conjugations, named according to the ending of the First Person Singular Present Indicative.

(1.) Verbs in -ω.   (2.) Verbs in -μι.

The Verb-stem is the shortest form in which the stem syllable is found in the Verb.

The Tense-stem consists of the Verb-stem with the addition of certain fixed characteristics of Tense and Mood.

Conjugation.—Of these Conjugations the Verbs in -ω are the more numerous, while the Verbs in -μι are the more ancient (in form), and for the most part express the simplest notions, such as—*being, saying, going, giving, sending.*

103. I. II.—*Persons and Numbers.*

The following Table shows the distinctions of Person and Number in different Tenses.

N.B.—The square brackets contain original forms which no longer exist in this shape.

	ACTIVE.		MIDDLE AND PASSIVE.	
	PRIMARY.	HISTORIC.	PRIMARY.	HISTORIC.
Sing. 1.	$(-\mu\iota)$	$[-\mu]$	$-\mu\alpha\iota$	$-\mu\eta\nu$
2.	$(-\sigma\iota)$	-s	$-\sigma\alpha\iota$	$-\sigma o$
3.	$(\tau\iota)$	$[-\tau]$	$-\tau\alpha\iota$	$-\tau o$
Dual 2.	$-\tau o\nu$		$(-\sigma)\theta o\nu$	
3.	$-\tau o\nu$	$-\tau\eta\nu$	$-(\sigma)\theta o\nu$	$(-\sigma)\theta\eta\nu$
Plur. 1.	$-\mu\epsilon\nu$		$-\mu\epsilon\theta\alpha$	
2.	$-\tau\epsilon$		$-(\sigma)\theta\epsilon$	
3.	$[-\nu\tau\iota]$	$[-\nu\tau]$	$-\nu\tau\alpha\iota$	$-\nu\tau o$

Compare with this table the Paradigms on pp. 66-71, which also illustrate the following notes.

104. *Persons.*—The Active Forms may be seen most clearly in the Present Tense of the verb εἰμί, *I am* (cp. **159**). The Passive Forms may be seen unaltered in the Perfect and Pluperfect Indicative, Middle and Passive, of λύ-ω (cp. **111**), but the σ is used *only after a vowel.* The Personal endings contain the roots of the Personal Pronouns (με, σε) and of the Demonstrative (τό). These appear plainly in the Singular, but in the other numbers are more obscure. With the Historic Personal endings compare throughout—*eram, eras, erat, eramus, eratis, erant;* but in Greek τ cannot stand at the end of a word, and is therefore dropped; for a similar reason μ in First Person Singular becomes ν. The σ in the termination of the Second Singular, Middle and Passive, is often omitted, and the vowels thus meeting contract:—ε-αι into ει (η), η-αι into η, ε-ο into ου, α-ο into ω.

III.—*Tenses.*

105. The meaning of the Tenses is the same as in Latin, the Aorist corresponding to the Indefinite Perfect, *e.g. I loosed.*

Historic Tenses have a prefix in the Indicative Mood, called the *Augment*, as λύ-ω, ἔ-λυ-ον. The Perfects, Pluperfects, and Future Perfect in all Moods prefix the *Reduplication* to the Stem, as λύ-ω, λέ-λυ-κα. Two forms, called *Strong* and *Weak*, are used of the Aorist, Perfect and Pluperfect Active, and Future Passive. The meaning is generally the same whether the Tense is Strong or Weak, but both forms are seldom found in *one voice* of the same Verb.

IV.—*The Moods.*

106. The Indicative and Imperative differ mainly in Termination.

The Terminations of the Imperative are as follows :—

ACT., -θι, -τω ; -τον, -των ; -τε. -ντων.
PASS., -σο, -σ-θω ; -σ-θον, -σ-θων ; -σ-θε, -σ-θων

but the σ between hyphens is used *only after a vowel.*

The Primary Conjunctive is distinguished from the Indicative by a long vowel.

The Historic Conjunctive adds ι (sometimes ιη or ιε) to the Indicative, and this ι forms a diphthong with the preceding hard vowel.

V.—*Verbal Adjectives.*

107. The Verbal Adjectives are two in number (*a.*) in -τός, -τή, -τόν ; (*b.*) in -τέος, -τέα, -τέον, not contracted.

These are passive in meaning—λυ-τός, *able,* or *fit, to be loosed ;* λυ-τέος, *necessary to be loosed.* The first is really a Passive Participle, cp. Latin *scrip-tus ;* the second corresponds to the Latin gerundive—πρακτέος, -τέα, -τεον, *faciendus, -a, -um.*

Augment.—The augment is the remnant of a demonstrative pronoun prefixed to the past tenses of the Indicative mood. It is in Greek the true sign of past time. **(122-125.)**

VI.— *Voice.*

108. The Middle Voice differs from the Passive only in the formation of the Future and Aorist Tenses. The meaning of the Active and Passive is the same as in Latin. The Middle Voice has various meanings, the prevailing idea being *self-advantage*, that is, the Subject of the Verb is also the Recipient or Remoter Object. Thus the chief uses are :—

(1.) ' To do a thing for one's-self.' Act., λύω τὸν ἵππον, *I loose the horse.* Mid., λύομαι τὸν ἵππον, *I loose my horse.*

(2.) ' To get a thing done for one's-self.' διδάσκομαι τὸν υἱόν, *I get my son taught.*

(3.) ' To do a thing to one's-self.' λούομαι, *I wash* (i.e. *myself*).

VERBS IN -ω.

109. Verbs in -ω may be classed according to the character of their Verb-stem.

> *N.B.*—The letters in brackets show the form which the Verb-stem often assumes in the Present and Imperfect Tenses. They are given to enable the learner to assign a Verb to its probable class.

I. *Vowel Stems.*

Hard Vowels (Contracted),	α, ε, o,	as τιμά-ω,	*I honour,*	τιμα.
Soft Vowels (Uncontr.),	{ ι, υ,	,, λύ-ω,	*I loose,*	λυ.
	{ αυ, ευ, ου,	,, λού-ω,	*I wash,*	λου.

II. *Consonant Stems.*

Guttural Mutes,	κ, γ, χ [σσ, ττ],	as πλέκ-ω,	*I weave,*	πλεκ.
Dental Mutes,	τ, δ, θ [ζ],	,, πείθ-ω,	*I persuade,*	πιθ.
Labial Mutes,	π, β, φ [πτ],	,, τύπ-τ-ω,	*I strike,*	τυπ.
Liquids and Nasals,	λ, ρ, μ, ν,	,, σπείρ-ω,	*I sow,*	σπρ.

TENSE.	Number.	Person.	INDICATIVE. Primary.	Historic.	IMPERATIVE.
PRESENT AND IMPERFECT.			*Present.*	*Imperfect.*	
	S.	1.	-ω [-ο-μι]	-ο-ν [-ο-μ] *A.*	
		2.	-εις [-ε-σι]	-ε-ς	-ε [-ε-θι]
		3.	-ει [-ε-τι]	-ε(ν) [-ε-τ]	-ε-τω
	D.	2.	-ε-τον	-ε-τον	-ε-τον
		3.	-ε-τον	-ε-την	-ε-των
	P.	1.	-ο-μεν	-ο-μεν	
		2.	-ε-τε	-ε-τε	-ε-τε
		3.	-ου-σι(ν) [-ο-ντι]	-ο-ν [-ο-ντ]	-ο-ντων
FUTURE.	S.	1.	-σ-ω		None.
		2.	-σ-εις		
		3.	-σ-ει		
			Etc., as Present.		
WEAK AORIST.	S.	1.		-σα *A.*	———
		2.		-σα-ς	-σον
		3.		-σε(ν)	-σα-τω
	D.	2.		-σα-τον	-σα-τον
		3.		-σα-την	-σα-των
	P.	1.		-σα-μεν	———
		2.		-σα-τε	-σα-τε
		3.		-σα-ν	-σα-ντων
WEAK PERFECT AND PLUPERFECT.			*Perfect.* *R.*	*Pluperfect.*	
	S.	1.	-κα	-κη *A.R.*	———
		2.	-κα-ς	-κη-ς	-κε *R.*
		3.	-κε(ν)	-κει	-κε-τω
	D.	2.	-κα-τον	-κει-τον	-κε-τον
		3.	-κα-τον	-κει-την	-κε-των
	P.	1.	-κα-μεν	-κει-μεν	———
		2.	-κα-τε	-κει-τε	-κε-τε
		3.	-κα-σι(ν) [-κα-ντι]	-κει-σαν} / -κε-σαν	-κο-ντων
STRONG AORIST.	S.	1.		-ο-ν *A.*	———
		2.		-ε-ς	-ε
		3.		-ε	-ε-τω
				Etc., as Imperf.	Etc., as Present.
STRONG PERFECT AND PLUPERFECT.			*Perfect.*	*Pluperfect.*	
	S.	1.	-α	-η *A. R.*	-ε *R.*
		2.	-α-ς	-η-ς	-ε-τω
		3.	-ε(ν)	-ει	Etc., as Weak Perfect.
			Etc., as Weak Perfect.	Etc., as Weak Pluperfect.	

A. Augmented Tenses.   *R.* Reduplicated Tenses.

| CONJUNCTIVE. | | VERB INFINITE. | |
Primary (Subj.)	Historic (Optative).	Subst. (Infin.)	Adj. (Participle).
-ω	-ο-ι-μι	-ειν	M. -ων
-ης	-ο-ι-ς		F. -ουσα
-η	-ο-ι		N. -ον
-η-τον	-ο-ι-τον		Stem -οντ
-η-τον	-ο-ι-την		
-ω-μεν	-ο-ι-μεν		
-η-τε	-ο-ι-τε		
-ω-σι(ν)	-ο-ιε-ν		
	-σο-ι-μι	-σειν	M. -σων
	-σο-ι-ς		F. -σουσα
None.	-σο-ι		N. -σον
	Etc., as Present.		Stem -σοντ
-σω	-σα-ι-μι	-σαι	M. -σας
-σης	-σα-ι-ς or σεια-ς		F. -σασα
-ση	-σα-ι or σειε		N. -σαν
-ση-τον	-σα-ι-τον		Stem -σαντ
-ση-τον	-σα-ι-την		
-σω-μεν	-σα-ι-μεν		
-ση-τε	-σα-ι-τε		
-σω-σι(ν)	-σα-ιε-ν or σεια-ν		
-κω R.	-κο-ι-μι R.	-κε-ναι R.	M. -κως R.
-κης	-κο-ι-ς		F. -κυια
-κη	-κο-ι		N. -κος
-κη-τον	-κο-ι-τον		Stem -κοτ
-κη-τον	-κο-ι-την		
-κω-μεν	-κο-ι-μεν		
-κη-τε	-κο-ι-τε		
-κω-σι(ν)	-κο-ιε-ν		
-ω	-ο-ι-μι	-ειν	M. -ων
-ης	-ο-ι-ς		F. -ουσα
-η	-ο-ι		N. -ον
Etc., as Present.	Etc., as Present.		Stem -οντ
-ω R.	-ο-ι-μι R.	-ε-ναι R.	M. -ως R.
-ης	-ο-ι-ς		F. -υια
-η	-ο-ι		N. -ος
Etc., as Weak Perfect.	Etc. as Weak Perfect.		Stem -οτ

A. Augmented Tenses. *R.* Reduplicated Tenses.

TENSE.	Number.	Person.	INDICATIVE.		IMPERATIVE.
			Primary.	Historic.	
			Present.	*Imperfect.*	
PRESENT AND IMPERFECT, MID. & PASS.	S.	1.	-ε-μαι	-ο-μην *A.*	———
		2.	-ει, η [-ε σαι]	-ου [-ε-σο]	-ου [-ε-σο]
		3.	-ε-ται	-ε-το	-ε-θω
	D.	2.	-ε-σθον	-ε-σθον	-ε-σθον
		3.	-ε-σθον	-ε-σθην	-ε-σθων
	P.	1.	-ο-μεθα	-ο-μεθα	
		2.	-ε-σθε	-ε-σθε	-ε-σθε
		3.	-ο-νται	-ο-ντο	-ε-σθων
WEAK FUTURE, PASSIVE.	S.	1.	-θη-σο-μαι		None.
		2.	-θη-σει, η		
		3.	-θη-σε-ται		
			Etc., as Present.		
WEAK AORIST, PASSIVE.	S.	1.		-θη-ν *A.*	
		2.		-θη-ς	-θη-τι [-θη-θι]
		3.		-θη	-θη-τω
	D.	2.		-θη-τον	-θη-τον
		3.		-θη-την	-θη-των
	P.	1.		-θη-μεν	
		2.		-θη-τε	-θη-τε
		3.		-θησαν	-θε-ντων
PERFECT AND PLUPERFECT, MID. & PASS.			*Perfect.*	*Pluperfect.*	
	S.	1.	-μαι *R.*	-μην *A.R.*	——— *R.*
		2.	-σαι	-σο	-σο
		3.	-ται	-το	-σθω
	D.	2.	-σθον	-σθον	-σθον
		3.	-σθον	-σθην	-σθων
	P.	1.	-μεθα	-μεθα	———
		2.	-σθε	-σθε	-σθε
		3.	-νται or -μενοι εἰσί(ν)	-ντο or -μενοι ἦσαν	-σθων
FUTURE PERFECT, MID. & PASS.	S.	1.	-σο-μαι *R.*		None.
		2.	-σει, η		
		3.	-σε-ται		
			Etc., as Present.		
STRONG FUTURE, PASSIVE.	S.	1.	-η-σο-μαι		None.
		2.	-η-σει, η		
		3.	-η-σε-ται		
			Etc., as Present.		
STRONG AORIST, PASSIVE.	S.	1.		-η-ν *A.*	
		2.		-η-ς	-η-θι
		3.		-η	-η-τω
				Etc.,, as Wk. Aor.	Etc., as Weak Aorist.

A. Augmented Tenses.   *R.* Reduplicated Tenses.

CONJUNCTIVE.		VERB INFINITE.	
Primary (Subjunc.)	Historic (Optative).	Subst. (Infin.)	Adj. (Participle).
-ω-μαι	-ο-ι-μην	-ε-σθαι	M. -ο-μενος
-ῃ [-η-σαι]	-ο-ι-ο [-οι σο]		F. -ο-μενη
-η-ται	-ο-ι-το		N. -ο-μενον
-η-σθον	-ο-ι-σθον		Stem -ομενο
-η-σθον	-ο-ι-σθην		
-ω-μεθα	-ο-ι-μεθα		
-η-σθε	-ο-ι-σθε		
-ω-νται	-ο-ι-ντο		
None.	-θη-σο-ι-μην	-θη-σε-σθαι	M. -θη-σο-μενος
	-θη-σο-ι-ο		F. -θη-σο-μενη
	-θη-σο-ι-το		N. -θη-σο-μενον
	Etc., as Present.		Stem -θησομενο
-θω	-θε-ιη-ν	-θη-ναι	M. -θεις
-θῃς	-θε-ιη-s		F. -θεισα
-θῃ	-θε-ιη		N. -θεν
-θη-τον	-θε-ιη-τον or -θειτον		Stem -θεντ
-θη-τον	-θε-ιη-την or -θειτην		
-θω-μεν	-θε-ιη-μεν or -θειμεν		
-θη-τε	-θε-ιη-τε or -θειτε		
-θω-σι(ν)	-θε-ιη-σαν or -θε-ιε-ν		
-μενος ὦ *R.*	-μενος εἴην *R.*	-σθαι *R.*	M. -μενος *R.*
-μενος ῇς	-μενος εἴης		F. -μενη
-μενος ῇ	-μενος εἴη		N. -μενον
-μενω ἦτον	-μενω εἴητον or εἶτον		Stem -μενο
-μενω ἦτον	-μενω εἰήτην or εἴτην		
-μενοι ὦμεν	-μενοι εἴημεν or εἶμεν		
-μενοι ἦτε	-μενοι εἴητε or εἶτε		
-μενοι ὦσι(ν)	-μενοι εἴησαν or εἶεν		
None.	-σο-ι-μην *R.*	-σε-σθαι *R.*	M. -σο-μενος *R.*
	-σο-ι-ο		F. -σο-μενη
	-σο-ι-το		N. -σο-μενον
	Etc., as Present.		Stem σομενο
None.	-η-σο-ι-μην	-η-σε-σθαι	M. -η-σο-μενος
	-η-σο-ι-ο		F. -η-σο-μενη
	-η-σο-ι-το		N. -η-συ-μενον
	Etc., as Present.		Stem -ησομενο
-ω	-ε-ιη-ν	-η-ναι	M. -εις
-ῃς	-ε-ιη-s		F. -εισα
-ῃ	-ε-ιη		N. -εν
Etc., as Weak Aorist.	Etc., as Weak Aorist.		Stem -εντ

CHARACTERISTIC MARKS OF

TENSES PECULIAR TO

TENSE.	Number.	Person.	INDICATIVE. Primary.	INDICATIVE. Historic.	IMPERATIVE.
FUTURE.	S.	1. 2. 3.	-σο-μαι -σει, ῃ[-σε-σαι] -σε·ται Etc., as Present.		None.
WEAK AORIST.	S. D. P.	1. 2. 3. 2. 3. 1. 2. 3.		-σα-μην *A.* -σω [-σα-σο] -σα-το -σα-σθον -σα-σθην -σα-μεθα -σα-σθε -σα-ντο	——— -σαι -σα-σθω -σα-σθον -σα-σθων ——— -σα-σθε -σα-σθων
STRONG AORIST.	S.	1. 2. 3.		-ο-μην *A.* -ου [-ε-σο] -ε-το Etc., as Imperf.	——— -ου [-ε-σο] -ε-σθω Etc., as Present.

R. Augmented Tenses.

Verbal adjectives—1. -τος, -τη, -τον.

2. -τεος, -τεα, -τεον.

MOOD, TENSE, AND PERSON.

THE MIDDLE VOICE.

CONJUNCTIVE.		VERB INFINITE.	
Primary (Subj.).	Historic (Optative).	Subst. (Infin.)	Adj. (Participle).
None.	-σο-ι-μην -σο-ι-ο [-σοι-σο] -σο-ι-το Etc., as Present.	-σε-σθαι	M. -σο-μενος F. -σο-μενη N. -σο-μενον Stem -σομενο
-σω-μαι -ση [-ση-σαι] -ση-ται -ση-σθον -ση-σθον -σω-μεθα -ση-σθε -σω-νται	-σα-ι-μην -σα-ι-ο [-σαι-σο] -σα-ι-το -σα-ι-σθον -σα-ι-σθην -σα-ι-μεθα -σα-ι-σθε -σα-ι-ντο	-σα-σθαι	M. -σα-μενος F. -σα-μενη N. -σα-μενον Stem -σαμενο
-ω-μαι -η [-η-σαι] -η-ται Etc., as Present.	-ο-ι-μην -ο-ι-ο [-οι-σο] -ο-ι-το Etc., as Present.	-ε-σθαι	M. -ο-μενος F. -ο-μενη N. -ο-μενον Stem -ομενο

111.

Tense.	Number.	Person.	INDICATIVE. Primary.	INDICATIVE. Historic.	IMPERATIVE.
			Present.	*Imperfect.*	
Present *I loose.* **Imperfect** *I was loosing.* Stem λῡ.	S.	1.	λύ-ω	ἔ-λῡ-ον	
		2.	λύ-εις	ἔ-λῡ-ες	λῦ-ε
		3.	λύ-ει	ἔ-λῡ-ε(ν)	λῡ-έτω
	D.	2.	λύ-ετον	ἐ-λύ-ετον	λύ-ετον
		3.	λύ-ετον	ἐ-λῑ-έτην	λῡ-έτων
	P.	1.	λύ-ομεν	ἐ-λύ-ομεν	
		2.	λύ-ετε	ἐ-λύ-ετε	λύ-ε-τε
		3.	λύ-ουσι(ν)	ἔ-λῡ-ον	λῡ-όντων
Future *I shall loose.* Stem λῡσ.	S.	1.	λύ-σω		
		2.	λύ-σεις		
		3.	λύ-σει		
	D.	2.	λύ-σετον		
		3.	λύ-σετον		
	P.	1.	λύ-σομεν		
		2.	λύ-σετε		
		3.	λύ-σουσι(ν)		
Weak Aorist *I loosed.* Stem λῦσα.	S.	1.		ἔ-λῡ-σα	
		2.		ἔ-λῡ-σας	λῦ-σον
		3.		ἔ-λῡ-σε(ν)	λῡ-σάτω
	D.	2.		ἐ-λύ-σατον	λύ-σατον
		3.		ἐ-λῡ-σάτην	λῡ-σάτων
	P.	1.		ἐ-λύ-σαμεν	
		2.		ἐ-λῑ-σατε	λύ-σατε
		3.		ἔ-λῡ-σαν	λῡ-σάντων
			Perfect.	*Pluperfect.*	(rare)
Weak Perf. *I have loosed.* **Pluperfect** *I had loosed* Stem λελῡκ	S.	1.	λέ-λῠ-κα	ἐ-λε-λύ-κη	
		2.	λέ-λῠ-κας	ἐ-λε-λύ-κης	λέ-λυ-κε
		3.	λέ-λῠ-κε(ν)	ἐ-λε-λύ-κει	λε-λῠ-κέτω
	D.	2.	λε-λύ-κατον	ἐ-λε-λῑ-κειτον	λε-λῠ-κέτον
		3.	λε-λύ-κατον	ἐ-λε-λῠ-κείτην	λε-λῠ-κέτων
	P.	1.	λε-λύ-καμεν	ἐ-λε-λῑ-κειμεν	
		2.	λε-λύ-κατε	ἐ-λε-λύ-κειτε	λε-λῠ-κετε
		3.	λε-λύ-κᾱσι(ν)	ἐ-λε-λύ-κεισαν ⎱ ἐ-λε-λῠ-κεσαν ⎰	λε-λῠ-κόντων
Strong Aorist.			Wanting in Vowel Stems.		
Strong Perfect and Pluperfect.			Wanting in Vowel Stems.		

CONJUNCTIVE.		VERB INFINITE.	
Primary (Subjunc.)	Historic (Optative).	Subst. (Infin.)	Adj. (Participle).
λύ-ω	λύ-οιμι	λύ-ειν	M. λύ-ων
λύ-ῃs	λύ-οιs		F. λύ-ουσα
λύ-ῃ	λύ-οι		N. λῦ-ον
λύ-ητον	λύ-οιτον		
λύ-ητον	λῡ-οίτην		Stem λῡοντ
λύ-ωμεν	λύ-οιμεν		
λύ-ητε	λύ-οιτε		
λύ-ωσι(ν)	λύ-οιεν		
	λύ-σοιμι	λύ-σειν	M. λύ-σων
	λύ-σοιs		F. λύ-σουσα
	λύ-σοι		N. λῦ-σον
	λύ-σοιτον		
	λῡ-σοίτην		Stem λυσοντ
	λύ-σοιμεν		
	λύ-σοιτε		
	λύ-σοιεν		
λύ-σω	λύ-σαιμι	λῦ-σαι	M. λύ-σαs
λύ-σῃs	λύ-σαιs or -σειαs		F. λύ-σασα
λύ-σῃ	λύ-σαι or -σειε(ν)		N. λῦ-σαν
λύ-σητον	λύ-σαιτον		
λύ-σητον	λῡ-σαίτην		Stem λυσαντ
λί-σωμεν	λύ-σαιμεν		
λύ-σητε	λύ-σαιτε		
λί-σωσι(ν)	λύ-σαιεν or -σειαν		
λε-λύ-κω	λε-λύ-κοιμι	λε-λυ-κέναι	M. λε-λῠ--κώs
λε-λῠ-κῃs	λε-λῠ-κοιs		F. λε-λῠ-κυῖα
λε-λῠ-κῃ	λε-λῠ-κοι		N. λε-λῐ-κόs
λε-λῠ-κητον	λε-λῐ-κοιτον		
λε-λῠ-κητον	λε-λῠ-κοίτην		Stem λελῠκοτ
λε-λῠ-κωμεν	λε-λῐ-κοιμεν		
λε-λῠ-κητε	λε-λῠ-κοιτε		
λε-λῠ-κωσι(ν)	λε-λῠ-κοιεν		

Tense.	Number.	Person.	INDICATIVE. Primary.	Historic.	IMPERATIVE.
Present Mid. *I loose for myself.*			*Present.*	*Imperfect.*	
	S.	1.	λύ-ομαι	ἐ-λυ-όμην	——
Pass. *I am being loosed.*		2.	λύ-ει, ῃ	ἐ-λύ ου	λύ-ου
		3.	λύ-εται	ἐ-λύ ετο	λῡ-έσθω
Imperfect Mid. *I was loosing for myself.*	D.	2.	λύ-εσθον	ἐ-λύ-εσθον	λύ-εσθον
		3.	λύ-εσθον	ἐ-λῑ-έσθην	λῡ-έσθων
	P.	1.	λυ-όμεθα	ἐ-λῑ-όμεθα	——
Pass. *I was being loosed.*		2.	λύ-εσθε	ἐ-λῡ-εσθε	λύ-εσθε
		3.	λύ-ονται	ἐ-λύ-οντο	λῡ-έσθων
Stem λῡ.					
Weak Fut. P. *I shall be loosed.*	S.	1.	λῠ-θήσομαι		
		2.	λῠ-θήσει, ῃ		
Stem λῠθησ.		3.	λῠ-θήσεται		
			Etc., as Present.		
	S.	1.		ἐ-λῠ-θην	——
		2.		ἐ-λῠ-θης	λῠ-θητι
Weak Aor. P. *I was loosed.*		3.		ἐ-λῠ-θη	λῠ-θήτω
	D.	2.		ἐ-λῑ-θητον	λύ-θητον
		3.		ἐ-λῑ-θήτην	λῠ-θήτων
Stem λῠθη.	P.	1.		ἐ-λύ-θημεν	——
		2.		ἐ-λύ-θητε	λῠ-θητε
		3.		ἐ-λῠ-θησαν	λῠ θέντων
Perfect Mid. *I have loosed for myself.*			*Perfect.*	*Pluperfect.*	
	S.	1.	λέ-λῠ-μαι	ἐ-λε-λύ-μην	
Pass. *I have been loosed.*		2.	λέ-λῠ-σαι	ἐ-λέ-λῠ-σο	λέ-λῠ-σο
		3.	λέ-λῠ-ται	ἐ-λέ-λῠ-το	λε-λύ-σθω
Pluperfect Mid. *I had loosed for myself.*	D.	2.	λέ-λυ-σθον	ἐ-λέ-λυ-σθον	λέ-λυ-σθον
		3.	λέ-λυ-σθον	ἐ-λε-λύ-σθην	λε-λύ-σθων
	P.	1.	λε-λύ-μεθα	ἐ-λε-λῑ-μεθα	——
Pass. *I had been loosed.*		2.	λέ-λυ-σθε	ἐ-λέ-λυ-σθε	λέ-λυ-σθε
		3.	λέ-λυ-νται	ἐ-λέ-λυ-ντο	λε-λύ-σθων
Stem λελῠ.					
Future Perf. Mid. *I shall have loosed for myself.* Pass. *I shall have been loosed.* Stem λελῡσ.	S.	1. 2. 3.	λε-λύ-σομαι λε-λύ-σει, -ῃ λε-λύ-σεται Etc., as Present.		
Strong Fut. P.			Wanting in Vowel Stems.		——
Strong Aor. P.					

CONJUNCTIVE.		VERB INFINITE.	
Primary (Subjunc.)	Historic (Optative).	Subst. (Infin.)	Adj. (Participle).
λύ-ωμαι	λῡ-οίμην	λύ-εσθαι	M. λῡ-όμενος
λύ-ῃ	λύ-οιο		F. λῡ-ομένη
λύ-ηται	λύ-οιτο		N. λῡ-όμενον
λύ-ησθον	λύ-οισθον		
λύ-ησθον	λῡ-οίσθην		Stem λυομενο
λῡ-ώμεθα	λῡ-οίμεθα		
λύ-ησθε	λύ-οισθε		
λύ-ωνται	λύ-οιντο		
	λῡ-θησοίμην	λῠ-θήσεσθαι	M. λῠ-θησόμενος
	λῠ-θήσοιο		F. λῠ-θησομένη
	λῠ-θήσοιτο		N. λῠ-θησόμενον
	Etc., as Present.		Stem λῠθησομενο
λῠ-θῶ	λῠ-θείην	λῠ-θῆναι	M. λῠ-θείς
λῠ-θῇς	λῠ-θείης		F. λῠ-θεῖσα
λῠ-θῇ	λῠ-θείη		N. λῠ-θέν
λῠ-θῆτον	λῠ-θείητον or -θείτον		
λῠ-θῆτον	λῠ-θειήτην or -θείτην		Stem λῠθεντ
λῠ-θῶμεν	λῠ-θείημεν or -θεῖμεν		
λῠ-θῆτε	λῠ-θείητε or -θεῖτε		
λῠ-θῶσι(ν)	λῠ-θεῖεν		
λε-λῠ-μένος ὦ	λε-λῠ-μένος εἴην	λε-λύ-σθαι	M. λε-λῠ-μένος
λε-λῠ-μένος ᾖς	λε-λῠ-μένος εἴης		F. λε-λῠ-μένη
λε-λῠ-μένος ᾖ	λε-λῠ-μένος εἴη		N. λε-λῠ-μένον
λε-λῠ-μένω ἦτον	λε-λῠ-μένω εἶτον		
λε-λῠ-μένω ἦτον	λε-λῠ-μένω εἴτην		Stem λελῠμενο
λε-λῠ-μένοι ὦμεν	λε-λῠ-μένοι εἶμεν		
λε-λῠ-μένοι ἦτε	λε-λῠ-μένοι εἶτε		
λε-λῠ-μένοι ὦσι(ν)	λε-λῠ-μένοι εἶεν		
	λε-λῠ-σοίμην	λε-λύ-σεσθ-αι	M. λε-λῠ-σόμενος
	λε-λύ-σοιο		F. λε-λῠ-σομένη
	λε-λύ-σοιτο		N. λε-λυ-σόμενον
	Etc., as Present.		
			Stem λελῠσομενο

Verbal Adjectives { λῠ-τός, -τή, -τόν, *able*, or *fit, to be loosed.*
λῠ-τέος, -τέα, -τέον, *necessary to be loosed.*

TENSE.	Number.	Person.	INDICATIVE. Primary.	INDICATIVE. Historic.	IMPERATIVE.
FUTURE MIDDLE. *I shall loose for myself.* Stem λῦσ.	S.	1. 2. 3.	λύ-σομαι λύ-σει, -σῃ λύ-σεται Etc., as Present.		None.
WEAK AORIST, MIDDLE. *I loosed for myself.* Stem λῦσα.	S. D. P.	1. 2. 3. 2. 3. 1. 2. 3.		ἐ-λῡ-σάμην ἐ-λύ-σω ἐ-λύ-σατο ἐ-λύ-σασθον ἐ-λῡ-σάσθην ἐ-λῡ-σάμεθα ἐ-λύ-σασθε ἐ-λύ-σαντο	—— λῦ-σαι λῡ-σάσθω λί-σασθον λῡ-σάσθων —— λύ-σασθε λῡ-σάσθων
STRONG AORIST, MIDDLE.			Wanting in Vowel Verbs.		

STRONG

EXAMPLES OF THE STRONG TENSES MAY

	Number.	Person.	Primary.	Historic.	Imperative.
STRONG AORIST, ACTIVE. *I persuaded.* Stem πιθ.	S.	1. 2. 3.		ἔ-πιθ-ον ἔ-πιθ-ες ἔ-πιθ-ε(ν) Etc., as Imperfect.	πίθ-ε πιθ-έτω Etc., as Present.
STRONG PERFECT, ACTIVE. *I have woven.* PLUPERFE T. *I had woven.* Stem πεπλεχ.	S.	1. 2. 3.	*Perfect.* πέ-πλεχ-α πέ-πλεχ-ας πέ-πλεχ-ε Etc., as Wk. Perf.	*Pluperfect.* ἐ-πε-πλέχ-η ἐ-πε-πλέχ-ης ἐ-πε-πλέχ-ει(ν) Etc., as Wk. Plupf.	πέ-πλέχ-ε πε-πλεχ-έτω Etc., as Weak Perfect.
STRONG FUTURE, PASSIVE. *I shall be woven.* Stem πλακησ.	S.	1. 2. 3.	πλάκ-ησομαι πλακ-ήσει, -ῃ πλακ-ήσεται Etc., as Wk. Fut.		
STRONG AORIST, PASSIVE. *I was woven.* Stem πλακη.	S.	1. 2. 3.		ἐ-πλάκ-ην ἐ-πλάκ-ης ἐ-πλάκ-η Etc., as Wk. Aorist.	πλάκ-ηθι πλακ-ήτω Etc., as Weak Aorist.
STRONG AORIST, MIDDLE. *I obeyed.* Stem πιθ.	S.	1. 2. 3.		ἐ-πιθ-όμην ἐ-πίθ-ου ἐ-πίθ-ετο Etc., as Imperfect.	πιθ-οῦ πιθ-έσθω Etc., as Present.

CONJUNCTIVE.		VERB INFINITE.	
Primary (Subj.)	Historic (Optative).	Subst. (Infin.)	Adj. (Participle).
None.	λῡ-σοίμην λῡ-σοιο λῡ-σοιτο Etc., as Present.	λῡ-σεσθαι	M. λῡ-σόμενος F. λῡ-σομένη N. λῡ-σόμενον Stem **λυσομενο**
λῡ-σωμαι λῡ-σῃ λῡ-σηται λῡ-σησθον λῡ-σησθον λῡ-σώμεθα λῡ-σησθε λῡ-σωνται	λῡ-σαίμην λῡ-σαιο λῡ-σαιτο λῡ-σαισθον λῡ-σαίσθην λῡ-σαίμεθα λῡ-σαισθε λῡ-σαιντο	λῡ-σασθαι	M. λῡ-σάμενος F. λῡ-σαμένη N. λῡ-σάμενον Stem **λυσαμενο**

TENSES.

BE TAKEN FROM CONSONANT VERBS (112).

πίθ-ω πίθ-ῃς πίθ-ῃ Etc., as Present.	πίθ-οιμι πίθ-οις πίθ-οι Etc., as Present.	πιθ-εῖν	M. πιθ-ών F. πιθ-οῦσα N. πιθ-όν Stem **πιθοντ**
πε-πλέχ-ω πε-πλέχ-ῃς πε-πλέχ-ῃ Etc., as Weak Perfect.	πε-πλέχ-οιμι πε-πλέχ-οις πε-πλέχ-οι Etc., as Weak Perfect.	πε-πλεχ-έναι	M. πε-πλεχ-ώς F. πε-πλεχ-υῖα N. πε-πλεχ-ός Stem **πεπλεχοτ**
	πλακ-ησοίμην πλακ-ήσοιο πλακ-ήσοιτο Etc., as Weak Future.	πλακ-ήσεσθαι	M. πλακ-ησόμενος F. πλακ-ησομένη N. πλακ-ησόμενον Stem **πλακησομενο**
πλακ-ῶ πλακ-ῇς πλακ-ῇ Etc., as Weak Aorist.	πλακ-είην πλακ-είης πλακ-είη Etc., as Weak Aorist.	πλακ-ῆναι	M. πλακ-είς F. πλακ-εῖσα N. πλακ-έν Stem **πλακεντ**
πίθ-ωμαι πίθ-ῃ πίθ-ηται Etc., as Present.	πιθ-οίμην πίθ-οιο πίθ-οιτο Etc., as Present.	πίθ-εσθαι	M. πιθ-όμενος F. πιθ-ομένη N. πιθ-όμενον Stem **πιθομενο**

FORMATION OF TENSES FROM THE VERB-STEM.

112. The Tenses may be arranged according to similarity of Tense-stem in *six* groups. **(129-145.)**

Group	Tense.	Formation.	Vowel Stems Verb Stem λυ
1	Present A.	Verb Stem -ω	λύ-ω
	Imperfect A.	Aug.-Verb Stem -ον	ἔ-λῦ-ον
	Pres. M. and P.	Verb Stem -ομαι	λύ-ομαι
	Impf. M. and P.	Aug.-Verb Stem -ομην	ἐ-λῦ-όμην
2	Strong Aor. A.	Aug.-Verb Stem -ον	—
	Strong Aor. M.	Aug.-Verb Stem -ομην	—
3	Future A.	Verb Stem -σω	λύ-σω
	Future M.	Verb Stem -σομαι	λύ-σομαι
4	Weak Aor. A.	Aug.-Verb Stem -σα	ἔ-λῦ-σα
	Weak Aor. M.	Aug.-Verb Stem -σαμην	ἐ-λῡ-σάμην
5	Strong. Perf. A.	Red.-Verb Stem -α	—
	Strong Plupf. A.	Aug.-Red.-Verb Stem -η	—
	Weak Perf. A.	Red.-Verb Stem -κα	λέ-λῠ-κα
	Weak Plupf. A.	Aug.-Red.-Verb Stem -κη	ἐ-λε-λῠ-κη
	Perf. M. and P.	Red.-Verb Stem -μαι	λέ-λῠ-μαι
	Plupf. M. and P.	Aug.-Red.-Verb Stem -μην	ἐ-λε-λῠ-μην
	Fut. Perf. M. and P.	Red.-Verb Stem -σομαι	λε-λύ-σομαι
6	Strong Aor. P.	Aug.-Verb Stem -ην	—
	Weak Aor. P.	Aug.-Verb Stem -θην	ἐ-λῠ-θην
	Strong Fut. P.	Verb Stem -ησομαι	—
	Weak Fut. P.	Verb Stem -θησομαι	λῠ-θήσομαι

The Tense-stems are formed from the Verb-stem by the addition of letters at the end, or by prefixing the reduplication. In many verbs the Verb-stem itself is altered also by the insertion or change of letters, especially in group 1 (Present and Imperfect Tenses), see **129.**

In the Strong Perfect the vowel of the stem is often strengthened, as πέ-ποιθ-α; sometimes also (especially in labial and guttural stems) the character is aspirated, as τέ-τυφ-α.

The Weak Perfect is the only form found in Vowel stems

and is the more common in dentals, liquids, and nasals. Where both forms occur, the Weak as a rule is Transitive and the Strong Intransitive.

N.B.—Many forms that are not found are given below in lighter type for the sake of completeness.

Group.	Guttural Stems. Verb-stem πλεκ. *Weave.*	Dental Stems. Verb-stem πιθ. *Persuade.*	Labial Stems. Verb-stem τυπ. *Strike.*	Liquid Stems. Verb-st. σπερ. *Sow.*
1	πλέκ-ω ἔ-πλεκ-ον πλέκ-ομαι ἐ-πλεκ-όμην	πείθ-ω ἔ-πειθ-ον πείθ-ομαι ἐ-πειθ-όμην	τύπτ-ω ἔ-τυπτ-ον τύπτ-ομαι ἐ-τυπτ-όμην	σπείρ-ω ἔ-σπειρ-ον σπείρ-ομαι ἐ-σπειρ-όμην
2	ἔ-πλακ-ον ἐ-πλακ-όμην	ἔ-πιθ-ον ἐ-πιθ-όμην	ἔ-τυπ-ον ἐ-τυπ-όμην	ἔ-σπαρ-ον ἐ-σπαρ-όμην
3	πλέξω πλέξομαι	πεί-σω πεί-σομαι	τύψω τύψομαι	σπερ-ῶ σπερ-οῦμαι
4	ἔ-πλεξα ἐ-πλεξάμην	ἔ-πει-σα ἐ-πει-σάμην	ἔ-τυψα ἐ-τυψάμην	ἔ-σπειρ-α ἐ-σπειρ-άμην
5	πέ-πλεχ-α ἐ-πε-πλέχη —— —— πέ-πλεγ-μαι ἐ-πε-πλέγ-μην πε-πλέξομαι	πέ-ποιθ-α ἐ-πε-ποίθ-η πέ-πει-κα ἐ-πε-πεί-κη πέ-πεισ-μαι ἐ-πε-πεισ-μην πε-πεί-σομαι	τέ-τυφ-α ἐ-τε-τύφ-η —— —— τέ-τυμ-μαι ἐ-τε-τύμ-μην τε-τύψομαι	—— —— ἔ-σπαρ-κα ἐ-σπάρ-κη ἔ-σπαρ-μαι ἐ-σπάρ-μην none
6	ἐ-πλάκ-ην ἐ-πλέχ-θην πλακ-ήσομαι πλεχ-θήσομαι	ἐ-πίθ-ην ἐ-πεισ-θην πιθ-ήσομαι πεισ-θήσομαι	ἐ-τύπ-ην ἐ-τύφ-θην τυπ-ήσομαι τυφ-θήσομαι	ἐ-σπάρ-ην ἐ-σπάρ-θην σπαρ-ήσομαι σπαρ-θήσομαι

The change of character, which takes place whenever the termination begins with a consonant, is explained on the next page. The above verbs may be conjugated in all their moods after the model of λύω without further change. The following tenses only require to be noticed, viz., Perfect and Pluperfect M. and P. (114), and groups 3 and 4 in liquid and nasal stems (115, 116, 117.)

RULES FOR THE CHANGE OF CONSONANTS IN VERBS.

113. The following are the Laws of Sound as far as they apply to the Formation of Tenses. For general rules see **11-27**.

Guttural and Labial Stems.

Hard letters must precede Hard.
Soft   „   „   „   Soft.
Aspirate   „   „   Aspirate.

Thus :—

Before σ $\begin{cases} \text{Labials become } \pi \text{ and form } \psi, \text{ as } \tau\acute{\upsilon}\psi\omega. \\ \text{Gutturals } \quad „ \quad \kappa \quad „ \quad \xi, \text{ as } \pi\lambda\acute{\epsilon}\xi\omega. \end{cases}$

Before θ $\begin{cases} \text{Labials become } \phi, \text{ as } \acute{\epsilon}\text{-}\tau\acute{\upsilon}\phi\text{-}\theta\eta\nu. \\ \text{Gutturals } \quad „ \quad \chi, \text{ as } \acute{\epsilon}\text{-}\pi\lambda\acute{\epsilon}\chi\text{-}\theta\eta\nu. \end{cases}$

Before μ $\begin{cases} \text{Labials become } \mu, \text{ as } \tau\acute{\epsilon}\text{-}\tau\upsilon\mu\text{-}\mu\alpha\iota. \\ \text{Gutturals } \quad „ \quad \gamma, \text{ as } \pi\acute{\epsilon}\text{-}\pi\lambda\epsilon\gamma\text{-}\mu\alpha\iota. \end{cases}$

Before τ $\begin{cases} \text{Labials become } \pi, \text{ as } \tau\acute{\epsilon}\text{-}\tau\upsilon\pi\text{-}\tau\alpha\iota. \\ \text{Gutturals } \quad „ \quad \kappa, \text{ as } \pi\acute{\epsilon}\text{-}\pi\lambda\epsilon\kappa\text{-}\tau\alpha\iota \end{cases}$

Dental Stems.

Dentals are dropped before σ or κ, as $\pi\epsilon\acute{\iota}\text{-}\sigma\omega$, $\pi\acute{\epsilon}\text{-}\pi\epsilon\iota\text{-}\kappa\alpha$. Before any other consonants they become σ, as $\acute{\epsilon}\text{-}\pi\epsilon\iota\sigma\text{-}\theta\eta\nu$, $\pi\acute{\epsilon}\text{-}\pi\epsilon\iota\sigma\text{-}\mu\alpha\iota$.

Liquid and Nasal Stems.

Liquids (λ, ρ) require no change.
Nasals (ν, μ) are very irregularly treated.
ν is usually dropped before σ, θ, μ, τ, κ, but from $\phi\alpha\acute{\iota}\nu\omega$ (Stem **φαν**) we have $\pi\acute{\epsilon}\text{-}\phi\alpha\nu\text{-}\sigma\alpha\iota$, $\acute{\epsilon}\text{-}\phi\acute{\alpha}\nu\text{-}\theta\eta\nu$, $\pi\acute{\epsilon}\text{-}\phi\alpha\sigma\text{-}\mu\alpha\iota$, $\pi\acute{\epsilon}\text{-}\phi\alpha\nu\text{-}\tau\alpha\iota$, $\pi\acute{\epsilon}\text{-}\phi\alpha\gamma\text{-}\kappa\alpha$.

114. *The Perfect and Pluperfect Middle and Passive of Consonant Verbs.*

	Number.	Person.	INDICATIVE.	IMPERATIVE.	OTHER MOODS.
Guttural Stems. πλεκ, *weave.*	S.	1.	πέ-πλεγ-μαι	———	
		2.	πέ-πλεξαι	πέ-πλεξο	Conj. Prim.
		3.	πέ-πλεκ-ται	πε-πλέχ-θω	πε-πλεγ-μένος ὦ
	D.	2.	πέ-πλεχ-θον	πέ-πλεχ-θον	Conj. Hist.
		3.	πέ-πλεχ-θον	πε-πλέχ-θων	πε-πλεγ-μένος εἴην
	P.	1.	πε-πλέγ-μεθα	———	Infin. πε-πλέχ-θαι
		2.	πέ-πλεχ-θε	πέ-πλεχ-θε	Partic. πε-πλεγ-μένος
		3.	πε-πλεγ-μένοι εἰσί(ν)	πε-πλέχ-θων	
Dental Stems. πιθ, *persuade.*	S.	1.	πέ-πεισ-μαι	———	
		2.	πέ-πει-σαι	πέ-πει-σο	Conj. Prim.
		3.	πέ-πεισ-ται	πε-πείσ-θω	πε-πεισ-μένος ὦ
	D.	2.	πέ-πεισ-θον	πέ-πεισ-θον	Conj. Hist.
		3.	πέ-πεισ-θον	πε-πείσ-θων	πε-πεισ-μένος εἴην
	P.	1.	πε-πείσ-μεθα	———	Infin. πε-πεῖσ-θαι
		2.	πέ-πεισ-θε	πέ-πεισ-θε	Partic. πε-πεισ-μένος
		3.	πε-πεισ-μένοι εἰσί(ν)	πε-πείσ-θων	
Labial Stems. τυπ, *strike.*	S.	1.	τέ-τυμ-μαι	———	
		2.	τέ-τυψαι	τέ-τυψο	Conj. Prim.
		3.	τέ-τυπ-ται	τε-τύφ-θω	τε-τυμ-μένος ὦ
	D.	2.	τέ-τυφ-θον	τέ-τυφ-θον	Conj. Hist.
		3.	τέ-τυφ-θον	τε-τύφ-θων	τε-τυμ-μένος εἴην
	P.	1.	τε-τύμ-μεθα	———	Infin. τε-τύφ-θαι
		2.	τέ-τυφ-θε	τέ-τυφ-θε	Part. τε-τυμ-μένος
		3.	τε-τυμ-μένοι εἰσί(ν)	τε-τύφ-θων	
Liquid & Nasal Stems. σπερ, *sow.*	S.	1.	ἔ-σπαρ-μαι	———	
		2.	ἔ-σπαρ-σαι	ἔ-σπαρ-σο	Conj. Prim.
		3.	ἔ-σπαρ-ται	ἐ-σπάρ-θω	ἐ-σπαρ-μένος ὦ
	D.	2.	ἔ-σπαρ-θον	ἔ-σπαρ-θον	Conj. Hist.
		3.	ἔ-σπαρ-θον	ἐ-σπάρ-θων	ἐ-σπαρ-μένος εἴην
	P.	1.	ἐ-σπάρ-μεθα	———	Infin. ἐ-σπάρ-θαι
		2.	ἔ-σπαρ-θε	ἔ-σπαρ-θε	Partic. ἐ-σπαρ-μένος
		3.	ἐ-σπαρ-μένοι εἰσί(ν)	ἐ-σπάρ-θων	

In the Pluperfects the same change of character takes place as in the perfect. The 3rd Person Plural is formed by ἦσαν with the participle (*scripti erant*).

LIQUID AND NASAL VERBS.

Future and Weak Aorist A. and M.

(1.) *The Future Active and Middle.*

115. In these Verbs the Future Active and Middle inserts ε between the Verb-stem and the terminations -σω, -σομαι; the σ is dropped out and contraction takes place as in γένους for γενεσ-ος (49), *e.g.*

Verb-stem ⎰ Fut. Act. φαν-ε-σω, φαν-εω, φᾰνῶ.
φαν, *show* ⎱ Fut. Mid. φαν-ε-σομαι, φαν-ε-ομαι, φᾰνοῦμαι.

In these futures the Verb-stem *is always short.*

	Number	Person	INDICATIVE.	HIST. CONJ. (OPTATIVE.)	VERB INFINITE.		
FUTURE ACTIVE.	S.	1.	φαν-ῶ	φαν-οίην	Infin. φαν-εῖν		
		2.	φαν-εῖς	φαν-οίης	Partic.		
		3.	φαν-εῖ	φαν-οίη	Nom.	M. φαν-ῶν	
	D.	2.	φαν-εῖτον	φαν-οῖτον		F. φαν-οῦσα	
		3.	φαν-εῖτον	φαν-οίτην		N. φαν-οῦν	
	P.	1.	φαν-οῦμεν	φαν-οῖμεν	Acc.	M. φαν-οῦντα	
		2.	φαν-εῖτε	φαν-οῖτε		F. φαν-οῦσαν	
		3.	φαν-οῦσι(ν)	φαν-οῖεν		N. φαν-οῦν	
FUTURE MIDDLE.	S.	1.	φαν-οῦμαι	φαν-οίμην	Infin. φαν-εῖσθαι		
		2.	φαν-εῖ, -ῇ	φαν-οῖο	Partic.		
		3.	φαν-εῖται	φαν-οῖτο		M. φαν-ούμενος	
	D.	2.	φαν-εῖσθον	φαν-οῖσθον		F. φαν-ουμένη	
		3.	φαν-εῖσθον	φαν-οίσθην		N. φαν-ούμενον	
	P.	1.	φαν-ούμεθα	φαν-οίμεθα			
		2.	φαν-εῖσθε	φαν-οῖσθε			
		3.	φαν-οῦνται	φαν-οῖντο			

116. Several Stems in ε(σ) and αδ similarly drop σ and contract, as τελέ-ω, I *accomplish*, St. τελε, Fut. τελῶ (for τελε-σω). βιβάζ-ω, I *bring*, St. βιβαδ, Fut. βιβῶ (for βιβαδ-σω); see **133** *b.*

Attic Future.—Some stems in ιδ insert ε *after* the σ of the future; hence κομίζ-ω, I *convey*, St. κομιδ, Fut. κομιῶ (for κομιδ-σεω), where the dental is dropped before σ, σ is dropped between two vowels, and εω contract into ω; see **133** *c.*

(2.) *The Weak Aorist, Active and Middle.*

117. In the Weak Aorist, Active and Middle, σ is dropped from the terminations -σα, -σαμην, and the *vowel of the stem is lengthened* in compensation ; thus :—

	VERB-STEM.	ENGLISH.	WK. AOR. A.	WK. AOR. M.
ă after ι or ρ becomes ᾱ	περᾰν	*penetrate*	ἐ-πέρᾱν-α	ἐ-περᾱν-άμην
ă otherwise becomes η	φᾰν	*show*	ἔ-φην-α	ἐ-φην-άμην
ε becomes ει	σπερ	*sow*	ἔ-σπειρ-α	ἐ-σπειρ-άμην
ῐ is lengthened	κρῐν	*judge*	ἔ-κρῑν-α	ἐ-κρῑν-άμην
ῠ is lengthened	ἀμῠν	*defend*	ἤμῡν-α	ἠμῡν-άμην

There is no further change in the conjugation of Tense or Mood.

Contracted Verbs.

118. HARD Vowel-stems (in -*a*, -*ε*, -*o*) undergo contraction in all Moods of the Present and Imperfect Tenses.

In the remaining Tenses, the Vowel character is lengthened, -*a* into -*η*,   *a* after ε, ι, or ρ into ᾱ, -*ε* into -*η*,   -*o* into -*ω*—thus :—

Verb-stem,	τιμα, *honour.*	Pres. Act.,	τιμάω, τιμῶ.	Fut.,	τιμή-σω.
,,	ἐα, *allow.*	,,	ἐάω, ἐῶ.	,,	ἐάσω.
,,	φιλε, *love.*	,,	φιλέω, φιλῶ.	,,	φιλή-σω.
,,	δηλο, *show.*	,,	δηλόω, δηλῶ.	,,	δηλώ-σω.

N.B.—These Verbs have no Strong Tenses.

Obs. Many of the contracted verbs are *derivatives*, formed from noun stems in -*a*, -*ε*, -*o*, as τιμά-ω, *I honour,* from τιμή, *honour,* stem τιμα.

In some, however, the contraction is due to the loss of the final consonant, as τελέ-ω for τελεσ-ω, πλέ-ω for πλεϜ-ω.

CONTRACTED

119   Stems in -α,

ACTIVE.

	Number.	Person.	Primary.		Historic.	
			Present.		*Imperfect.*	
	S.	1.	τιμῶ	(ά-ω)	ἐτίμων	(α-ον)
		2.	τιμᾷς	(ά-εις)	ἐτίμᾱς	(α-ες)
		3.	τιμᾷ	(ά-ει)	ἐτίμᾱ	(α-ε)
Indicative.	D.	2.	τιμᾶτον	(ά-ετον)	ἐτιμᾶτον	(ά-ετον)
		3.	τιμᾶτον	(ά-ετον)	ἐτιμάτην	(α-έτην)
	P.	1.	τιμῶμεν	(ά-ομεν)	ἐτιμῶμεν	(ά-ομεν)
		2.	τιμᾶτε	(ά-ετε)	ἐτιμᾶτε	(ά-ετε)
		3.	τιμῶσι(ν)	(ά-ουσι)	ἐτίμων	(α-ον)
	S.	2.	τίμα	(α-ε)		
		3.	τιμάτω	(α-έτω)		
Imperative.	D.	2.	τιμᾶτον	(ά-ετον)		
		3.	τιμάτων	(α-έτων)		
	P.	2.	τιμᾶτε	(ά-ετε)		
		3.	τιμώντων	(α-όντων)		
			(Subjunctive.)		*(Optative.)*	
	S.	1.	τιμῶ	(ά-ω)	τιμῴην	(α-οίην)
		2.	τιμᾷς	(ά-ῃς)	τιμῴῃς	(α-οίης)
		3.	τιμᾷ	(ά-ῃ)	τιμῴη	(α-οίη)
Conjunc-tive.	D.	2.	τιμᾶτον	(ά-ητον)	τιμῷτον	(ά-οιτον)
		3.	τιμᾶτον	(ά-ητον)	τιμῴτην	(α-οίτην)
		1.	τιμῶμεν	(ά-ωμεν)	τιμῷμεν	(ά-οιμεν)
		2.	τιμᾶτε	(ά-ητε)	τιμῷτε	(ά-οιτε)
		3.	τιμῶσι(ν)	(ά-ωσι)	τιμῷεν	(ά-οιεν)

Infinitive, $\begin{cases} τιμᾶν. \\ (α-εεν) \end{cases}$ Participle, $\begin{cases} τιμῶν, & τιμῶσα, & τιμῶν \\ (ά-ων) & (ά-ουσα) & (ά-ον) \end{cases}$

Contractions of A *Verbs* (11).

α with ε or η becomes ᾱ (the first prevailing).
α with o or ω   ,,   ω (the o sound prevailing).
ι is *subscript*; ν disappears.

Obs. Some stems in -α contract into η instead of ᾱ, as ζάω, *I live* (ζῇς, ζῇ, ζῆν), πεινάω, *I hunger*, διψάω, *I thirst*, χράομαι, *I use*, and a few others.

VERBS,

τιμά-ω, *I honour*, Verb-stem τιμα.

MIDDLE AND PASSIVE.

	Number.	Person.	PRIMARY.		HISTORIC.	
			Present.		*Imperfect.*	
INDICATIVE.	S.	1.	τιμῶμαι	(ά-ομαι)	ἐτιμώμην	(α-όμην)
		2.	τιμᾷ	(ά-ῃ)	ἐτιμῶ	(ά-ου)
		3.	τιμᾶται	(ά-εται)	ἐτιμᾶτο	(ά-ετο)
	D.	2.	τιμᾶσθον	(ά-εσθον)	ἐτιμᾶσθον	(ά-εσθον)
		3.	τιμᾶσθον	(ά-εσθον)	ἐτιμάσθην	(α-έσθην)
	P.	1.	τιμώμεθα	(α-όμεθα)	ἐτιμώμεθα	(α-όμεθα)
		2.	τιμᾶσθε	(ά-εσθε)	ἐτιμᾶσθε	(ά-εσθε)
		3.	τιμῶνται	(ά-ονται)	ἐτιμῶντο	(ά-οντο)
IMPERATIVE.	S.	2.	τιμῶ	(ά-ου)		
		3.	τιμάσθω	(α-έσθω)		
	D.	2.	τιμᾶσθον	(ά-εσθον)		
		3.	τιμάσθων	(α-έσθων)		
	P.	2.	τιμᾶσθε	(ά-εσθε)		
		3.	τιμάσθων	(α-έσθων)		
			(Subjunctive).		*(Optative.)*	
CONJUNCTIVE.	S.	1.	τιμῶμαι	(ά-ωμαι)	τιμῴμην	(α-οίμην)
		2.	τιμᾷ	(ά-ῃ)	τιμῷο	(ά-οιο)
		3.	τιμᾶται	(ά-ηται)	τιμῷτο	(ά-οιτο)
	D.	2.	τιμᾶσθον	(ά-ησθον)	τιμῷσθον	(ά-οισθον)
		3.	τιμᾶσθον	(ά-ησθον)	τιμῴσθην	(α-οίσθην)
	P.	1.	τιμώμεθα	(α-ώμεθα)	τιμῴμεθα	(α-οίμεθα)
		2.	τιμᾶσθε	(ά-ησθε)	τιμῷσθε	(ά-οισθε)
		3.	τιμῶνται	(ά-ωνται)	τιμῷντο	(ά-οιντο)

Infinitive, { τιμᾶσθαι. (ά-εσθαι) }   Participle, { τιμώμενος, -η, -ον. (α-όμενος, -η, -ον). }

	ACTIVE.	MIDDLE.	PASSIVE.
FUTURE.	τιμή-σω	τιμή-σομαι	τιμη-θήσομαι
WEAK AORIST.	ἐ-τίμη-σα	ἐ-τιμη-σάμην	ἐ-τιμή-θην
PERFECT.	τε-τίμη-κα	τε-τίμη-μαι	τε-τίμη-μαι

CONTRACTED

120.   Stems in -ε,

ACTIVE.

	Number.	Person.	PRIMARY.		HISTORIC.	
			Present.		*Imperfect.*	
INDICATIVE.	S.	1.	φιλῶ	(έ-ω)	ἐφίλουν	(ε-ον)
		2.	φιλεῖς	(έ-εις)	ἐφίλεις	(ε-ες)
		3.	φιλεῖ	(έ-ει)	ἐφίλει	(ε-ε)
	D.	2.	φιλεῖτον	(έ-ετον)	ἐφιλεῖτον	(έ-ετον)
		3.	φιλεῖτον	(έ-ετον)	ἐφιλείτην	(ε-έτην)
	P.	1.	φιλοῦμεν	(έ-ομεν)	ἐφιλοῦμεν	(έ-ομεν)
		2.	φιλεῖτε	(έ-ετε)	ἐφιλεῖτε	(έ-ετε)
		3.	φιλοῦσι(ν)	(έ-ουσι)	ἐφίλουν	(ε-ον)
IMPERATIVE.	S.	2.	φίλει	(ε-ε)		
		3.	φιλείτω	(ε-έτω)		
	D.	2.	φιλεῖτον	(έ-ετον)		
		3.	φιλείτων	(ε-έτων)		
	P.	2.	φιλεῖτε	(έ-ετε)		
		3.	φιλούντων	(ε-όντων)		
			(Subjunctive).		*(Optative.)*	
CONJUNCTIVE.	S.	1.	φιλῶ	(έ-ω)	φιλοίην	(ε-οίην)
		2.	φιλῇς	(έ-ῃς)	φιλοίης	(ε-οίης)
		3.	φιλῇ	(έ-ῃ)	φιλοιη	(ε-οίη)
	D.	2.	φιλῆτον	(έ-ητον)	φιλοῖτον	(έ-οιτον)
		3.	φιλῆτον	(έ-ητον)	φιλοίτην	(ε-οίτην)
	P.	1.	φιλῶμεν	(έ-ωμεν)	φιλοῖμεν	(έ-οιμεν)
		2.	φιλῆτε	(έ-ητε)	φιλοῖτε	(έ-οιτε)
		3.	φιλῶσι(ν)	(έ-ωσι)	φιλοῖεν	(έ-οιεν)

Infinitive, { φιλεῖν. (ε-εεν) }   Participle, { φιλῶν   φιλοῦσα   φιλοῦν. (ε-ων)   (έ-ουσα)   (έ-ον) }

Contractions of E *Verbs* (cp. 11).

εε becomes ει ; εο becomes ου.

ε followed by a long vowel or diphthong is absorbed.

Obs. Stems in -ε of one syllable have only the contraction in ει (from ε-ε or ε-ει), as πλέ-ω, *I sail,* δεῖ, *it is necessary :*

	Indic.	*Imper.*	*Conj. Prim.*	*Conj. Hist.*	*Infin.*	*Partic*
Pres. and {	πλέ-ω, ἔ-πλε-ον	πλεῖ	πλέ-ω	πλέ-οιμι	πλεῖν	πλέ-ων
Impf. {	δεῖ, ἔ-δει	—	δέ-ῃ	δέ-οι	δεῖν	δέο-ν

But δέω, *I bind,* contracts throughout.

VERBS.

φιλέ-ω, *I love*, Verb-stem **φιλε**.

MIDDLE AND PASSIVE.

	Number.	Person.	PRIMARY.		HISTORIC.	
			Present.		*Imperfect.*	
INDICATIVE.	S.	1.	φιλοῦμαι	(έ-ομαι)	ἐφιλούμην	(ε-όμην)
		2.	φιλεῖ or -ῇ	(έ-ειορέ-η)	ἐφιλοῦ	(έ-ου)
		3.	φιλεῖται	(έ-εται)	ἐφιλεῖτο	(έ-ετο)
	D.	2.	φιλεῖσθον	(έ-εσθον)	ἐφιλεῖσθον	(έ-εσθον)
		3.	φιλεῖσθον	(έ-εσθον)	ἐφιλείσθην	(ε-έσθην)
	P.	1.	φιλούμεθα	(ε-όμεθα)	ἐφιλούμεθα	(ε-όμεθα)
		2.	φιλεῖσθε	(έ-εσθε)	ἐφιλεῖσθε	(έ-εσθε)
		3.	φιλοῦνται	(έ-ονται)	ἐφιλοῦντο	(έ-οντο)
IMPERATIVE.	S.	2.	φιλοῦ	(έ-ου)		
		3.	φιλείσθω	(ε-έσθω)		
	D.	2.	φιλεῖσθον	(έ-εσθον)		
		3.	φιλείσθων	(ε-έσθων)		
	P.	2.	φιλεῖσθε	(έ-εσθε)		
		3.	φιλείσθων	(ε-έσθων)		
			(Subjunctive.)		*(Optative.)*	
CONJUNCTIVE.	S.	1.	φιλῶμαι	(έ-ωμαι)	φιλοίμην	(ε-οίμην)
		2.	φιλῇ	(έ-η)	φιλοῖο	(έ-οιο)
		3.	φιλῆται	(έ-ηται)	φιλοῖτο	(έ-οιτο)
	D.	2.	φιλῆσθον	(έ-ησθον)	φιλοῖσθον	(έ-οισθον)
		3.	φιλῆσθον	(έ-ησθον)	φιλοίσθην	(ε-οίσθην)
	B.	1.	φιλώμεθα	(ε-ώμεθα)	φιλοίμεθα	(ε-οίμεθα)
		2.	φιλῆσθε	(έ-ησθε)	φιλοῖσθε	(ε-οισθε)
		3.	φιλῶνται	(έ-ωνται)	φιλοῖντο	(ε-οιντο)

Infinitive, { φιλεῖσθαι (έ-εσθαι)   Participle, { φιλούμενος, -η, -ον (ε-όμενος, -η, -ον)

	ACTIVE.	MIDDLE.	PASSIVE.
FUTURE,	φιλή-σω	φιλή-σομαι	none
WEAK AORIST,	ἐ-φίλη-σα	ἐ-φιλη-σάμην	ἐ-φιλή-θην
PERFECT,	none	πε-φίλη-μαι	πε-φίλη-μαι

121.　　　　　　　　　　　

ACTIVE.

	Number.	Person.	PRIMARY.		HISTORIC.	
			Present.		*Imperfect.*	
	S.	1.	δηλῶ	(ό-ω)	ἐδήλουν	(ο-ον)
		2.	δηλοῖς	(ό-εις)	ἐδήλους	(ο-ες)
		3.	δηλοῖ	(ό-ει)	ἐδήλου	(ο-ε)
INDICA- TIVE.	D.	2.	δηλοῦτον	(ό-ετον)	ἐδηλοῦτον	(ό-ετον)
		3.	Οηλοῦτον	(ό-ετον)	ἐδηλούτην	(ο-έτην)
	P.	1.	δηλοῦμεν	(ό-ομεν)	ἐδηλοῦμεν	(ό-ομεν)
		2.	δηλοῦτε	(ό-ετε)	ἐδηλοῦτε	(ό-ετε)
		3.	δηλοῦσι(ν)	(ό-ουσι)	ἐδήλουν	(ο-ον)
	S.	2.	δήλου	(ο-ε)		
		3.	δηλούτω	(ο-έτω)		
IMPERA- TIVE.	D.	2.	δηλοῦτον	(ό-ετον)		
		3.	δηλούτων	(ο-έτων)		
	P.	2.	δηλοῦτε	(ό-ετε)		
		3.	δηλούντων	(ο-όντων)		
			(Subjunctive.)		*(Optative.)*	
	S.	1.	δηλῶ	(ό-ω)	δηλοίην	(ο-οίην)
		2.	δηλοῖς	(ό-ῃς)	δηλοίης	(ο-οίης)
		3.	δηλοῖ	(ό-ῃ)	δηλοίη	(ο-οίη)
CONJUNC- TIVE.	D.	2.	δηλῶτον	(ό-ητον)	δηλοῖτον	(ό-οιτον)
		3.	δηλῶτον	(ό-ητον)	δηλοίτην	(ο-οίτην)
	P.	1.	δηλῶμεν	(ό-ωμεν)	δηλοῖμεν	(ό-οιμεν)
		2.	δηλῶτε	(ό-ητε)	δηλοῖτε	(ό-οιτε)
		3.	δηλῶσι(ν)	(ό-ωσι)	δηλοῖεν	(ό-οιεν)

Infinitive, { δηλοῦν (ο-εεν). }　　Participle, { δηλῶν　δηλοῦσα　δηλοῦν (ό-ων)　(ό-ουσα)　(ό-ον). }

Contractions of O *Verbs* (cp. 11).

o with a long vowel becomes ω.

o ,, short ,, ου.

Any combination with ι **becomes** οι.

VERBS.

δηλό-ω, *I show*, Verb-stem, **δηλο**.

MIDDLE AND PASSIVE.

	Number.	Person.	PRIMARY.		HISTORIC.	
			Present.		*Imperfect.*	
INDICA-TIVE.	S.	1.	δηλοῦμαι	(ό-ομαι)	ἐδηλούμην	(ο-όμην)
		2.	δηλοῖ	(ό-ῃ)	ἐδηλοῦ	(ό-ου)
		3.	δηλοῦται	(ό-εται)	ἐδηλοῦτο	(ό-ετο)
	D.	2.	δηλοῦσθον	(ό-εσθον)	ἐδηλοῦσθον	(ό-εσθον)
		3.	δηλοῦσθον	(ό-εσθον)	ἐδηλούσθην	(ο-έσθην)
	P.	1.	δηλούμεθα	(ο-όμεθα)	ἐδηλούμεθα	(ο-όμεθα)
		2.	δηλοῦσθε	(ό-εσθε)	ἐδηλοῦσθε	(ό-εσθε)
		3.	δηλοῦνται	(ό-ονται)	ἐδηλοῦντο	(ό-οντο)
IMPERA-TIVE.	S.	2.	δηλοῦ	(ό-ου)		
		3.	δηλούσθω	(ο-έσθω)		
	D.	2.	δηλοῦσθον	(ό-εσθον)		
		3.	δηλούσθων	(ο-έσθων)		
	P.	2.	δηλοῦσθε	(ό-εσθε)		
		3.	δηλούσθων	(ο-έσθων)		
			(Subjunctive.)		*(Optative.)*	
CONJUNC-TIVE.	S.	1.	δηλῶμαι	(ό-ωμαι)	δηλοίμην	(ο-οίμην)
		2.	δηλοῖ	(ό-ῃ)	δηλοῖο	(ό-οιο)
		3.	δηλῶται	(ό-ηται)	δηλοῖτο	(ό-οιτο)
	D.	2.	δηλῶσθον	(ό-ησθον)	δηλοῖσθον	(ό-οισθον)
		3.	δηλῶσθον	(ό-ησθον)	δηλοίσθην	(ο-οίσθην)
	P.	1.	δηλώμεθα	(ο-ώμεθα)	δηλοίμεθα	(ο-οίμεθα)
		2.	δηλῶσθε	(ό-ησθε)	δηλοῖσθε	(ό-οισθε)
		3.	δηλῶνται	(ό-ωνται)	δηλοῖντο	(ο-οιντο)

Infinitive, { δηλοῦσθαι (ό-εσθαι). } Participle, { δηλούμενος, -η, -ον (ο-όμενος, -η, -ον. }

	ACTIVE.	MIDDLE.	PASSIVE.
FUTURE,	δηλώ-σω	δηλώ-σομαι	δηλω-θήσομαι
WEAK AORIST,	ἐ-δήλω-σα	ἐ-δηλω-σάμην	ἐ-δηλώ-θην
PERFECT,	δε-δήλω-κα	δε-δήλω-μαι	δε-δήλω-μαι

Augment.

122. THE Augment is prefixed to all Historic Tenses in the Indicative Mood.

I. The Syllabic Augment prefixes ε to Stems beginning with a consonant, as :—

λύ-ω, *I loose.*　Imperfect, ἔ-λυ-ον.

Obs. 1. ρ is doubled, as ῥίπτ-ω, *I throw.* Impf. ἔρριπτ-ον.
Obs. 2. βούλομαι, δύναμαι, and μέλλω take either ε or η.

II. The Temporal Augment lengthens a short initial vowel :—

α into	η	as	ἄγ-ω, *I lead.*	Impf.	ἦγ-ον.
ε	„	η	„	ἐθέλ-ω, *I wish.*	„	ἤθελ-ον.
ο	„	ω	„	ὀνομάζ-ω, *I name.*	„	ὠνόμαζ-ον.
ῐ	„	ῑ	„	ἱκετεύ-ω, *I beseech.*	„	ἱκέτευ-ον.
ῠ	„	ῡ	„	ὑβρίζ-ω, *I insult.*	„	ὕβριζ-ον.

The Diphthongs αι, οι, αυ are similarly augmented :—

αι into	η	as	αἱρέ-ω, *I take.*	Impf.	ἤρουν.
οι	„	ῳ	„	οἰκτείρ-ω, *I pity.*	„	ᾤκτειρ-ον.
αυ	„	ηυ	„	αὐξάν-ω, *I increase.*	„	ηὔξαν-ον.

Other Diphthongs, as ει, ευ, are not usually augmented.

123. *Obs.* 1. In nine Verbs ει is found instead of η from ε. These are :—

ἐάω, *I permit.*	ἐργάζομαι, *I work.*
ἐθίζω, *I accustom.*	ἕρπω, *I creep.*
ἑλίσσω, *I roll.*	ἑστιάω, *I feast (trans.)*
ἕλκω, *I drag.*	ἔχω, *I have.*
ἕπομαι, *I follow.*	

These Verbs originally began with a consonant and took the Syllabic Augment, but, the consonant being lost, ει has resulted from the contraction of ε with ε : thus ἕρπω = σερπω (Lat. *serpo*), Impf. εἷρπον for ἐ(σ)ερπ-ον. So εἰργαζόμην for ἐ(F)εργαζομην and εἶχον for ἐ(σ)εχον.

Obs. 2. In a few Verbs, for the same reason, the Syllabic Augment ε stands before a vowel, ὠθέω, *I thrust,* ἐώθουν.

A few have both Augments, as ὁράω, *I see,* ἑώρων.

Augment in Compound Words.

124. Verbs compounded with a preposition insert the Augment between the preposition and the stem, as :—

εἰσ-φέρ-ω, *I carry to.*   Impf. εἰσ-έ-φερ-ον.
ἐκ-βάλλω, *I cast out.*   „   ἐξ-έ-βαλλ-ον.
συλ-λέγω, *I gather.*   „   συν-έ-λεγ-ον.

The final vowel of a preposition is cut off before the Augment, as, ἀπο-βάλλ-ω, *I cast away*, ἀπ-έ-βαλλ-ον : περί and πρό are exceptions, *e.g.* περι-βάλλ-ω, *I cast around*, περι-έ-βαλλ-ον ; προ-βάλλω *I cast before,* προ-έ-βαλλ-ον, or (by crasis) προὔβαλλον.

125. *Obs.* Verbs compounded with δυs- augment before it, if the stem begins with a consonant or a long vowel, as, δυσ-φορέ-ω, *I am impatient*, ἐ-δυσ-φόρουν, δυσ-ωνέ-ω, *I haggle*, ἐ-δυσ-ώνουν ; but after it, if the stem begins with a short vowel, as, δυσ-ἄρεστέ-ω, *I am ill-pleased*, δυσ-ηρέστουν. For verbs compounded with εὖ, no rule can be given. All other compounds take the augment at the beginning, as, οἰκο-δομέω, *I build a house*, ᾠκο-δόμουν.

Reduplication.

126. Reduplication is a means of prolonging the sound of the Stem, to signify continuance in the action of the Verb (but it is found in Substantives as well as verbs). The Reduplication marks the Perfect-stem, and is therefore found in all Moods of the Perfects, Pluperfects, and Future Perfect.

I. If the stem begins with a single consonant, this consonant is repeated with ε, as Verb-stem λυ. Perfect-stem, λε-λυ. But if the first consonant is an aspirate (χ, θ, φ), the corresponding hard letter (κ, τ, π), is used in reduplication, as :—

θυω, *I sacrifice.*   Verb-stem, θυ.   Perfect, τέ-θῠ-κα.

II. If the stem begins

    (1) with two consonants, *the second being a mute,*

    (2) with a double consonant (ψ, ξ, ζ),

    (3) with ρ,

    ε only is prefixed, ρ being doubled, as :—

κτείνω, *I kill.*   Verb-stem, κτεν   Perfect, ἔ-κτον-α.

στερέω, *I deprive.*   „   στερε   „   ἐ-στέρη-κα.

ζητέω, *I seek.*   „   ζητε   „   ἐ-ζήτη-κα.

ῥίπτω, *I throw.*   „   ῥιπ   ,.   ἔῤ-ῥιφ-α.

But if the second consonant is λ, ρ, μ, or ν, the first consonant is usually repeated, as :—

πλήσσω, *I strike.*   Verb-stem, πλαγ   Perfect, πέ-πληγ-α.

γρεφω, *I write.*   „   γραφ   „   γέ-γραφ-α.

III. If the stem begins with a vowel, the vowel is length-ened as in the case of the Temporal Augment :—

ἀγγέλλω, *I announce.* Verb-stem, ἀγγελ. Perf ἠγγελ-κα.

N.B.—In Compound Verbs the position of Reduplication is the same as that of the Augment (cp. 124).

127. *Attic Reduplication.*—Some stems beginning with a, ε, o, take the Attic Reduplication, which lengthens the initial vowel, and also prefixes the first two letters of the stem, as :—

    ἀλείφω, *I anoint.* Verb-stem, ἀλιφ   Perf. ἀλ-ήλιφ-α.

    ἐλαύνω, *I drive.*   „   ἐλα   „   ἐλ-ήλα-κα.

    ὀρύσσω, *I dig.*   „   ὀρυχ   „   ὀρ-ώρυγ-μαι.

128. *Reduplication with* ι.—This form of Reduplication is found in the Present-stem Tenses of some Verbs in -μι of the First Class, and some others :—

    Verb-stem, θε   Present, τί-θη-μι, *I put.*

    „   ἑ   „   ἵ-η-μι, *I send.*

    „   στα   „   ἵ-στη-μι (for σι-στη-μι), *I place.*

    „   δο   „   δί-δω-μι, *I give.*

    „   γνω   ..   γι-γνώ-σκω, *I know.*

Formation of Tenses.

129. THE stems for the various tenses are formed from the Verb-stem (cp. 102) by the addition of letters at the end of the stem, *e.g.* Verb-stem λῠ, Fut. stem λῡ-σ ; or by altering the vowel of the stem, *e.g.* Verb-stem λῐπ, Pres. stem λειπ ; or by reduplication, *e.g.* Verb-stem λῠ, Perf. stem, middle, λε-λῠ. In many forms the letters added at the end of the stems have coalesced with the final consonant of the stem, as in the nouns.

Group i.—*Present-stem.*

130. *N.B.*—The Present-*stem* includes the Present and Imperfect *tenses*.

The formations of the Present-stem may be arranged under six heads, as in the following paradigm :—

Formation.	Verb-stem.	Present-stem.	Present.	Imperfect.
1.	ἀγ τιμα λῠ	ἀγ- τιμα- λῠ-	ἄγ-ω τιμά-ω λῠ-ω	ἦγ-ο-ν ἐ-τίμα-ο-ν ἐ-λῡ-ο-ν
2.	λῐπ φῠγ τᾰκ	λειπ- φευγ- τηκ-	λείπ-ω φεύγ-ω τήκ-ω	ἔ-λειπ-ο-ν ἔ-φευγ-ο-ν ἔ-τηκ-ο-ν
3.	τῠπ βλᾰβ	τυπ-τ- βλαπ-τ-	τύπ-τ-ω βλάπ-τ-ω	ἔ-τυπ-τ-ο-ν ἔ-βλαπ-τ-ο-ν
4.	φυλακ κρᾱγ φρᾰδ βᾰλ	φυλασσ- κραζ- φραζ- βαλλ-	φυλάσσ-ω κράζ-ω φράζ-ω βάλλ-ω	ἐ-φύλασσ-ον ἔ-κραζ-ο-ν ἔ-φραζ-ο-ν ἔ-βαλλ-ο-ν
5.	γηρα(s)	γηρα-σκ-	γηράσκ-ω	ἐ-γήρασκ-ο-ν
6.	λᾰβ	λα-μ-β-αν-	λαμβάν-ω	ἐ-λάμβαν-ο-ν

(1.) *Unenlarged Formation.*—The Verb-stem is used for the Present-stem without any change,

as ἄγω, *I lead*, Verb-stem, ἀγ.

But ῐ and ῠ become ῑ and ῡ, as λύ-ω, *I loose*, Verb-stem, λῡ.

Obs. The origin of this lengthening is doubtful; it may be the remains of a lost iota, in which case these presents would belong to class 4.

(2.) *Lengthened Formation.*—The Verb-stem is lengthened by flexional lengthening (cp. 14), *e.g.* λείπ-ω, *I leave*, Verb-stem, λῐπ.

Examples.—φεύγω, *I fly*; πείθω, *I persuade*; τήκω, *I melt.*

(3.) **T** *Formation.*—The Verb-stem is increased by the addition of τ, *e.g.* τύπτ-ω, *I strike*, Verb-stem, τῠπ.

Examples.—κόπτω, *I beat*; βάπτω, *I dip*; βλάπτω, *I harm.*

Obs. With the exception of τίκτ-ω this formation is confined to labial stems.

(4.) **I** *Formation.*—The Verb-stem is increased by the addition of ι. This ι coalesces with the final consonant of the stem according to certain laws of sound.

γ, κ, or χ	with	ι=σσ,	*e.g.* φυλάσσω, *I guard*,	for	φυλακι-ω.
γ	,,	ι= ζ,	*e.g.* κράζω, *I cry*,	,,	κραγι-ω.
τ	,,	ι=σσ,	*e.g.* πλάσσω, *I mould*,	,,	πλατι-ω.
δ	,,	ι= ζ,	*e.g.* φράζω, *I tell*,	,,	φραδι-ω.
λ	,,	ι=λλ,	*e.g.* βάλλω, *I throw*,	,,	βαλι-ω.

ν and ρ transfer the ι into the preceding syllable (*epenthesis*), *i.e.* νι, ρι, become ιν, ιρ.

Thus κτείνω, *I slay*,	for	κτενι-ω.	
φθείρω, *I destroy*,	,,	φθερι-ω.	
κρίνω, *I judge*,	,,	κρῐνι-ω.	

Obs. So, exceptionally, one λ Verb, ὀφείλω, *I owe*, for ὀφελι-ω.

Examples.

ταράσσω, *I disturb* (ταραχι-ω), τάσσω, *I arrange* (ταγι-ω).
ἐρέσσω, *I row* (ἐρετι-ω), βράσσω, *I roast* (βρατι-ω).
σαλπίζω, *I blow a trumpet* (σαλπιγγι-ω), στάζω, *I drop* (σταγι-ω).
ἀγγέλλω, *I announce* (ἀγγελι-ω).

(5.) *Inceptive Formation.*—The letters σκ are added to the Verb-stem, which is sometimes reduplicated,

e.g. ἡβά-σκ-ω, *I grow young*,   Verb-stem, ἡβα
     δι-δρά-σκ-ω, *I run*,   Verb-stem, δρα

From the meaning of "beginning to do or be," conveyed by some of these verbs, the class is called inceptive (*incipere*, *to begin*).

(6.) *Nasal Formation.*—The letters ν, αν, νε (νι), are added to the Verb-stem,

e.g. δάκ-ν-ω, *I bite*,   Verb-stem, δακ
     ἁμαρτ-άν-ω, *I err*,   „   ἁμαρτ
     ἱκ-νέ-ομαι, *I come*,   „   ἱκ
     βαίνω (βα-νι-ω), *I come*, „   βα

Or, ν (γ, μ) is inserted in the Stem and αν is added,

     τυγχ-άν-ω, *I hit*,   Verb-stem, τυχ
     λαμβ-άν-ω, *I take*,   „   λαβ

For examples see 167.

Parallels to these classes may easily be supplied from Latin, *e.g.*

Class i. *ag-o, reg-o, amo* (for *ama-o*).

   ii. *dūco*, older *douco*, stem *dŭc*.

   iii. *plec-t-o, flec-t-o.*

   iv. *cap-i-o, fac-i-o, jac-i-o.*

   v. *ap-i-sc-or, pa-sc-o*, and, with inceptive meaning, *pube-sc o, invetera-sc-o.*

   vi. *ju-n-go, ju-n-xi, ju-n-ctum* (cp. *jug-um*).
       fi-n-go, fi-n-xi, fic-tum.
       ta-n-go tetig-i, tac-tum.

131. *Group* ii.—*The Strong Aorist, Active and Middle.*

The strong Aorist Active adds -ο-ν to the Verb-stem.
The Strong Aorist Middle adds -ό-μην to the Verb-stem.

The Augment is prefixed in the Indicative Mood.

The terminations are the same as those of the Imperfect Active and Middle, and therefore in Verbs of the First or Unenlarged formation, in which the Verb-stem and Present-stem are the same, there is, as as a rule, no Strong Aorist, for it would be identical with the Imperfect. In any of the other five formations the tense may occur, *e.g.*:—

Formation—

	Verb-stem.	Active.	Middle.
(2.) λείπω, *I leave,*	λιπ	ἔλιπον	ἐλιπόμην
(3.) τίκτω, *I bring forth,*	τεκ	ἔτεκον	ἐτεκόμην
(4.) βάλλω, *I cast,*	βαλ	ἔβαλον	ἐβαλόμην
(5.) εὑρίσκω, *I find,*	εὑρ	εὗρον	εὑρόμην
(6.) ἁμαρτάνω, *I err,*	ἁμαρτ	ἥμαρτον	ἡμαρτόμην

Obs. In a few instances a Strong Aorist is formed from verbs of the first formation by (1.) change of the vowels of the stem; (2.) omission of the vowels; (3.) reduplication, *e.g.* :—

	Verb-stem	Active	Middle
(1.) πλέκω, *I weave,*	πλεκ	ἔ-πλακ-ο-ν	ἐ-πλακ-ό-μην
τρέπω, *I turn,*	τρεπ	ἔ-τραπ-ο-ν	ἐ-τραπ-ό-μην
(2.) ἔχω, *I have,*	σεχ	ἔ-σχ-ο-ν	ἐ-σχ-ό-μην
ἕπομαι, *I follow,*	σεπ		ἐ-σπ-ό-μην
(3.) ἄγω, *I lead,*	ἀγ	ἤγ-αγ-ο-ν	ἠγ-αγ-ό-μην

Strong and Weak.—Tenses are relatively *Strong* or *Weak* according as they rely, less or more, on external additions to the Verb-stem.

132. *Group* iii.—*The Future Active and Middle.*

The Future Active adds -σω to the Verb-stem,

The Future Middle adds -σομαι to the Verb-stem,

e.g. ἄγω, *I lead*, Verb-stem, ἀγ, ἄξω, ἄξομαι (ξ for γσ).
κόπτω, *I beat*, Verb-stem, κοπ, κόψω (ψ for πσ).

A short final vowel is lengthened before σ, *e.g.* λῠ,
λύσω, τιμᾰ, τιμήσω. Except αἰνέω and others, see list, 161.

A dental is omitted before σ, φράζω, φράσω (φραδ-σω).

Obs. a if preceded by ε, ι, or ρ, becomes ᾱ not η,
  e.g. ἐάω, *I allow*, fut. ἐάσω.
    ἰάομαι, *I heal*, fut. ἰάσομαι.
    δράω, *I do*, fut. δράσω.

As the Future is formed from the *Verb-stem*, not from
the Present-stem, the additional elements used in forming
the Present-stem in formations 3, 4, 5, 6, are dropped in
the Future; but the *lengthened stem* in formation 2 is
retained in the Future, *e.g.* λείπω, λείψω.

Contracted Future.

133. (1.) *Futures without* σ.

(*a.*) Verbs with liquid or nasal characters reject σ in
the Future (115), and are conjugated as contracted verbs
like φιλέω, *e.g.*:—

  κρίνω, *I judge*, Verb-stem, κρῐν, fut. κρῐνῶ, -εῖς, -εῖ, etc.
  νέμω, *I distribute*, Verb-stem, νεμ, fut. νεμῶ, -εῖς, -εῖ, etc.
  σφάλλω, *I overthrow*, Verb-stem, σφᾰλ, fut. σφᾰλῶ,
    -εῖς, -εῖ, etc.

(*b.*) In some Futures σ is omitted and the final vowel of the stem contracts with -ω of the termination, *e.g.* :—

τελῶ (-εω), *I accomplish*, fut. τελῶ (τελέσω), εῖς, εῖ, etc.
ὄλλυμι, *I destroy*, fut. ὀλῶ (ὀλέσω), -εῖς, -εῖ, etc.
ἐλαύνω, *I drive*, fut. ἐλῶ (ἐλάσω), -ᾷς, -ᾷ, etc.
Verbs in -άζω usually keep σ in the future, as

σκευάζω, *I prepare*, fut. -άσω, στεγάζω, fut. -άσω,
but πελάζω, *I come near*, has fut. πελῶ, -ᾷς, -ᾷ.

(*c.*) The same formation of the Future is also found in verbs in -ίζω (-ιδιω), of more than two syllables (*Attic future*, cp. 116), *e.g.* :—

κομίζω, *I bring near*, Verb-st. **κομιδ**, fut. κομιῶ, -εῖς, -εῖ.

134. (2.) *Futures with σ.*

A few verbs have a Future Middle in -σοῦμαι, beside the common form in -σομαι (*Doric future*).

πνέω, *I blow*, πνευσοῦμαι (πνεύσομαι).
πλέω, *I sail*, πλευσοῦμαι (πλεύσομαι).
φεύγω, *I fly*, φευξοῦμαι (φεύξομαι).

135. In verbs which signify a bodily or personal activity, the Future Middle has frequently an active meaning : such are, ᾄδω, *I sing* ; ἀκούω, *I hear* ; ἀπολαύω, *I enjoy* ; βαδίζω, *I walk* ; βοάω, *I call* ; γελάω, *I laugh* ; οἰμώζω, *I wail* ; σιγάω and σιωπάω, *I keep silence*. Compare also the lists of irregular verbs (**163**).

136. In some verbs the Future Middle can have a passive sense ; the most common are τιμήσομαι, ἀδικήσομαι, οἰκήσομαι, ὠφελήσομαι, στερήσομαι. Futures in -οῦμαι are rare in the passive sense.

137. *Group* iv.—*The Weak Aorist, Active and Middle.*

The Weak Aorist Active adds -σα to the Verb-stem.

The Weak Aorist Middle adds -σάμην to the Verb-stem.

The Augment is prefixed in the Indicative Mood.

The rules given for the lengthening of the vowel and change of consonants before -σω and -σομαι of the Future, apply to -σα and -σάμην of the Aorist.

Verbs with liquid or nasal characters reject σ in the Weak Aorist, and lengthen the vowel in compensation (cp. 15) *e.g.* :—

σφάλλω, *I overthrow,* (ἐ-σφαλ-σα) ἔσφηλα.
νέμω, *I distribute,* (ἐ-νεμ-σα) ἔνειμα.
κρίνω, *I judge,* (ἐ-κριν-σα) ἔκρῑνα.
φθείρω, *I destroy,* (ἐ-φθερ-σα) ἔφθειρα.

The Weak Aorist is found in verbs of all formations; it is the usual Aorist in the first formation; less common in the others, especially in the nasal formation.

138. *Group* v.—*The Perfects, Pluperfects, and Future Perfect.*

The stems of these tenses are distinguished by reduplication.

A.—*The Perfects Active (Strong and Weak).*

The Perfect Active is formed in two ways :- -

I. The Strong Perfect adds -a to the reduplicated Verb-stem, and the vowel of the stem is (as a rule) strengthened; *e.g.* :—

Verb-stem,	φαν, *shew*,	Perfect,	πέ-φην-α.
„	πραγ, *do*,	„	πέ-πρᾱγ-α.
„	λιπ, *leave*,	„	λέ-λοιπ-α.
„	τρεφ, *nourish*,	„	τέ-τροφ-α.
„	γραφ, *write*,	„	γέ-γρᾰφ-α.

In some guttural and labial stems the character is aspirated :—

Verb-stem,	τρεπ, *turn*,	Perfect,	τέ-τροφ-α.
„	πλεκ, *weave*,	„	[πέ-πλεχ-α.]
„	βλαβ, *harm*,	„	βἔ-βλᾰφ-α.

Obs. πράσσω, *I do* (stem πραγ), has both forms, πέπρᾱγα, and πέπρᾱχα. The unaspirated perfect is *intransitive, I have fared;* the aspirated is *transitive, I have done.*

139. II. The Weak Perfect adds -κα to the reduplicated Verb-stem. The quantity of the stem-vowel is generally the same as in the Future.

The Weak Perfect is the only form found in vowel-stems, and is the commoner form in dental, liquid, and nasal stems.

Before κ the Dental Mutes are dropped.
    „   the Liquids (λ, ρ) remain unchanged.
    „   the Nasal ν becomes Nasal γ (=ng).

Verb-stem,	τιμα, *honour*,	Perfect,	τε-τίμη-κα.
„	κομιδ, *convey*,	„	κε-κόμῐ-κα.
„	πιθ, *advise*,	„	πέ-πει-κα.
„	ἀγγελ, *announce*,	„	ἤγγελ-κα.
„	φᾰν *shew*,	„	[πέ-φαγ-κα.]

Obs. When a Verb has both a Strong and a Weak Perfect, the first is generally intransitive, the second transitive, *e.g.* :—

Strong, πέποιθα, *I trust.*   Weak, πέπεικα, *I have persuaded.*

  „   πέφηνα, *I have appeared.*   „   [πέφαγκα,] *I have shown.*

140.   **B.**—*The Pluperfects Active (Strong and Weak).*

The stems of the Pluperfects are formed as those of the Perfects. To this stem the Pluperfect prefixes the augment, and adds the termination η in place of the Perfect *a*, *e.g.* :—

Perfect, πέ-ποιθ-α,   Pluperfect, ἐ-πε-ποίθη.

    „   τε-τίμη-κα,   „   ἐ-τε-τιμή-κη.

Obs. A later form of the 1st sing. Pluperfect ends in -ειν.

141.   **C.**—*The Perfects, Middle and Passive.*

The Perfects, Middle and Passive, which have the same form, add -μαι to the reduplicated Verb-stem, *e.g.* Verb-stem λυ, Perfect, Middle and Passive, λέλὔ-μαι.

In Verbs of the second or lengthened class the lengthened form of the Present is often retained in the Perfect Passive, *e.g.* :—

Verb-stem, πιθ, Pres. πείθω, Perf. M. and P. πέ-πεισ-μαι.

    „   λιπ,   „   λείπω,   „   „   λέ-λειμ-μαι.

Obs. The final consonant of the stem here comes into direct collision with the initial consonant of the terminations, -μαι, -σαι, -ται, etc. This gives rise to a variety of changes, for which see the Paradigm of the Perfect Passive, and the rules in **113, 114.**

142.   **D.**—*The Pluperfect, Middle and Passive.*

As in the Active, the Pluperfect follows the Perfect; the stem is the same, but the Augment is prefixed, and the historical termination -μην takes the place of -μαι, *e.g.* :—

Perfect, λέ-λὔ-μαι.   Pluperfect, ἐ-λε-λύ-μην.

143.   **E.—*The Future Perfect.***

The Future Perfect, Middle and Passive, is formed from the Perfect stem by the addition of -σομαι, the termination of the Future. The stem-vowel, if short, is lengthened, as in the Future, *e.g.* :—

Perf. stem, γεγράφ, *write.*   Fut. Perf. γεγράψομαι.
   „   λελῠ, *loose.*   „   λελῡσομαι.

An Active Form of this Future is sometimes found, *e.g.* πεπράξω, *I shall do* (*have done*).

144.   *Group* vi.—*The Aorists and Futures Passive.*

There are two formations of the Aorist Passive.

I. (*a.*) The Strong Aorist Passive is marked by the addition of ε (which generally becomes η) to the Verb-stem. The terminations are those of the Active Historic Tenses.

In the Indicative Mood the Augment is prefixed.

Ex. Verb-stem, τῠπ, *strike.*   Str. Aor. Pass., ἐ-τῠπ-η-ν.
    „   στᾰλ, *send.*   „   ἐ-στᾰλ-η-ν.

This form is rarely found in Verbs which have a Strong Aorist Active.

(*b.*) The Strong Future Passive is formed by adding -ήσομαι to the Verb-stem, *e.g.* :—

Verb-stem, τῠπ, *strike.* Str. Fut. Pass., τῠπ-ήσομαι.
    „   στᾰλ, *send.*   „   στᾰλ-ήσομαι.

145. II. (*a.*) The Weak Aorist Passive adds θε, which generally becomes θη, to the Verb-stem. In other respects the formation is the same as the Strong Aorist, *e.g.* :—

Verb-stem, λῦ, *loose.*   Weak Aor. Pass. ἐ-λῠ́-θη-ν.
    „   παιδευ, *instruct.*   „   ἐ-παιδεύ-θη-ν.

Obs. An aspirate may be transposed, 22 (*b.*), *e.g.* verb-stem θυ, *sacrifice.* Weak Aor. Pass., ἐ-τῠ́-θη-ν.

(*b.*) The Weak Future Passive adds -θήσομαι to the Verb-stem, *e.g.* :—

Verb-stem, λῦ, *loose.*   Weak Fut. Pass. λῠ-θήσομαι.
    „   παιδευ, *instruct.*   „   παιδευ-θήσομαι.

Accentuation of Verbs.

146. *General Rule.*—The accent is placed as far back as possible.

Peculiarities of accent will be best noted under each Mood :—

Indicative.—The Presents of εἰμί and φημί are oxytone, but (except in 2 Sing.) are usually enclitic.

N.B.—Contracted Futures are circumflexed, as φανῶ. If the accent fall on the Temporal Augment, it must be a circumflex if possible, as ἦγε.

Imperative.—The Strong Aor. Mid. is perispomenon, as λιποῦ.

The following are oxytone :—ἐλθέ, εὑρέ, ἰδέ, λαβέ, εἰπέ.

Conjunctive Primary.—The Aorists Passive of Verbs in -ω, and all tenses of the -μι conjugation, have the circumflex (perispomenon or properispomenon).

Conjunctive Historic.—All Pass. Tenses of the -μι conjugation have the circumflex where possible. Final αι and οι are considered long.

Infinitive.—(*a.*) The following accent the last syllable but one, if short with the acute, if long with the circumflex :—

> The Weak Aor. Act., as νομίσαι, ποιῆσαι.
> The Strong Aor. Mid., as λιπέσθαι.
> The Perf. Mid. and Pass., as λελύσθαι, πεποιῆσθαι.
> All that end in -ναι, as λελυκέναι, τιθέναι, εἶναι.

(*b.*) The Strong Aor. Act. is perispomenon, as λιπεῖν.

Participle.—(*a.*) The following are oxytone :—

> The Strong Aor. Act., as λιπών.
> All of the Third Decl. that end in -ς (except the Weak Aor. Act.), as λελυκώς, λυθείς, ἱστάς, διδούς.

(*b.*) The Perf. Mid. and Pass. and the Verbal in -τέος are paroxytone throughout. as τετυμμένος, λυτέος.

N.B.—In all paroxytone words, the vowel on which the accent falls is short; if the vowel is long, the word is properispomenon.

Verbs in -μι.

147. VERBS in -μι differ from verbs in -ω only in the Present, Imperfect, and Strong Aorist Tenses Active and Middle. In these tenses the personal endings are added to the Verb-stem or Present-stem without the connecting vowel (*o*, *ε*) which is found in the same tenses of verbs in -ω.

Formation of Tenses.

Present	Pres.-Stem.	**Active** -μι	**Middle** -μαι	
Imperfect	Aug., Pres.-Stem.	,, -ν	,, -μην	
Strong Aor.	Aug., Verb-Stem.	,, -ν	,, -μην	

A few verbs differ also in the Perfect. The remaining tenses are the same in both conjugations.

Verbs in -μι are divided into two classes according to the formation of the Present-stem :—

FIRST CLASS.—Verbs in which the Verb-stem, or the Verb-stem reduplicated with ι, is used as the Present-stem, as φη-μί, *I say*, Verb-stem φα. δίδω-μι, *I give*, Verb-stem δο.

N.B.—Verbs of the first class lengthen the vowel in the sing. of the Active tenses.

SECOND CLASS.—Verbs in which the syllable -νυ is added to the Verb-stem to form the Present-stem, as δείκνυ-μι, *I show*, Verb-stem δεικ. (This class includes the Consonant-stems.)

In three verbs of the first class, τίθημι, ἵημι, and δίδωμι the Weak Aorist ends in -κα—ἔθηκα, ἧκα, ἔδωκα. These forms are peculiar to the Indicative, and are generally found in the sing. only.

---

148. Many verbs have a Present and Imperfect in the ω conjugation, and follow the μι conjugation only in the Aorist, as γιγνώσκω, *I know*, aor. ἔ-γνω-ν. βαίνω, *I go*, aor. ἔ-βη-ν. διδράσκω, *I run*, aor. ἔ-δρα-ν. κτείνω, *I kill*, aor. ἔ-κτα-ν. φθάνω. *I anticipate*, aor. ἔ-φθη-ν.

149.

τί-θη-μι, *I place,*

ACTIVE

Tense.	Number.	Person.	INDICATIVE. Primary.	INDICATIVE. Historic.	IMPERATIVE.
			Present.	*Imperfect.*	
PRESENT AND IMPERFECT. Stem τιθε.	S.	1.	τί-θη-μι	ἐ-τί-θη-ν	——
		2.	τί-θη-ς	ἐ-τί-θεις *	τί-θει *
		3.	τί-θη-σι(ν)	ἐ-τί-θει *	τι-θέ-τω
	D.	2.	τί-θε-τον	ἐ-τί-θε-τον	τί-θε-τον
		3.	τί-θε-τον	ἐ-τι-θέ-την	τι-θέ-των
	P.	1.	τί-θε-μεν	ἐ-τί-θε-μεν	——
		2.	τί-θε-τε	ἐ-τί-θε-τε	τί-θε-τε
		3.	τι-θέ-ᾱσι(ν)	ἐ-τί-θε-σαν	τι-θέ-ντων
				Strong. *Weak.*	
AORIST. Stem θε.	S.	1.		ἔ-θη-κα	
		2.		ἔ-θη-κας	θέ-ς
		3.		ἔ-θη-κε(ν)	θέ-τω
	D.	2.		ἔ-θε-τον	θέ-τον
		3.		ἐ-θέ-την	θέ-των
	P.	1.		ἔ-θε-μεν	——
		2.		ἔ-θε-τε	θέ-τε
		3.		ἔ-θε-σαν ἔ-θη-καν	θέ-ντων

MIDDLE

	Number.	Person.	Primary.	Historic.	IMPERATIVE.
			Present.	*Imperfect.*	
PRESENT AND IMPERFECT. Stem τιθε.	S.	1.	τί-θε-μαι	ἐ-τι-θέ-μην	——
		2.	τί-θε-σαι	ἐ-τί-θε-σο	τί-θε-σο
		3.	τί-θε-ται	ἐ-τί-θε-το	τι-θέ-σθω
	D.	2.	τί-θε-σθον	ἐ-τί-θε-σθον	τί-θε-σθον
		3.	τί-θε-σθον	ἐ-τι-θέ-σθην	τι-θέ-σθων
	P.	1.	τι-θέ-μεθα	ἐ-τι-θέ-μεθα	——
		2.	τί-θε-σθε	ἐ-τί-θε-σθε	τί-θε-σθε
		3.	τί-θε-νται	ἐ-τί-θε-ντο	τι-θέ-σθων
STRONG AORIST. Stem θε.	S.	1.		ἐ-θέ-μην	——
		2.		ἔ-θου	θοῦ
		3.		ἔ-θε-το	θέ-σθω
				Etc., as Imperfect.	Etc., as Present.

* Formed as from Verb in -ω.   Impf. rarely ἐ-τίθη-ς, ἐ-τίθη.

Verb-stem **θε.**

VOICE.

CONJUNCTIVE.		VERB INFINITE.	
Primary (Subjunc.)	Historic (Optative).	Subst. (Infin.)	Adj. (Participle).
τι-θῶ	τι-θείην	τι-θέ-ναι	M. τι-θεί-ς
τι-θῇ-ς	τι-θείης		F. τι-θεῖ-σα
τι-θῇ	τι-θείη		N. τι-θέ-ν
τι-θῆ-τον	τι-θεῖτον		
τι-θῆ-τον	τι-θείτην		Stem τιθεντ
τι-θῶ-μεν	τι-θεῖμεν		
τι-θῆ-τε	τι-θεῖτε		
τι-θῶ-σι(ν)	τι-θεῖεν		
θῶ	θείην	θεῖ-ναι	M. θεί-ς
θῇς	θείης		F. θεῖ-σα
θῇ	θείη		N. θέ-ν
θῆ-τον	θεῖτον		
θῆ-τον	θείτην		Stem θεντ
θῶ-μεν	θεῖμεν		
θῆ-τε	θεῖτε		
θῶ-σι(ν)	θεῖεν		

VOICE.

τι-θῶ-μαι	τι-θεί-μην	τί-θε-σθαι	M. τι-θέ-μενος
τι-θῇ	τι-θεῖ-ο		F. τι-θε-μένη
τι-θῆ-ται	τι-θεῖ-το		N. τι-θέ-μενον
τι-θῆ-σθον	τι-θεῖ-σθον		
τι-θῆ-σθον	τι-θεί-σθην		Stem τιθεμενο
τι-θώ-μεθα	τι-θεί-μεθα		
τι-θῆσ-θε	τι-θεῖ-σθε		
τι-θῶ-νται	τι-θεῖ-ντο		
θῶ-μαι	θεί-μην	θέ-σθαι	M. θέ-μενος
θῇ	θεῖ-ο		F. θε-μένη
θῆ-ται	θεῖ-το		N. θέ-μενον
Etc., as Present.	Etc., as Present.		Stem θεμενο

150.

ἵ-η-μι, *I send,*

ACTIVE

TENSE.	Number.	Person.	INDICATIVE.		IMPERATIVE.
			Primary.	Historic.	
			Present.	*Imperfect.*	
PRESENT AND IMPERFECT. Stem ἱε.	S.	1.	ἵ-η-μι	ἵ-ειν	—
		2.	ἵ-η-s	ἵ-εις*	ἵ-ει *
		3.	ἵ-η-σι(ν)	ἵ-ει*	ἱ-έ-τω
	D.	2.	ἵ-ε-τον	ἵ-ε-τον	ἵ-ε-τον
		3.	ἵ-ε-τον	ἱ-έ-την	ἱ-έ-των
	P.	1.	ἵ-ε-μεν	ἵ-ε-μεν	—
		2.	ἵ-ε-τε	ἵ-ε-τε	ἵ-ε-τε
		3.	ἱ-ᾶ-σι(ν)	ἵ-ε-σαν	ἱ-έ-ντων

TENSE.	Number.	Person.	INDICATIVE. Historic.		IMPERATIVE.
			Strong.	Weak.	
AORIST. Stem ἑ.	S.	1.		ἧ-κα	—
		2.		ἧ-κας	ἕ-s
		3.		ἧ-κε(ν)	ἕ-τω
	D.	2.	εἷτον		ἕ-τον
		3.	εἵ-την		ἕ-των
	P.	1.	εἷ-μεν		—
		2.	εἷ-τε		ἕ-τε
		3.	εἷ-σαν	ἧκαν	ἕ-ντων

MIDDLE

TENSE.	Number.	Person.	Present.	Imperfect.	IMPERATIVE.
PRESENT AND IMPERFECT. Stem ἱε.	S.	1.	ἵ-ε-μαι	ἱ-έ-μην	—
		2.	ἵ-ε-σαι	ἵ-ε-σο	ἵ-ε-σο, ἵου
		3.	ἵ-ε-ται	ἵ-ε-το	ἱ-έ-σθω
	D.	2.	ἵ-ε-σθον	ἵ-ε-σθον	ἵ-ε-σθον
		3.	ἵ-ε-σθον	ἱ-έ-σθην	ἱ-έ-σθων
	P.	1.	ἱ-έ-μεθα	ἱ-έ-μεθα	—
		2.	ἵ-ε-σθε	ἵ-ε-σθε	ἵ-ε-σθε
		3.	ἵ-ε-νται	ἵ-ε-ντο	ἱ-έ-σθων
STRONG AORIST. Stem ἑ.	S.	1.		εἵ-μην	—
		2.		εἷ-σο	οὗ
		3.		εἷ-το	ἕ-σθω
				Etc., as Imperfect.	Etc., as Present.

* Formed as from Verb in -ω. Impf. rarely ἵ-η-ν, ἵ-η-s, ἵ-η.

Verb-stem **ε**.

VOICE.

CONJUNCTIVE.		VERB INFINITE.	
Primary (Subjunc.)	Historic (Optative).	Subst. (Infin.)	Adj. (Participle).
ἱ-ῶ	ἱ-είην	ἱ έ-ναι	M. ἱ-εί-ς
ἱ-ῇ-ς	ἱ-είης		F. ἱ-εῖ-σα
ἱ-ῇ	ἱ-είη		N. ἱ-έ-ν
ἱ-ῆ-τον	ἱ-εῖτον		
ἱ-ῆ-τον	ἱ-είτην		Stem ἱεντ
ἱ-ῶ-μεν	ἱ-εῖμεν		
ἱ-ῆ-τε	ἱ-εῖτε		
ἱ-ῶ-σι(ν)	ἱ-εῖεν		
ὧ	εἴην	εἶ-ναι	M. εἴ-ς
ᾖ-ς	εἴης		F. εἶ-σα
ᾖ	εἴη		N. ἔ-ν
ἦ-τον	εἶτον		
ἦ-τον	εἴτην		Stem ἐντ
ὧ-μεν	εἶμεν		
ἦ-τε	εἶτε		
ὧ-σι(ν)	εἶεν		

VOICE.

ἱ-ῶ-μαι	ἱ-εί-μην	ἵ-ε-σθαι	M. ἱ-έ-μενος
ἱ-ῇ	ἱ-εῖ-ο		F. ἱ-ε-μένη
ἱ-ῆ-ται	ἱ-εῖ-το		N. ἱ-έ-μενον
ἱ-ῆ-σθον	ἱ-εῖ-σθον		
ἱ-ῆ-σθον	ἱ-εί-σθην		Stem ἱεμενο
ἱ-ώ-μεθα	ἱ-εί-μεθα		
ἱ-ῆ-σθε	ἱ-εῖ-σθε		
ἱ-ῶ-νται	ἱ εῖ-ντο		
ὧ-μαι	εἴ-μην	ἔ-σθαι	M. ἔ-μενος
ᾖ	εἶ-ο		F. ἐ-μένη
ἦ-ται	εἶ-το		N. ἔ-μενον
Etc., as Present.	Etc.		
			Stem ἐμενο

151.   ἵ-στη-μι, *I place,*

ACTIVE

TENSE.	Number.	Person.	INDICATIVE. Primary.	INDICATIVE. Historic.	IMPERATIVE.
			Present.	*Imperfect.*	
PRESENT AND IMPERFECT. Stem ἱστᾰ.	S.	1.	ἵ-στη-μι	ἵ-στη-ν	—
		2.	ἵ-στη-s	ἵ-στη-s	ἵ-στη
		3.	ἵ-στη-σι(ν)	ἵ-στη	ἱ-στά-τω
	D.	2.	ἵ-στα-τον	ἵ-στα-τον	ἵ-στα-τον
		3.	ἵ-στα-τον	ἱ-στά-την	ἱ-στά-των
	P.	1.	ἵ-στα-μεν	ἵ-στα-μεν	—
		2.	ἵ-στα-τε	ἵ-στα-τε	ἵ-στα-τε
		3.	ἱ-στᾶ-σι(ν)	ἵ-στα-σαν	ἱ-στά-ντων
STRONG AORIST. Stem στα.	S.	1.		ἔ-στη-ν	—
		2.		ἔ-στη-s	στῆ-θι
		3.		ἔ-στη	στή-τω
	D.	2.		ἔ-στη-τον	στῆ-τον
		3.		ἐ-στή-την	στή-των
	P.	1.		ἔ-στη-μεν	
		2.		ἔ-στη-τε	στῆ-τε
		3.		ἔ-στη-σαν	στά-ντων
PERFECT AND PLUPERFECT.	Weak.		*Perfect* ἕστη-κα	*Pluperfect.* εἱστή-κη	ἕστη-κε
	Strong.		(See 156)		ἕστα-θι

MIDDLE

	Number.	Person.	Present.	Imperfect.	
	S.	1.	ἵ-στα-μαι	ἱ-στά-μην	—
		2.	ἵ-στα-σαι	ἵ-στα-σο	ἵ-στα-σο
		3.	ἵ-στα-ται	ἵ-στα-το	ἱ-στά-σθω
PRESENT AND IMPERFECT. Stem ἱστα.	D.	2.	ἵ-στα-σθον	ἵ-στα-σθον	ἵ-στα-σθον
		3.	ἵ-στα-σθον	ἱ-στά-σθην	ἱ-στά-σθων
	P.	1.	ἱ-στά-μεθα	ἱ-στά-μεθα	—
		2.	ἵ-στα-σθε	ἵ-στα-σθε	ἵ-στα-σθε
		3.	ἵ-στα-νται	ἵ-στα-ντο	ἱ-στά-σθων

N.B.—In the Present, Future and Weak Aorist, ἵστημι has a transitive force, *I make to stand ;* in the Strong Aorist and Perfect it is intransitive ; Strong Aorist, ἔστην, *I stood ;* the Perfect ἕστηκα has the meaning of a Present, *I stand.* The Middle means *I place*

Verb-stem **στᾰ.**

VOICE.

CONJUNCTIVE.		VERB INFINITE.	
Primary (Subjunc.).	Historic (Optative).	Subst. (Infin.).	Adj. (Participle).
ἱ-στῶ	ἱ-σταίην	ἱ-στά-ναι	M. ἱ-στά-ς
ἱ-στῇ-ς	ἱ-σταίης		F. ἱ-στᾶ-σα
ἱ-στῇ	ἱ-σταίη		N. ἱ-στά-ν
ἱ-στῆ-τον	ἱ-σταῖτον		
ἱ-στῆ-τον	ἱ-σταίτην		Stem **ἱσταντ**
ἱ-στῶ-μεν	ἱ-σταῖμεν		
ἱ-στῆ-τε	ἱ-σταῖτε		
ἱ-στῶ-σι(ν)	ἱ-σταῖεν		
στῶ	σταίην	στῆ-ναι	M. στά-ς
στῇ-ς	σταίης		F. στᾶσ-α
στῇ	σταίη		N. στά-ν
στῆ-τον	σταῖτον		
στῆ-τον	σταίτην		Stem **σταντ**
στῶ-μεν	σταῖμεν		
στῆ-τε	σταῖτε		
στῶ-σι(ν)	σταῖεν		
ἑστή-κω	ἑστή-κοιμι	ἑστη-κέναι	ἑστη-κώς
ἑστῶ	ἑσταίην	ἑστάναι	ἑστώς

VOICE.

ἱ-στῶ-μαι	ἱ-σταί-μην	ἵ-στα-σθαι	M. ἱ-στά-μενος
ἱ-στῇ	ἱ-σταῖ-ο		F. ἱ-στα-μένη
ἱ-στῆ-ται	ἱ-σταῖ-το		N. ἱ-στά-μενον
ἱ-στῆ-σθον	ἱ-σταῖ-σθον		
ἱ-στῆ-σθον	ἱ-σταί-σθην		Stem **ἱσταμενο**
ἱ-στώ-μεθα	ἱ-σταί-μεθα		
ἱ-στῆ-σθε	ἱ-σταῖ-σθε		
ἱ-στῶ-νται	ἱ-σταῖ-ντο		

myself or *place for myself.* There is no Strong Aorist Middle and the Perfect ἕσταμαι is rare. Weak Aorist Middle ἐστησάμην always *I placed for myself.* For other Tenses see **154.**

152.　　　　　　　　　　　　　　　　δί-δω-μι, *I give,*

ACTIVE

Tense.	Number.	Person.	INDICATIVE.		IMPERATIVE.
			Primary.	Historic.	
			Present.	*Imperfect.*	
PRESENT AND IMPERFECT. Stem διδο.	S.	1.	δί-δω-μι	ἐ-δί-δουν*	——
		2.	δί-δω-ς	ἐ-δί-δους*	δί-δου*
		3.	δί-δω-σι(ν)	ἐ-δί-δου*	δι-δό-τω
	D.	2.	δί-δο-τον	ἐ-δί-δο-τον	δί-δο-τον
		3.	δί-δο-τον	ἐ-δι-δό-την	δι-δό-των
	P.	1.	δί-δο-μεν	ἐ-δί-δο-μεν	——
		2.	δί-δο-τε	ἐ-δί-δο-τε	δί-δο-τε
		3.	δι-δό-ᾱσι(ν)	ἐ-δί-δο-σαν	δι-δό-ντων
				Strong.　Weak.	
AORIST. Stem δο.	S.	1.		ἔ-δω-κα	——
		2.		ἔ-δω-κας	δό-ς
		3.		ἔ-δω-κε	δό-τω
	D.	2.		ἔ-δο-τον	δό-τον
		3.		ἐ-δό-την	δό-των
	P.	1.		ἔ-δο-μεν†	
		2.		ἔ-δο-τε	δό-τε
		3.		ἔ-δο-σαν	δό-ντων

MIDDLE

	Number.	Person.	Present.	Imperfect.	
	S.	1.	δί-δο-μαι	ἐ-δι-δό-μην	
		2.	δί-δο-σαι	ἐ-δί-δο-σο	δί-δο-σο
PRESENT AND IMPERFECT. Stem διδο.		3.	δί-δο-ται	ἐ-δί-δο-το	δι-δό-σθω
	D.	2.	δί-δο-σθον	ἐ-δί-δο-σθον	δί-δο-σθον
		3.	δί-δο-σθον	ἐ-δι-δό-σθην	δι-δό-σθων
	P.	1.	δι-δό-μεθα	ἐ-δι-δό-μεθα	
		2.	δί-δο-σθε	ἐ-δί-δο-σθε	δί-δο-σθε
		3.	δί-δο-νται	ἐ-δί-δο-ντο	δι-δό-σθων
STRONG AORIST. Stem δο.	S.	1.		ἐ-δό-μην	
		2.		ἔ-δου	δοῦ
		3.		ἔ-δο-το	δό-σθω
				Etc., as Imperfect.	Etc., as Present.

* Formed as from Verb in -ω.　　　† Weak Plur. (ἐδώκαμεν, etc.) is rare.

Verb Stem δο.

VOICE.

CONJUNCTIVE.		ERB INFINITE.	
Primary (Subj.)	Historic (Optative).	Subst. (Infin.)	Adj. (Participle).
δι-δῶ	δι-δοίην	δι-δό-ναι	M. δι-δού-ς
δι-δῷ-ς	δι-δοίης		F. δι-δοῦ-σα
δι-δῷ	δι-δοίη		N. δι-δό-ν
δι-δῶ-τον	δι-δοῖτον		Stem διδοντ.
δι-δῶ-τον	δι-δοίτην		
δι-δῶ-μεν	δι-δοῖμεν		
δι-δῶ-τε	δι-δοῖτε		
δι-δῶ-σι(ν)	δι-δοῖεν		
δῶ	δοίη-ν	δοῦ-ναι	M. δού-ς
δῷ-ς	δοίη-ς		F. δοῦ-σα
δῷ	δοίη		N. δό-ν
δῶ-τον	δοῖ-τον		Stem δοντ.
δῶ-τον	δοί-την		
δῶ-μεν	δοῖ-μεν		
δῶ-τε	δοῖ-τε		
δῶ-σι(ν)	δοῖ-εν		

VOICE

δι-δῶ-μαι	δι-δοί-μην	δί-δο-σθαι	M. δι-δό-μενος
δι-δῷ	δι-δοῖ-ο		F. δι-δο-μένη
δι-δῶ-ται	δι-δοῖ-το		N. δι-δό-μενον
δι-δῶ-σθον	δι-δοῖ-σθον		Stem διδομενο.
δι-δῶ-σθον	δι-δοί-σθην		
δι-δώ-μεθα	δι-δοί-μεθα		
δι-δῶ-σθε	δι-δοῖ-σθε		
δι-δῶ-νται	δι-δοῖ-ντο		
δῶ-μαι	δοί-μην	δό-σθαι	M. δό-μενος
δῷ	δοῖ-ο		F. δο-μένη
δῶ-ται	δοῖ-το		N. δό-μενον
Etc., as Present.	Etc., as Present.		Stem δομενο.

153.   δείκ-νυ-μι, *I shew*,

ACTIVE

TENSE.	Number.	Person.	INDICATIVE. Primary.	INDICATIVE. Historic.	IMPERATIVE.
			Present.	*Imperfect.*	
PRESENT AND IMPERFECT. Stem δεικνυ.	S.	1.	δείκ-νῡ-μι	ἐ-δείκ-νῡ-ν	——
		2.	δείκ-νῡ-ς	ἐ-δείκ-νῡ-ς	δείκ-νῡ
		3.	δείκ-νύ-σι(ν)	ἐ-δείκ-νῡ	δεικ-νύ-τω
	D.	2.	δείκ-νῠ-τον	ἐ-δείκ-νῠ-τον	δείκ-νῠ-τον
		3.	δείκ-νῠ-τον	ἐ-δείκ-νῠ-την	δεικ-νῠ-των
	P.	1.	δείκ-νῠ-μεν	ἐ-δείκ-νῠ-μεν	——
		2.	δείκ-νῠ-τε	ἐ-δείκ-νῠ-τε	δείκ-νῠ-τε
		3.	δεικ-νύ-ᾱσι(ν)	ἐ-δείκ-νῠ-σαν	δεικ-νύ-ντων

MIDDLE

	Number.	Person.	Primary.	Historic.	IMPERATIVE.
PRESENT AND IMPERFECT. Stem δεικνυ.	S.	1.	δείκ-νῠ-μαι	ἐ-δεικ-νῠ-μην	——
		2.	δείκ-νῠ-σαι	ἐ-δείκ-νῠ-σο	δείκ-νῠ-σο
		3.	δείκ-νῠ-ται	ἐ-δείκ-νῠ-το	δεικ-νύ-σθω
	D.	2.	δείκ-νυ-σθον	ἐ-δείκ-νυ-σθον	δείκ-νυ-σθον
		3.	δείκ-νυ-σθον	ἐ-δεικ-νύ-σθην	δεικ-νύ-σθων
	P.	1.	δεικ-νῠ-μεθα	ἐ-δεικ-νῠ-μεθα	——
		2.	δείκ-νυ-σθε	ἐ-δείκ-νυ-σθε	δείκ-νυ-σθε
		3.	δείκ-νυ-νται	ἐ-δείκ-νυ-ντο	δεικ-νύ-σθων

154.   OTHER TENSES OF

CLASS I.	STEM.	Future.	Wk. Aorist.	Perf. Act.
τί-θη-μι	θε	θή-σω	ἔ-θη-κα	τέ-θη-κα
ἵ-η-μι	ἑ	ἥ-σω	ἧ-κα	εἷ-κα
ἵ-στη-μι	στα	στή-σω / στή-σομαι	ἔ-στη-σα / ἐ-στη-σάμην	ἕστη-κα
δί-δω-μι	δο	δώ-σω	ἔ-δω-κα	δέ-δω-κα
CLASS II. δείκ-νυ-μι	δεικ	δείξω	ἔ-δειξα	δέ-δειχ-α

Verb-stem **δεικ.**

VOICE.

| CONJUNCTIVE. | | VERB INFINITE. | |
Primary (Subjunc.)	Historic (Optative).	Subst. (Infin.)	Adj. (Participle).
δεικ-νύ-ω	δεικ-νύ-οιμι	δεικ-νύ-ναι	M. δεικ-νύ-ς
δεικ-νύ-ῃς	δεικ-νύ-οις		F. δεικ-νῦ-σα
δεικ-νύ-ῃ	δεικ-νύ-οι		N. δεικ-νύ-ν
δεικ-νύ-ητον	δεικ-νύ-οιτον		
δεικ-νύ-ητον	δεικ-νυ-οίτην		Stem δεικνυντ
δεικ-νύ-ωμεν	δεικ-νύ-οιμεν		
δεικ-νύ-ητε	δεικ-νύ-οιτε		
δεικ-νύ-ωσι(ν)	δεικ-νύ-οιεν		

VOICE.

			M. δεικ-νύ-μενος
δεικ-νύ-ωμαι	δεικ-νυ-οίμην	δείκ-νυ-σθαι	F. δεικ-νύ-μένη
δεικ-νύ-ῃ	δεικ-νύ-οιο		N. δεικ-νύ-μενον
δεικ-νύ-ηται	δεικ-νύ-οιτο		
δεικ-νύ-ησθον	δεικ-νύ-οισθον		Stem δεικνυμενο
δεικ-νύ-ησθον	δεικ-νυ-οίσθην		
δεικ-νυ-ώμεθα	δεικ-νυ-οίμεθα		
δεικ-νύ-ησθε	δεικ-νύ-οισθε		
δεικ-νύ-ωνται	δεικ-νύ-οιντο		

VERBS IN -μι.

Perf. Mid. and Pass.	Wk. Aorist Pass.	Wk. Future Pass.	Verb Adj.
τέ-θει-μαι	ἐ-τέ-θην	τε-θήσομαι	θε-τέος
εἶ-μαι	εἴ-θην	ἐ-θήσομαι	ἐ-τέος
——	ἐ-στά-θην	στα-θήσομαι	στα-τέος
δέ-δο-μαι	ἐ-δό-θην	δο-θήσομαι	δο-τέος .
δέ-δειγ-μαι	ἐ-δείχ-θην	δειχ-θήσομαι	δεικ-τέος

155.   *Notes on the Paradigms of Verbs in -μι.*

(i) *Pres. Indic. Act. 3 Plur.* τιθέᾱσι is for τιθε-αντι, τ
becoming σ, and ν being dropped out.   A shorter form τιθεῖσι,
not used in Attic Greek, is for τιθε-ντι, τιθε-νσι (compare λύουσι
for λυ-οντι).

(ii.) *Imperat. Pres. 2 Sing.*   τίθει, ἵει, δίδου, δείκνυ are contractions for τίθεε, ἵεε, δίδοε, δείκνυε, as if from Verbs in -ω.
In the Strong Aorist, θές, ἕς, δός are for θε-θι, ἑ-θι, δο-θι.   The
termination -θι remains in στῆ-θι and ἕστα-θι from ἵστημι, and
is found also in γνῶ-θι from γιγνώσκω, *I know*, βῆ-θι from
βαίνω, *I go*, etc.   Compare the Aor. Imper. Pass. of verbs in -ω.
3 Plur.   The termination -σαν in Hist. Conj. and Imperf.
Indic. is probably due to composition.   -σαν is from ἔσαν
for ᾖσαν the 3 Plur. of ἦι (from εἰμί, *I am*), the ε being lost,
or from ἔσαντι, a form of the 3 Plur. Pres.

(iii.) *Infinitive.*   The form in -ναι must be compared with
the Perf. Infin. of verbs in -ω, as λελυκέναι.   The termination is
probably ι, the sign of the locative case, and the Infinitive
is a case of a verbal substantive signifying the action of the
verb, as τιθέναι (stem τιθενα), *in placing.*

(iv.) *Middle 2 Sing.*   The σ of -σαι and -σο of the present
(and imperfect) in the Indic. and Imperat. is rarely elided as
in verbs in -ω ; but in the Conjunctive present and in all moods
of the Strong Aorist it is always elided.

156.   *The Perfect and Pluperfect Active.*

The Perfect and Pluperfect Active are usually the same as the
Weak Perfect and Pluperfect of verbs in -ω, but some verbs have
a strong form in the dual and plural of the Indic., and in
all persons of the other moods, as ἕστηκα, *I stand.*

Perfect Indicative.

S.	1.	ἕστηκα	D.	1.	——	P.	1.	ἕστα-μεν
	2.	ἕστηκας		2.	ἕστα-τον		2.	ἕστα-τε
	3.	ἕστηκε(ν)		3.	ἕστα-τον		3.	ἑστᾶ-σι(ν)

Pluperfect.

S.			D.			P.		
	1.	εἰστήκη		1.	——		1.	ἔστα-μεν
	2.	εἰστήκης		2.	ἔστα-τον		2.	ἔστα-τε
	3.	εἰστήκει		3.	ἐστά-την		3.	ἔστᾰ-σαν.

Imperat., ἔστᾰ-θι.   **Conj. Prim.**, ἐστῶ.   **Conj. Hist.**, ἐσταίην.

Infin., ἐστᾰ-ναι.   **Partic. Nom.**, ἐστώς, -ῶσα, -ός.
  Acc., ἐστῶτα, -ῶσαν, -ός.

Obs. Some verbs of the ω conjugation have similar Perfects, as τέθνηκα from θνήσκω, βέβηκα from βαίνω, δέδιᾰ (or δέδοικα) from (δείδω).

157. To the First Class of Verbs in -μι belong εἰμί, *I am;* εἶμι, *I shall go;* φημί, *I say.*

(1.) εἰμί, *I am*, Verb-stem **ἐς.**

		INDICATIVE.		IMPERA-TIVE.	CONJUNCTIVE.	
		Primary.	Historic.		Prim. (Subj.).	Hist. (Opt.)
		Present.	*Imperfect.*			
S.	1.	εἰ-μί	ἦν or ἦ	—	ὦ	εἴην
	2.	εἶ	ἦσθα	ἴσθι	ᾖς	εἴης
	3.	ἐσ-τί(ν)	ἦν	ἔστω	ᾖ	εἴη
D.	2.	ἐσ-τόν	ἦστον	ἔστον	ἦτον	εἶτον
	3.	ἐσ-τόν	ἤστην	ἔστων	ἦτον	εἴτην
P.	1.	ἐσ-μέν	ἦμεν	—	ὦμεν	εἶμεν
	2.	ἐσ-τέ	ἦτε	ἔστε	ἦτε	εἶτε
	3.	εἰσί(ν)	ἦσαν	ὄντων	ὦσι(ν)	εἶεν

Infinitive, εἶναι.   *Participle,* ὤν, οὖσα, ὄν, Stem **ὀντ.**

Future Indicative.

S. 1. ἔσομαι	D. 1. ——	P. 1. ἐσόμεθα
2. ἔσῃ or ἔσει	2. ἔσεσθον	2. ἔσεσθε
3. ἔσται	3. ἔσεσθον	3. ἔσονται

Conj. Hist. ἐσοίμην, *Infin.* ἔσεσθαι, *Partic.* ἐσόμενος, -η, -ον.

Obs. 1. The Present Indicative, with the exception of the 2 Sing., is enclitic.

Obs. 2. Pres. Indic. 1 Sing. εἰ-μί is for ἐσ-μι (compare Latin *sum* for *es-u-mi*), the diphthong ει resulting from compensatory lengthening for the loss of s. 2 Sing. εἶ is for ἐσ-σι, ἐσι. 3 Plur. εἰ-σί for ἐσ-ντι. Conj. Primary 1 Sing. ὦ is for ἐσ-ω, 2 Sing. ῇς for ἐσ-ῃς, etc. Conj. Historic 1 Sing. εἴην is for ἐσ-ιη-ν (compare τιθε-ίη-ν, and *siem* old Latin for *sim*). Impf. 1 Sing. ἦν is for ἐσ-αμ, ἐαμ, ἐαν (compare Latin *eram* from *sum*. where *r* is for *s*). Sometimes ν is dropped, and we find ἦ, old Greek ἔα, in the 1 Sing. The Augment may also be absorbed in the η. The Fut. 3 Sing. ἔσται is for ἐσ-εται, by *syncope*.

158.   (2.) εἶμι, *I shall go*, Verb-stem ἰ.

	INDICATIVE.		IMPERA- TIVE.	CONJUNCTIVE.	
	Primary.	Historic.		Prim. (Subj.)	Historic (Opt.)
	Present.	*Imperfect.*			
S. 1.	εἶ-μι	ᾔειν or ᾖα	—	ἴω	ἴοιμι
2.	εἶ	ᾔεισθα	ἴθι	ἴῃς	ἴοις
3.	εἶ-σι(ν)	ᾔει	ἴτω	ἴῃ	ἴοι
D. 2.	ἴ-τον	ᾖτον	—	ἴητον	ἰοίτον
3.	ἴ-τον	ᾔτην	—	ἴητον	ἰοίτην
P. 1.	ἴ-μεν	ᾖμεν	—	ἴωμεν	ἴοιμεν
2.	ἴ-τε	ᾖτε	ἴτε	ἴητε	ἴοιτε
3.	ἴ-ᾱσι(ν)	ᾖεσαν or ᾖσαν	ἰόντων	ἴωσι(ν)	ἴοιεν

Infinitive, ἰέναι.   *Participle,* ἰών, ἰοῦσα, ἰόν, Stem ἰοντ.

Obs. In the Present Indicative 1, 2, 3 Singular, the diphthong ει may be compared with λείπω, from Verb-stem λιπ. It is confined to the Singular, like the long vowel in τίθημι, etc. The Imperfect resembles a Pluperfect in form. The -α in ᾖα is the same as in ἔα, ᾖ (Lat. *eram*), and ᾖα is therefore for ᾔισα (= ἐ + ει + σα).

159. (3.) φημί, *I say*, Verb-stem **φα.**

		INDICATIVE.		IMPERA-TIVE.	CONJUNCTIVE.		VERB INFIN.	
		Primary.	Historic.		Prim. (Sub.)	Hist. (Op.)	Infin.	Part.
		Present.	*Imperfect.*				φᾰ́ναι	(φάς)*
S.	1.	φημί	ἔφην	—	φῶ	φαίην	φᾰ́ναι	(φάς)*
	2.	φῄς	ἔφησθα	φᾰθί	φῇς	φαίης		
	3.	φησί(ν)	ἔφη	φᾰ́τω	φῇ	φαίη		
D.	2.	φατόν	ἔφατον	—	φῆτον	φαῖτον		
	3.	φατόν	ἐφάτην	—	φῆτον	φαίτην		
P.	1.	φαμέν	ἔφαμεν	—	φῶμεν	φαῖμεν		
	2.	φατέ	ἔφατε	φάτε	φῆτε	φαῖτε		
	3.	φᾱσί(ν)	ἔφᾰσαν	—	φῶσι(ν)	φαῖεν		

Future, φήσω. *Weak Aorist,* ἔφησα. *Part. Mid.* φάμενος.

* φάσκων, from φάσκω, is commonly used, and an Imperfect ἔφασκε is used for a strong or reiterated assertion.

Obs. The forms of the Present Indicative are enclitic, except in the 2 Singular.

160. Οἶδα, the Perfect of the stem ἰδ (Strong Aorist εἶδον) is thus conjugated:—

οἶδα, *I know,* Verb-stem ἰδ.

		INDICATIVE.		IMPERA-TIVE.	CONJUNCTIVE.	
		Primary.	Historic.		Prim. (Subj.)	Hist. (Opt.)
		Perfect.	*Pluperfect.*			
S.	1.	οἶδα	ᾔδη	—	εἰδῶ	εἰδείην
	2.	οἶσθα	ᾔδησθα	ἴσθι	εἰδῇς	εἰδείης
	3.	οἶδε(ν)	ᾔδει(ν)	ἴστω	εἰδῇ	εἰδείη
D.	2.	ἴστον	ᾖστον	—	εἰδῆτον	εἰδεῖτον
	3.	ἴστον	ᾖστην	—	εἰδῆτον	εἰδείτην
P.	1.	ἴσμεν	ᾖσμεν	—	εἰδῶμεν	εἰδεῖμεν
	2	ἴστε	ᾖστε	ἴστε	εἰδῆτε	εἰδεῖτε
	3.	ἴσᾱσι(ν)	ᾔδεσαν ⎰ ᾖσαν ⎱	—	εἰδῶσι(ν)	εἰδεῖεν

Infinitive, εἰδέναι. *Participle,* εἰδώς, εἰδυῖα, εἰδός, Stem ἰδοτ

Obs. With the form οἶδα from ἰδ compare λέλοιπα from λιπ, and with the εἰ of the conjunctive compare λείπω from λιπ and εἶμι from ἰ. The 2 Sing. οἶσθα is for οἰδ-θα (the dental becoming σ), and ἴστον, ἴσμεν are for ἰδ-τον, ἰδ-μεν. The 3 Plur. ἴσᾱσι(ν) is probably for ἰδ-σαντι. The η in the Plupf. is due to the augment, ᾔδ- being for ἐ-ειδ-.

161. Irregular Verbs.

	Future.	Aorist.	Perf. Act.	Perf. Pass.	Aor. Pass.
-ἄγνυμι, break (tr.)	-ἄξω	-ἔαξα	-ἔᾱγα (intr.)		-ἐάγην
ἄγω, lead	ἄξω	ἤγαγον	ἦχα	ἦγμαι	ἤχθην
ᾄδω, sing	ᾄσομαι	ᾖσα		ᾖσμαι	ᾔσθην
αἰδοῦμαι (ε-ω), reverence	αἰδέσομαι,	[1]		[1]	ᾐδέσθην
ἐπ- -αἰνῶ (ε-ω),[2] praise	-αἰνέσω	-ῄνεσα		-ῄνημαι	-ῃνέθην
αἱρῶ (ε-ω),[3] take	αἱρήσω	εἷλον	ᾕρηκα	ᾕρημαι	ᾑρέθην
αἰσθάνομαι, perceive	αἰσθήσομαι	ᾐσθόμην		ᾔσθημαι (dep.)	
ἀκούω, hear	ἀκούσομαι	ἤκουσα	ἀκήκοα		ἠκούσθην
ἁλίσκομαι, am caught	ἁλώσομαι	ἑάλων[4] ἥλων	ἑάλωκα ἥλωκα		
ἁμαρτάνω, err	ἁμαρτήσομαι	ἥμαρτον	ἡμάρτηκα	ἡμάρτημαι	ἡμαρτήθην
ἀμφι-έννυμι, clothe	ἀμφιῶ	ἠμφίεσα		ἠμφίεσμαι	
ἀνᾱλίσκω, spend	ἀνᾱλώσω	ἀνήλωσα ἀνάλωσα	ἀνήλωκα ἀνάλωκα	ἀνήλωμαι ἀνάλωμαι	ἀνηλώθην[5]

[1] Aor. ᾐδεσάμην, Poet. Perf. ᾔδεσμαι, rare.

[2] The simple verb is poetic, ἐπαινῶ being used in prose. Perf. ἐπ-ῄνεκα only in Isocrates.

[3] ἁλίσκομαι supplies a Pres., Impf., Fut., Aor., and Perf., Passive. The mid. αἱροῦμαι, means *I choose*, Fut. αἱρήσομαι, Aor. εἱλόμην, Perf. ᾕρημαι, *I have chosen*, or *I have been chosen*, Aor. ᾑρέθην, *I was chosen*.

[4] The moods are ἑάλων, or ἥλων, ἁλῶ, ἁλοίην, ἁλῶναι, ἁλούς.

[5] Aor. Pass. ἀνᾱλώθην, rare.

	Future.	Aorist.	Perf. Act.	Perf. Pass.	Aor. Pass.
ἀπεχθάνομαι am hated	ἀπεχθήσομαι	ἀπηχθόμην		ἀπήχθημαι	
ἀρέσκω please		ἤρεσα			
ἀρκῶ (ε-ω), suffice	ἀρκέσω	ἤρκεσα			
αὐξάνω, ⎱ αὔξω, ⎰ increase (tr.)	αὐξήσω	ηὔξησα	ηὔξηκα	ηὔξημαι	ηὐξήθην
ἄχθομαι, am vexed	ἀχθέσομαι				ἠχθέσθην
βαίνω, go	βήσομαι	ἔβην [1]	βέβηκα		
βάλλω, throw	βαλῶ	ἔβαλον	βέβληκα	βέβλημαι	ἐβλήθην
βιβάζω, bring	βιβῶ	ἐβίβασα			
βιβρώσκω, eat			βέβρωκα	βέβρωμαι	ἐβρώθην
βλαστάνω, bud	βλαστήσω	ἔβλαστον			
βόσκω, feed	βοσκήσω				
βούλομαι, wish	βουλήσομαι			βεβούλημαι	ἐβουλήθην ἠβουλήθην M.
γαμῶ (ε-ω),[2] marry	γαμῶ	ἔγημα	γεγάμηκα		
γελῶ (α-ω), laugh	γελάσομαι	ἐγέλἄσα			ἐγελάσθην
γηράσκω, grow old	γηράσω γηράσομαι	ἐγήρᾶσα	γεγήρᾱκα		

[1] The moods are ἔβην, βῆθι, βῶ, βαίην, βῆναι, βάς (mostly ἀπο-).
[2] Mid. γαμοῦμαι (of the woman), *nubo*.

	Future.	Aorist.	Perf. Act.	Perf. Pass.	Aor. Pass.
γίγνομαι, become	γενήσομαι	ἐγενόμην	γέγονα	γεγένημαι	
γιγνώσκω, ascertain	γνώσομαι	ἔγνων [1]	ἔγνωκα	ἔγνωσμαι	ἐγνώσθην
δάκνω, bite	δήξομαι	ἔδακον [2]		δέδηγμαι	ἐδήχθην
-δαρθάνω, sleep		-ἔδαρθον [3]	-δεδάρθηκα		
δεῖ (ε-ει), it is necessary	δεήσει	ἐδέησε			
δέομαι, M., entreat	δεήσομαι				ἐδεήθην
διδάσκω, teach	διδάξω	ἐδίδαξα	δεδίδαχα	δεδίδαγμαι	ἐδιδάχθην
ἀπό -διδράσκω, run	-δρᾱσομαι	-ἔδρᾱν	-δέδρᾱκα		
δοκῶ (ε-ω),[4] seem	δόξω	ἔδοξα		δέδογμαι	
δύναμαι, can	δυνήσομαι			δεδύνημαι	ἐδυνήθην ἠδυνήθην
δύω, enter, put on	δύσω	ἔδῡσα ἔδῡν(intr.)	δέδῡκα (intr.)	δέδῠμαι	ἐδύθην
ἐγείρω, rouse	ἐγερῶ	ἤγειρα	ἐγρήγορα [5]	ἐγήγερμαι	ἠγέρθην
ἐθέλω, will	ἐθελήσω	ἠθέλησα	ἠθέληκα		
ἐθίζω, accustom	ἐθιῶ	εἴθισα	εἴθικα	εἴθισμαι	εἰθίσθην
ἐλαύνω, drive	ἐλῶ	ἤλασα	ἐλήλακα	ἐλήλαμαι	ἠλάθην
ἐλίσσω, roll	ἐλίξω	εἴλιξα		εἴλιγμαι	εἰλίχθην

[1] The St. Aor. Act. moods are ἔγνων, γνῶθι, γνῶ, γνοίην, γνῶναι, γνούς.
[2] Wk. Aor. ἔδηξα, rare.   [3] Str. Aor. ἔδραθον, poet.
[4] Fut. δοκήσω, Aor. ἐδόκησα, Perf. δεδόκηκα, Aor. Pass. ἐδοκήθην, all poet.
[5] Perf. Intr. *I am awake.*

	Future.	Aorist.	Perf. Act.	Perf. Pass.	Aor. Pass.
ἕλκω, drag	ἕλξω	εἵλκῠσα	εἵλκῠκα	εἵλκυσμαι	εἱλκύσθην
ἐπίσταμαι, understand	ἐπιστήσομαι				ἠπιστήθην
ἕπομαι,[1] follow	ἕψομαι	ἑσπόμην			
ἕρρω, go away	ἐρρήσω	ἤρρησα	ἤρρηκα		
ἔρχομαι, go, come	εἶμι [2]	ἦλθον	ἐλήλυθα		
ἐσθίω, eat	ἔδομαι	ἔφαγον	[3]		
καθ- -εύδω, sleep	εὐδήσω				
εὑρίσκω, find	εὑρήσω	εὗρον	εὕρηκα	εὕρημαι	εὑρέθην
ἔχω,[4] have	ἕξω σχήσω	ἔσχον	ἔσχηκα	[5]	
ἕψω, cook	ἑψήσομαι	ἥψησα		[6]	
ἐῶ (α-ω),[7] allow	ἐάσω	εἴᾱσα	εἴᾱκα	εἴᾱμαι	εἰᾱθην
ζέω, boil	ζέσω	ἔζεσα			
ζεύγνυμι, yoke	ζεύξω	ἔζευξα		ἔζευγμαι	ἐζεύχθην
ζῶ (α-ω), live	βιώσομαι [8]	ἐβίων	βεβίωκα		
ἡβάσκω, grow up	[9]	ἥβησα	ἥβηκα		

[1] Impf. εἱπόμην, Aor. M. Inf. σπέσθαι.
[2] εἶμι supplies Imperf. and Moods of Pres., see **160**. ἐλεύσομαι, poet. and rare. ἥκω, *I am come*, supplies an alternative Perf.
[4] Impf. εἶχον.
[3] Perf. Act. ἐδήδοκα, Perf. Pass. ἐδήδεσμαι, rare.
[5] Perf. Pass. ἔσχημαι, used in compounds.
[6] Perf. Pass. ἥψημαι, Aor. Pass. ἑψήθην, rare.
[7] Impf. εἴων.
[8] Fut. ζήσω, rare.
[9] Fut. ἐφ-ηβήσω, rare.

	Future.	Aorist.	Perf. Act.	Perf. Pass.	Aor. Pass.
ἥδομαι, delight in	ἡσθήσομαι, M.				ἥσθην, M.
θάπτω, bury	θάψω	ἔθαψα		τέθαμμαι	ἐτάφην
θιγγάνω, touch	θίξομαι	ἔθιγον			
ἀπο -θνήσκω, die	-θἄνοῦμαι	-ἔθἄνον	τέθνηκα		
-θρώσκω, leap	-θοροῦμαι	-ἔθορον			
ἀφ- -ικνοῦμαι(ε-ο), come	-ἵξομαι	-ἱκόμην		-ῖγμαι	
ἱλάσκομαι, propitiate	ἱλἄσομαι	ἱλἄσάμην			
καθαίρω, cleanse,	καθαρῶ	ἐκάθηρα		κεκάθαρμαι	ἐκαθάρθην
καθέζομαι, sit down, sit	καθεδοῦμαι				
καθίζω, set, also sit	καθιῶ	ἐκάθῐσα [1]			
κάθημαι, [2] sit					
καίω, burn	καύσω	ἔκαυσα [3]	κέκαυκα	κέκαυμαι	ἐκαύθην
καλῶ (-ε-ω), call	καλῶ	ἐκάλεσα	κέκληκα	κέκλημαι	ἐκλήθην
κάμνω, toil	κᾰμοῦμαι	ἔκᾰμον	κέκμηκα		
κεῖμαι, [4] lie	κείσομαι				

[1] Aor. κάθῐσα, poet.
[2] The Moods are κάθημαι, κάθησο, καθῶμαι, καθοίμην, καθῆσθαι, καθήμενος, Impf. ἐκαθήμην.
[3] Aor. ἔκεα, poet.
[4] The Moods are κεῖμαι, κεῖσο, (κέωμαι rare) κεοίμην, κεῖσθαι, κείμενος.

	Future.	Aorist.	Perf. Act.	Perf. Pass.	Aor. Pass.
κεράννῡμι, mix	[1]	ἐκέρᾱσα		κέκρᾱμαι	ἐκρᾱ́θην
κερδαίνω, gain	κερδᾰνῶ	ἐκέρδᾱνα	[2]		
κιγχᾰ́νω,[3] find	κιχήσομαι	ἔκιχον			
κλαίω,[4] weep	κλαύσομαι	ἔκλαυσα		κέκλαυμαι	
κλέπτω, steal	κλέψω	ἔκλεψα	κέκλοφα	κέκλεμμαι	ἐκλάπην
κλῑ́νω, bend	κλῐνῶ	ἔκλῑνα	κέκλῐκα	κέκλῐμαι	ἐκλίθην [5]
κρέμαμαι, hang (intr.)	κρεμήσομαι				
κρεμάννῡμι, hang (tr.)	κρεμῶ	ἐκρέμασα			ἐκρεμάσθην
κρῑ́νω, judge	κρῐνῶ	ἔκρῑνα	κέκρῐκα	κέκρῐμαι	ἐκρῐ́θην
κτῶμαι (α-ο), acquire	κτήσομαι	ἐκτησάμην		κέκτημαι [6]	ἐκτήθην
-κτείνω, kill	-κτενῶ	-έκτεινα [7]	-έκτονα		
λαγχάνω, obtain by lot	λήξομαι	ἔλαχον	εἴληχα [8]	εἴληγμαι	ἐλήχθην
λαμβάνω, take	λήψομαι	ἔλαβον	εἴληφα	εἴλημμαι	ἐλήφθην
λανθάνω, lie hid	λήσω	ἔλαθον	λέληθα	[9]	
λάσκω, cry	λακήσομαι	ἔλᾰκον	λέλᾱκα [10]		

[1] Fut. κεράσω, late.   Aor. Pass. ἐκεράσθην, rare.
[2] Perf. Act. -κεκέρδηκα, in compounds.   [3] Only in poetry.   Epic form κῑχάνω.
[4] Also κλάω.   Fut. Act. κλαήσω, rare.   [5] Wk. Aor. Pass. ἐκλίνθην, poet.
[6] Perf. κέκτημαι, *I possess.*   Another form, ἔκτημαι, is rare in Attic except in Plato.
[7] Str. Aor. Act. ἔκτᾰνον, poet.   For the Passive voice ἀπο-θνήσκω is used (*q.v.*).
[8] Perf. Act. λέλογχα, poet.
[9] Perf. Mid. λέλησμαι, *I forget,* Aor. ἐλήσθην, *I forgot.*
[10] Str. P. λέληκα, Epic.

	Future.	Aorist.	Perf. Act.	Perf. Pass.	Aor. Pass.
λέγω, φημί, ἀγορεύω,[1] say	λέξω ἐρῶ	ἔλεξα [2] εἶπον, εἶπα	εἴρηκα	-λέλεγμαι -εἴλεγμαι εἴρημαι	ἐλέχθην ἐρρήθην
μανθάνω, learn	μᾰθήσομαι	ἔμᾰθον	μεμάθηκα		
μάχομαι, fight	μαχοῦμαι	ἐμαχεσάμην		μεμάχημαι	
μεθύσκω, intoxicate		[3]			ἐμεθύσθην
μέλει, it is a care	μελήσει	ἐμέλησε	μεμέληκε		
μέλλω, intend	μελλήσω	ἐμέλλησα[4]			
μένω, remain	μενῶ	ἔμεινα	μεμένηκα		
μίγνυμι, mix	μίξω	ἔμῐξα		μέμῑγμαι	ἐμίχθην
-μιμνήσκω,[5] remind	-μνήσω	-ἔμνησα		μέμνημαι I remember	ἐμνήσθην
νέμω, allot	νεμῶ	ἔνειμα	νενέμηκα	νενέμημαι	ἐνεμήθην
νέω, swim	νεύσομαι	ἔνευσα	νένευκα		
οἴγω,[6] οἴγνυμι, } open	οἴξω	ἔῳξα		ἔῳγμαι	
ἀνοίγνυμι,	ἀνοίξω	ἀνέῳξα	ἀνέῳχα	ἀνέῳγμαι	ἀνεῴχθην
οἴομαι, think	οἰήσομαι				ᾠήθην (as Mid.)
οἴχομαι, am gone	οἰχήσομαι		[7]		

[1] ἀγορεύω takes the place of λέγω in compounds.
[2] Wk. Aor. Act. ἔλεξα, rare in Plato and the Orators.
[3] Wk. Aor. Act. ἐμέθῠσα, poet.
[4] Impf. and Aor. sometimes augment with η.
[5] Simple Verb is poet. in Act. Voice.
[6] οἴγω is the more common form. The double augment occurs chiefly in compounds.
[7] Perf. οἴχωκα or ᾤχωκα, poet.

	Future.	Aorist.	Perf. Act.	Perf. Pass.	Aor. Pass.
ὀλισθάνω, *slip*		ὤλισθον			
-ὄλλυμι,[1] *destroy*	-ὀλῶ	-ώλεσα	-ὀλώλεκα -ὄλωλα (intr.)		
ὄμνυμι, *swear*	ὀμοῦμαι	ὤμοσα	ὀμώμοκα		ὠμόθην
ὀμόργνυμι, *wipe*	ὀμόρξω	ὤμορξα			ὠμόρχθην
ὄρνυμι, *rouse*	ὄρσω	ὦρσα	ὄρωρα (intr.)		
ὁρῶ (α-ω),[2] *see*	ὄψομαι	εἶδον[3]	ἑώρᾱκα[4]	ἑώρᾱμαι ὦμμαι	ὤφθην
ὀσφραίνομαι, *smell* (tr.)	ὀσφρήσομαι	ὠσφρόμην			
ὀφείλω, *owe*	ὀφειλήσω	ὤφελον			
ὀφλισκάνω, *owe*	ὀφλήσω,	ὦφλον	ὤφληκα		
παίζω, *sport*	παίξομαι	ἔπαισα	πέπαικα	πέπαισμαι	
πάσχω, *suffer*	πείσομαι	ἔπᾰθον	πέπονθα		
πετάννυμι, *spread*	πετῶ	ἐπέτᾰσα		πέπτᾰμαι	ἐπετάσθην
πέτομαι, *fly*	πτήσομαι[5]	ἐπτόμην			

[1] Simple Verb is poet. ; in prose usually ἀπ-όλλυμι. Str. Perf. ὄλωλα, *I am undone.* Str. Aor. Mid. ὠλόμην, *I perished.*
[2] Impf. ἑώρων.
[3] Str. Aor. Act. Moods are εἶδον, ἰδέ, ἴδω, ἴδοιμι, ἰδεῖν, ἰδών.
[4] Str. Perf. ὄπωπα, usually poet.
[5] Fut. πετήσομαι, poet. and late prose. Fut. πτήσομαι is from ἵπτημι, which also supplies an Aor. ἔπτην.

	Future.	Aorist.	Perf. Act.	Perf. Pass.	Aor. Pass.
πίμπλημι,[1] fill	πλήσω	ἔπλησα		πέπλησμαι	ἐπλήσθην
πίμπρημι,[2] burn (tr.)	-πρήσω	-ἔπρησα		-πέπρημαι -πέπρησμαι	-ἐπρήσθην
πίνω, drink	πίομαι	ἔπιον	πέπωκα	πέπομαι	ἐπόθην
πίπτω, fall	πεσοῦμαι	ἔπεσον	πέπτωκα [3]		
πλέω, sail	πλεύσομαι [4]	ἔπλευσα	πέπλευκα		
πνέω, breathe	πνεύσομαι [5]	ἔπνευσα	πέπνευκα		
πυνθάνομαι, ascertain	πεύσομαι	ἐπυθόμην		πέπυσμαι	
πωλῶ (ε-ω), ἀποδίδομαι, sell	πωλήσω ἀποδώσομαι	ἐπώλησα ἀπεδόμην	πέπρᾱκα [6]	πέπρᾱμαι	ἐπράθην
ῥέω, flow	[7]		ἐρρύηκα		ἐρρύην (act.)
ῥήγνυμι, break (tr.)	ῥήξω	ἔρρηξα	ἔρρωγα (intr.)	[8]	ἐρράγην
ῥώννυμι, strengthen	[9]	ἔρρωσα		ἔρρωμαι	ἐρρώσθην
σβέννυμι, extinguish	σβέσω	ἔσβεσα ἔσβην (intr.)	ἔσβηκα (intr.)	ἔσβεσμαι	ἐσβέσθην
σκεδάννυμι, scatter	σκεδῶ	ἐσκέδᾰσα		ἐσκέδασμαι	ἐσκεδάσθην

[1] In compounds, if μ precedes, the μ of the stem is dropt, as ἐμ-πίπλημι, but ἐν-επίμπλην.
[2] In compounds, treated as πίμπλημι above.
[3] Perf. Part. also πεπτώς.
[4] Fut. also πλευσοῦμαι, rare. Perf. Pass. πέπλευσμαι, rare.
[5] Fut. also πνευσοῦμαι, rare.
[6] Pres. πιπράσκω, rare. πωλῶ is the commonest Pres., ἀποδώσομαι the commoner Fut.
[7] Fut. ῥεύσομαι and ῥυήσομαι, rare   Wk. Aor. ἔρρευσα, rare.
[8] Perf. Pass. ἔρρηγμαι, rare.   [9] Fut. ῥώσω, rare.

	Future.	Aorist.	Perf. Act.	Perf. Pass.	Aor. Pass.
στερίσκω, *deprive*	στερήσω	ἐστέρησα	ἐστέρηκα	ἐστέρημαι	ἐστερήθην
στρέφω, *turn* (tr.)	στρέψω	ἔστρεψα		ἔστραμμαι	ἐστράφην
τείνω, *stretch*	τενῶ	ἔτεινα	τέτᾰκα	τέτᾰμαι	ἐτᾰθην
τελῶ (ε-ω), *accomplish*	τελῶ	ἐτέλεσα	τετέλεκα	τετέλεσμαι	ἐτελέσθην
τέμνω, *cut*	τεμῶ	ἔτεμον	τέτμηκα	τέτμημαι	ἐτμήθην
τίκτω, *bring forth*	τέξομαι	ἔτεκον	τέτοκα		
τίνω, *pay*	τίσω	ἔτῑσα	[1]		
τιτρώσκω, *wound*	τρώσω	ἔτρωσα		τέτρωμαι	ἐτρώθην
τρέπω, *turn* (tr.)	τρέψω	ἔτρεψα[2]	τέτροφα	τέτραμμαι	ἐτρέφθην[2]
τρέφω, *nourish*	θρέψω	ἔθρεψα	τέτροφα	τέθραμμαι	ἐτράφην
τρέχω, *run*	δραμοῦμαι	ἔδραμον	δεδράμηκα		
τυγχάνω, *hit*	τεύξομαι	ἔτῠχον	τετύχηκα[4]		
ὑπισχνοῦμαι, *promise*	ὑποσχήσομαι	ὑπεσχόμην		ὑπέσχημαι	
φάσκω, *say*	φήσω	ἔφησα			
φέρω, *bear*	οἴσω	ἤνεγκα[5]	ἐνήνοχα	ἐνήνεγμαι	ἠνέχθην
φθάνω, *anticipate*	φθήσομαι	ἔφθην ἔφθᾰσα	ἔφθᾰκα		

[1] Perf. Act. τέτῑκα, Perf. Pass. τέτισμαι, Wk. Aor. Pass. ἐτίσθην, all rare.
[2] All the Aorists are found. Str. Aor. Act. ἔτραπον, poet., Str. Aor. Mid. ἐτραπόμην, *I turned myself, fled*, but Wk. Aor. ἐτρεψάμην, usually *I turned from myself, routed*. Str. Aor. Pass. ἐτράπην, usually Mid. Intrans.
[3] Tenses from obsolete δρέμω.   [4] Perf. Act. τέτευχα, rarer.
[5] Tenses from οἴω. ἐνέγκω. Str. Aor. ἤνεγκον, commoner, but poet.

	Future.	Aorist.	Perf. Act.	Perf. Pass.	Aor. Pass.
φθίνω, *waste*(intr.)		ἐφθίμην		ἔφθιμαι	
φύω, *grow* (tr.)	φύσω	ἔφῡσα (tr.) ἔφυν(intr.)	πέφῡκα (intr.)		
χαίρω, *rejoice*	χαιρήσω		[1]	[1]	ἐχάρην
χᾰλω (α-ω), *loosen*		ἐχάλᾰσα			ἐχαλάσθην
χάσκω, *gape*	χᾰνοῦμαι	ἔχᾰνον	κέχηνα		
χέω, *pour*	χέω	ἔχεα		κέχῠμαι	ἐχῠθην
χρή,[2] *it is necessary*	χρήσει				
χρῶμαι (α-ο), *use*	χρήσομαι	ἐχρησάμην		κέχρημαι	ἐχρήσθην
ὠθῶ (ε-ω), *push*	ὤσω[3]	ἔωσα		ἔωσμαι	ἐώσθην
ὠνοῦμαι[4](ε-ο), *buy*	ὠνήσομαι	ἐπρῐάμην[5]		ἐώνημαι	ἐωνήθην

[1] Perf. Act. κεχᾰρηκα and Perf. Pass. κεχᾰρημαι, poet.
[2] The Moods are χρή, Impf. χρῆν or ἐχρῆν, χρῇ, χρείη, χρῆναι, χρεών (indecl.).
[3] Fut. Act. ὠθήσω, poet.
[4] Impf. is ἐωνούμην.
[5] Str. Aor. from obsolete πρίαμαι. The Moods are ἐπρῐάμην, πρίω, πρίωμαι, πριαίμην, πρίασθαι, πριάμενος.

APPENDIX I.

162.

Words differing in meaning according to their Accent.

ἄγος, Ionic ἅγος, *curse, pollution.*　ἀγός, *leader.*
ἄγων, participle from ἄγω.　ἀγών, *a contest.*
αἶνος, *a tale, story.*　αἰνός, *dreadful.*
ἀλλά, *but.*　ἄλλα, neut. plur. from ἄλλος.
ἀνά, *up.*　ἄνα, vocative of ἄναξ, and for ἀνάστηθι.
ἄνω, *up, upwards.*　ἀνῶ, str. aor. conj. prim. from ἀνίημι.
ἄρα, *igitur.*　ἆρα (interrog.) sometimes *igitur.*　ἀρά, *a prayer* or *curse.*
αὕτη, nom. sing. fem. from οὗτος, *this.*　αὐτή for ἡ αὐτή.

βασίλεια, *a queen.*　βασιλεία, *a kingdom.*
βίος, *life.*　βιός, *a bow.*
βροτός, *mortal.*　βρότος, *gore.*

δῆμος, *people.*　δημός, *fat.*
διά, *through.*　Δία, acc. of Ζεύς.　δῖα, fem. of δῖος, *divine.*

εἰ, *if.*　εἶ, *thou art,* from εἰμί, or *thou wilt go,* from εἶμι.
εἶα, *on! up!*　εἴα, 3 sing. imperf. act. from ἐάω.
εἴκω, *I yield.*　εἰκώ, accus. sing. of εἰκών, *an image.*
εἰμί, *I am.*　εἶμι, *I shall go.*
εἶπε, *he said.*　εἰπέ, *say.*
εἷς, *one.*　εἵς, aor. part. from ἵημι.
εἰσί, 3 plur. from εἰμί.　εἶσι, 3 sing. from εἶμι.
εἴτε, *whether.*　εἶτε for εἴητε, 3 plur. pres. conj. hist. from εἰμί.
ἔνι for ἔνεστι.　ἐνί for ἐν.
ἔνος and ἕνος, *a year old.*　ἑνός, gen. sing. of εἷς, *one.*
ἐξαίρετος, *choice, chosen.*　ἐξαιρετός, *that can be taken out.*

ἔπαινος, *praise.* ἐπαινός, *awful, dread.*

ἔστι, *he is (exists),* ἐστί *(enclitic), is,* etc. (cp. **146**).

ἐφεῦρε, *he discovered.* ἔφευρε, *find out.*

ἤ, *or, than.* ἦ, *verily, truly;* also 3 sing. imperf. from (ἠμί), *I say.*

ἡ, *fem. from the article* ὁ. ᾗ, *fem. from relat. pron.* ὅς.

ᾗ, *dat. fem. from* ὅς. ᾖ, 3 sing. pres. conj. from εἰμί.

ἠμέν, *conjunction.* ἦμεν, 1 plur. imperf. from εἰμί.

ἤν, *conjunction and interjection.* ἦν, 1 and 3 sing., imperf. from εἰμί, and 1 sing. imperf. from (ἠμί).

ἦτε, 2 plur. imperf. or pres. subj. from εἰμί. ᾖτε, 2 plur. imperf. from εἶμι.

θεά, *goddess.* θέα, *spectacle.*

θεῶν, gen. plur. of θεός, *a god.* θέων, *participle from* θέω, *I run.*

ἰδού, *interjection.* ἰδοῦ, *imperat. of* εἰδόμην.

κάλως, *a cable.* καλῶς, *beautifully.*

κλείς, *a key.* κλεῖς, for κλεῖδες, *nom. plur. of the same word.*

μένω, *I remain.* μενῶ, *I shall remain.*

μῆτις, *wisdom.* μήτις, *lest any one.*

μυρίοι, *countless numbers.* μύριοι, *ten thousand.*

μύσος, *abomination.* μυσός, *abominable.*

νεός, *fallow land.* νέος, *young.*

νεῶν, gen. plur. from ναῦς. νέων, gen. plur. from νέος, *new.* νεών, acc. sing. or gen. plur. from νεώς, *temple.*

νομός, *pasture.* νόμος, *law.*

νῦν, *now, at this time.* νυν, (enclitic) *then, therefore.*

οἱ, *nom. masc. plur. of the article* ὁ. οἵ, *nom. plur. masc. of the relative pron.* ὅς. οἷ, *whither.*

οἴκοι, *at home.* οἶκοι, *houses.*

οἶος, *alone.* οἰός, *gen. from* οἶς, *a sheep.* οἷος, *qualis.*

ὅμως, *yet, still.* ὁμῶς, *equally, together*

πάρα, for πάρεστι. παρά, *by.*

πέρι, for περίεστι.   περί, *about.*

ποῖος, *of what nature?*   ποιός, *of a certain nature.*

πῶς, *how?*   πως, *in some way.*

σίγα, imperat. of σιγάω.   σῖγα, *silently.*

ταὐτά, for τὰ αὐτά.   ταῦτα, nom. pl. from οὗτος.

τροπός, *a thong.*   τρόπος, *a turn, manner.*

τροχός, *a hoop.*   τρόχος, *a running.*

φασί, 3 plur. pres. ind. from φημί.   φᾶσι, dat. plur. of φάς,
   pres. part. of the same.

φυγών, participle, str. aor. from φεύγω.   φυγῶν, gen. plur. from
   φυγή, *flight.*

φῶς, τό, *light.*   φώς, ὁ, *a man.*

ὦ, with the voc. of a noun.   ὤ, an independent interjection.

ὤμοι, *alas!*   ὦμοι, nom. plur. of ὦμος, *a shoulder.*   ὠμοί, nom.
   plur. masc. of ὠμός, *raw.*

ὦμος, *a shoulder.*   ὠμός, *raw.*

ὥς, *so, thus.*   ὡς, *as.*

For the rules of accentuation, cp. 10, 28-31, 51, 146, and
foot of p. 27.

APPENDIX II.

Notes on the Case-Endings.

163. The following is a table of Case-endings, which in the First and Second Declension must be given with the Stem-vowel.

	FIRST DECLENSION.		SECOND DECLENSION.		THIRD DECLENSION.	
SING.	M.	F.	M.F.	N.	M.F.	N.
Nom.	-ᾱς or -ης	-α or -η	-ος	-ον	-ς (often lost)	—
Voc.	-ᾰ or -η	-α or -η	-ε	-ον	(Stem or Nom.)	—
Acc.	-ᾱν or -ην	-αν or -ην	-ον	-ον	-α(-ν after vowel)	—
Gen.	-ου	-ας or -ης	-ου		-ος	
Dat.	-ᾳ or -η	-ᾳ or -η	-ῳ		-ι	
DUAL						
N.V.A.	-ᾱ		-ω		-ε	
G.D.	-αιν		-οιν		-οιν	
PLUR.						
N.V.	-αι		-οι	-α	-ες	-ᾰ
Acc.	-ᾱς		-ους	-α	-ας	-ᾰ
Gen.	-ων		-ων		-ων	
Dat.	-αις or -αισι(ν)		-οις or -οισι(ν)		-σι(ν)	

Obs. 1. The terminations that mark the various cases were probably in the first instance pronouns added to the end of the stem (as *-ward* in English *home-ward*). By constant use with the stems they gradually lost all separate existence.

Obs. 2. The difference in the cases of the various declensions is partly real and partly apparent.

Nom. Sing.—ς is added, which in the Third Declension is often absorbed, as ποιμήν for ποιμεν-ς. Neuters in the Second Declension take the acc. termination for the nominative, perhaps because they were regarded as objects rather than agents.

Nom. Plur.—In the First and Second Declensions ι is found, in the Third -ες. Either the difference is real, or in the former case we must suppose that ς is lost, as λόγοι for λογο-ις. Neuters take acc. termination -α.*

---

* The form in -ι (if it is really different from -ες, and λόγοι is not for λογο-ις) was apparently first used in the pronouns, and from these it was borrowed in Latin and Greek for the First and Second Declension.

Voc. Sing.—The pure stem or the nominative is used for the vocative, which is not really a case but only a noun-interjection. The ε in λόγε is merely a weakened form of o, the character.

Acc. Sing.—All Declensions have -ν for m (cp. 24 a, and Latin acc. sing.); the -a found in consonant nouns is perhaps = -αν (for -αμ). Neuters of the Third Declension have the stem only.

Acc. Plur.—s is added to the acc. sing. Hence νεανίᾱς for νεανιαν-s, λόγους for λογον-s, λαμπάδας for λαμπαδαν-s. Neuters have -a in all Declensions (compare Latin *carmin-a*).

Gen. Sing.—First Decl. -ας, -ης, -ου, Second -ου, Third -ος. These result from two forms, (1.) ας, (2.) σγα.

(1.) μουσα-ας becomes μούσης. λαμπαδ-ας becomes λαμπάδ-ος (o for a).

(2.) κριτα-σγο, κριτᾱ-ο, κριτεο, κριτοῦ. λογο-σγο, λόγοιο, λογοο, λόγου.

Gen. Plur.—The termination in the First and Second Decl. was -σων (compare *-rum* in Latin) and σ is dropped, μουσα-σων, μουσά-ων, μουσῶν.* In the Third it was -ων.

Dat. Sing.—Here also there are two formations, (1.) -αι, (2.) -ι.

(1.) μουσα -αι makes μούσῃ; λογο-οι makes λόγῳ.

(2.) λαμπάδ-ι. In adverbs we find a similar formation from A and O stems, as χαμα-ί, *on the ground*, οἴκο-ι, *at home*. This -ι was strictly the sign of the locative case, and -αι the sign of the dative proper.

Dat. Plur.—The termination is -σι in all Declensions, but in A and O stems, -αις is for -α-σι, and -οις for -o-σι (by *epenthesis*). Thus μουσα-σι becomes μούσαισι, μούσαις, and λογο-σι becomes λόγοισι, λόγοις. The case is strictly a locative; the genuine dative is represented by the *-bus* in Latin (*nubi-bus*).

The *Neuter Plural* and the cases of the *Dual* cannot be explained satisfactorily, but in μούσᾱ, οἴκω, ε (compare λαμπάδ-ε) has probably been absorbed.

---

* Here also Latin and Greek seem to have transferred to the First and Second Declension a form originally found in the pronouns.

Notes on the Declensions.

164.   *First Declension. A Nouns.*

Feminines.—(a.) The following rules will be found useful in determining the Nominative from any of the Oblique cases, or from the stem :—

(i.) All stems in which the character is preceded by ε, ι, or ρ form the nominative in -α, as acc. σοφίαν, nom. σοφίᾱ, dat. plur. πέτραις, nom. πέτρα.

(ii.) All stems in which the character is preceded by σ or by the double consonants ξ, ζ, ψ, σσ, ττ, λλ, form the nominative in -α, as nom. plur. ἅμαξαι, nom. sing. ἅμαξα.

(iii.) After any other vowel or consonant, the -α of the stem usually becomes η in the nominative, as acc. plur. βοάς, nom. sing. βοή, nom. plur. πύλαι, nom. sing. πύλη.

To these rules there are a few exceptions.

(b.) As χώρᾱ are declined some proper names in ᾱ, as Λήδα, 'Αθηνᾶ, and μνᾶ, contracted from μνάα.

(c.) In the nom. and acc. sing. α pure is always long, every other α is short.   Exceptions are :—

Feminine designations in -εια or -τρια, as βασίλειᾰ, *queen*, ψάλτριᾰ, *player ;* all words in -εια derived from adjectives in -ης, as ἀλήθειᾰ, *truth ;* and several words which have a diphthong in the last syllable but one, as εὔνοιᾰ, *good-will*, μοῖρᾰ, *fate*, etc.

165.   *Second Declension. O Nouns.*

(a.) θεός has voc. θεός, compare Latin *deus.*

(b.) *Attic Declension.*—In most of these words ω is preceded by ε, and the lengthening of the last syllable is due to the transfer of quantity from one vowel to another. Thus, λαό-ς is the older form of λεώς (compare βασιλέως, 172 (d.)). Possibly the original form was λαϜ-ος so that when the Ϝ was dropped, compensation was made sometimes in one vowel, sometimes in another. Several words of this declension omit -ν in the acc. sing., *e.g.* ἕως, *dawn* : ἅλως, *threshing-floor*, etc.

(c.) In some stems there is a confusion between the Second and Third Declensions (stems in o, and in ες). Thus, the usual dat. plur. of δένδρον, τό, *tree*, is δένδρεσι(ν) and conversely of πῦρ, τό, *fire*, the dat. plur. is πῠροῖς. σκότος, *darkness*, is generally an -o noun, but sometimes treated as from a stem σκοτες, making a gen. sing. σκότους.

Third Declension.

166. Soft Vowel Stems.

(a.) All vowel stems, masc. or fem., take -ν in the acc. except stems in -ευ, as βασιλεύς, where έᾱ is = εϜαν. All monosyllables use nominative as vocative.

(b.) σῦς is the usual type of substantive-stems in -υ. Adjectives are declined like πῆχυς.

Most stems in -ι are like πόλις. These, and a few stems in υ, as πῆχυς, weaken the character into ε in gen. and dat. sing., and all cases of the dual and plural.

(c.) Isolated forms are κίς, *worm*, and a diphthong-stem οῖς (from ὄϊς for ὄϜις, Latin *ovis*), *sheep*, which keep ι throughout. So also the adjective ἴδρις, ἴδρι, *knowing*.

(d.) The *Attic* genitive, -ως for -ος, is probably accounted for by the loss of a consonant, which represented part of the ι or υ before a vowel, and passed either into the preceding or following vowel, thus:—

> Stem πολι, gen. πολεγ-ος, becomes πόλη-ος (Homer), and πόλε-ως (Attic).
>
> Stem πηχυ, gen. πηχεϜ-ος, becomes πήχεως (Attic).
>
> Stem βασιλευ, gen. βασιλεϜ-ος, becomes βασιλῆ-ος (Homer), and βασιλέ-ως (Attic).

Compare also the declension of ναῦς (52) where the variations of quantity are to be similarly explained.

(*e*) With βοῦς compare Latin *bos.* Before vowel-endings υ became F and was afterwards lost, βοϜ-ος, *bovis.* Acc. plur. βοῦς for βου-ν-ς.

167. CONSONANT STEMS.

(*a.*) *Gutturals.*—In this class must be noticed the stem τριχ, *hair,* which replaces on the first letter the aspirate which is lost in nom. and dat. plur., θρίξ, θριξί(ν). γυνή, *woman,* stem γυναικ, has voc. γύναι, acc. γυναῖκα, dat. plur. γυναιξί(ν).

(*b.*) *Dentals.*—πούς, ὁ, *foot,* stem ποδ, is lengthened in nom. sing. contrary to rule (23). Dat. plur., ποσί(ν).

κλείς, ἡ, *key,* stem κλειδ, acc. κλεῖν. Acc. plur., κλεῖς or κλεῖδας. The Old Attic forms, κλῄς, κλῇδα, κληδός, κλῃδί, are always used in Tragedy. παῖς, *boy,* stem παιδ, has voc. παῖ. ἄναξ, *king,* stem ἀνακτ, voc. ἄνα. Most neuters are declined as σῶμα, merely dropping the dental; a few, as φῶς, *light,* stem φωτ, change τ into ς in N.V.A. sing., and some of these, as γῆρας, *age,* κνέφας, *gloom,* κρέας, *meat,* σέλας, *flash,* reject τ in all other cases, having only the contracted forms. οὖς, *ear,* stem ὠτ, is irregular in the nom. γάλα, *milk,* stem γαλακτ, drops κτ.

To this class belong also stems in -ρτ, as δάμαρ, *wife,* stem δαμαρτ, some of which reject either ρ or τ in every case. These are ἧπαρ, τό, *liver,* stem ἡπαρτ, gen. ἥπᾰτος, dat. plur. ἥπασι(ν); φρέαρ, τό, *well,* stem φρεαρτ, gen. φρέατος; ἄλειφαρ, τό, *salve.* Also ὕδωρ, τό, *water,* stem ὑδαρτ, gen. ὕδᾰτος, and σκῶρ, τό, *dirt.* (**55.**)

The stems γονατ, *knee,* and δορατ, *spear,* become γόνυ and δόρυ in nom. voc. and acc. sing.

(*c.*) *Liquids.*—χείρ, ἡ, *hand,* stem χειρ, often drops ι as acc. sing. χέρ-α, and the short form only is found in χερ-οῖν, χερ-σί(ν). ἀστήρ, ὁ, *star,* stem ἀστερ, is like πατήρ in dat. plur. only. ἀστράσι(ν), μάρτυς, ὁ, *witness,* stem μαρτυρ, drops ρ in nom. sing. and dat. plur., μάρτυσι(ν). Neuters of this class take the stem as nom., voc., acc. sing.

The monosyllable πῦρ, *fire*, stem πῦρ, lengthens the stem-vowel.

(*d.*) *Nasals.*—The monosyllable κτείς, ὁ, *comb*, stem κτεν, lengthens the vowel in nom. and voc. sing.; compare πούς.

κύων, *dog*, has voc. κύον.   The other cases are from a stem κυν, as acc. κύν-α, gen. κυν-ός, etc.

Ποσειδῶν, *Poseidon*, stem Ποσειδων, has acc. Ποσειδῶνα or Ποσειδῶ, and Ἀπόλλων, *Apollo*, stem Ἀπολλων, acc. Ἀπόλλωνα or Ἀπόλλω.

(*e.*) *Spirants.*—Proper names in -ης are derivatives from neuters in -ος like γένος, as Δημοσθένης, stem Δημοσθενες, from σθένος, *strength*, stem σθενες.   Many of these names take also an acc. sing. in -ην, as if from a stem in α, Σωκράτης, *Socrates*, acc. Σωκράτη and Σωκράτην.   Ἡρακλῆς, *Heracles*, and other compounds of κλέος, *glory*, are contracted in every case, and undergo a double contraction in the dat. sing.   Nom. Ἡρακλῆς (ης), Voc. Ἡράκλεις (εες), Acc. Ἡρακλέᾱ (εα), Gen. Ἡρακλέους (εος), Dat. Ἡρακλεῖ (εεϊ, εει).

APPENDIX III.

168. Derivation and Composition.

WORDS are either simple, and formed by derivation, or compound, and formed by composition.

A.—*Derivation.*

Simple words are formed or derived from a single stem, by means of one or more terminations (suffixes) ; *e.g.* stem, ἀρχ, ἄρχω, *I rule,* ἀρχή, *rule ;* stem ἀρχα, ἀρχα-ῖο-ς, *ancient.*

Obs. 1. Words formed immediately from verb-stems, as ἄρχω, ἀρχή, are called primitive ; those formed from noun-stems like ἀρχα-ῖο-ς, are called derivative.

Obs. 2. In a great number of these terminations or suffixes we can trace a more or less definite signification ; *e.g.,* from ποιέω, *I make,* ποιη-τής, *poet (mak-er),* ποίη-μα, *poem (thing made).*

The following are the most common suffixes for forming substantives, adjectives, and verbs.

169. (*a.*) Substantives.

(1.) Nouns signifying the *doer* or *agent* are formed by -ευ, -τηρ, -τορ, -τα (Nom. -εύς, -τήρ, -τωρ, -τής), masculine ; -τειρα, -τρια, -τριδ, -τιδ (Nom. -τειρα, -τρια, -τρίς, -τις) feminine ; *e.g.*
Primitive—

    Verb-stem σω, σω-τήρ, σώ-τειρα, *saviour.*
       ,,   ῥε, ῥή-τωρ, *speaker.*
       ,,   αὐλε, αὐλη-τής, αὐλη-τρίς, *flute-player.*
Derivative—

    Noun-stem οικο, οἰκέ-της, οἰκέ-τις, *servant.*
       ,,   δρομο, δρομεύς, *runner.*

Obs. τα (της) is also used to denote the country of a person, *e.g.* Αἰγινήτης, *an Aeginetan.*

(2.) Nouns signifying an *action* are formed by -τι, -σι (Nom. -τις, -σις). These are all primitive, *e.g.*—

Verb-stem πιθ, πίσ-τις, *trust.*
,,   μιμε, μίμη-σις, *imitation.*
,,   φυ, φύ-σις, *growth, nature.*
,,   πραγ, πρᾶξις, *action.*

(3.) The *result of an action* is signified by the suffix, -ματ (Nom. μα). These nouns are also all primitive, *e.g.*—

Verb-stem ποιε, ποίη-μα, *poem.*
,,   ρε, ρῆ-μα, *speech.*
,,   βα, βῆ-μα, *step*

(4.) The *instrument* is signified by the termination -τρο (neut. -τρον). Nouns in -τρον are also primitives, *e.g.*

Verb-stem ἀρο, ἄρο-τρον, *plough.*
,,   λυ, λύ-τρον, *ransom.*

Obs. Nouns in -τρον or -θρον also signify *place, e.g.* λέκτρον (λεγ), *bed* ; and some of these are derivatives, *e.g.* πτολί-ε-θρον (πτολι), *citadel* ; θύρ-ε-θρον (θυρα), *doorway.*

(5.) The *place* is signified by the suffixes, -τηριο, -ειο (neut. -τήριον, -εῖον). The first of these are primitives, the second derivatives, *e.g.*—

(1.) Verb-stem δικαδ, δικασ-τήριο-ν, *judgment-hall.*
(2.) Noun-stem κουρευ, κουρ-εῖο-ν,   *barber's shop.*
,,   μουσα, μουσ-εῖο-ν,   *museum.*

Obs. Places in which a plant grows, apartments, and the like, are denoted by -ών, *e.g.* ἀμπελών, *vineyard* ; ἀνδρών, *men's apartment.*

(6.) *Abstract qualities* are denoted—

By the suffix -τητ (nom. -της),	Noun-stem νεο,	νεό-της,	*youth.*
	,, βαρυ,	βαρύ-της,	*weight.*
or -συνα, (nom. -συνη),	,, δικαιο,	δικαιο-σύνη,	*justice.*
or -ια,	,, σοφο,	σοφ-ία,	*wisdom.*
	,, εὐδαιμον,	εὐδαιμον-ία,	*happiness.*

Before -ια a final σ of the stem is omitted, *e.g.*—

    Noun-stem ἀληθε(ς), ἀλήθε-ια, *truth*.
           ,,   εὐσεβε(ς), εὐσέβε-ια, *piety*.

(7.) Diminutives are formed by -ιο, -ισκο, -ισκα, -ιδιο, -αριο, etc., *e.g.*—

    Noun-stem παιδ,   παιδ-ίον,   *child*.
         ,,   ,,   παιδ-ίσκη,   *girl*.
         ,,   Ἑρμα,   Ἑρμ-ίδιον,   *little Hermes*.
         ,,   παιδ,   παιδ-άριον,   *child*.

(8.) Patronymics, or substantives signifying the origin of a person, are formed chiefly by the suffix -δα (Nom. -δης), *e.g.*—

    Noun-stem Βορεα,   Βορεά-δης, *son of Boreas*.
         ,,   Κρονο,   Κρονί-δης (ι for ο), *son of Cronos*.
         ,,   Πηλευ,   Πηλεί-δης (ι for υ), *son of Peleus*.

A rare form of the patronymic ends in -ιων, *e.g.* Κρονίων. The feminines are formed by -αδ (Nom. -ας), as Βορεάς, *a Boread*, or more rarely by -ινα (Nom. -ίνη), Εὐηνίνη (*daughter of Euenus*).

(b.) Adjectives.

170. Adjectives are formed

(1.) By the suffix -ιο (Nom. -ιος).

These adjectives denote a general connection with the substantives from which they are derived, *e.g.*—

    Noun-stem οὐρανο, οὐράν-ιος, *heavenly*.
         ,,   ἀγορα, ἀγορα-ῖος, *of the marketplace*.
         ,,   δημο, δήμ-ιος,   *of the people*.

(2.) By the suffix -κο (Nom. -κός) *e.g.*—

    Noun-stem ἀρχ,   ἀρχι-κός, *able to rule*.
         ,,   φύσι,   φυσι-κός, *natural*.

When derived from verbs or nouns of action, these adjectives mean *able to do* this or that.

(3.) By the suffixes -εο and -ινο (Nom. -εος, -ινος), *e.g.*

    Noun-stem χρυσο, χρύσ-εος, *golden*.
         ,,   λιθο,   λίθ-ινος, *of stone*.

These signify the *material* of which a thing is formed.
Other terminations of adjectives are -λος, -μος, -σιμος.

(c.) Verbs.

171. The forms of derivative verbs (*i.e.* verbs derived from nouns) in common use are—

Verbs in a-ω, as τιμά-ω,　*I honour,* noun-stem τιμα.

　　　,,　ε-ω,　,,　φιλέ-ω,　*I love,*　　　　,,　　φιλο.

　　　,,　ο-ω,　,,　δηλό-ω,　*I show,*　　　,,　　δηλο.

　　　,,　ευ-ω,　,,　βουλεύ-ω, *I advise,*　　,,　　βουλα.

　　　,,　ιζ-ω,　,,　ἐλπί-ζω,　*I hope,*　　　,,　　ἐλπιδ.

　　　,,　αζ-ω,　,,　δικά-ζω,　*I judge,*　　　..　　δικα.

Obs. (1.) Verbs in -οω are generally transitive in meaning, as opposed to verbs in -εω, which are intransitive; *e.g.* πολεμέω, *I am at war;* πολεμόω, *I make hostile.*

Obs. (2.) For verbs in -σκω, see Irregular Verbs (166).

To these may be added the desideratives in -σείω, *e.g.* stem δρα, δρασείω, *I desire to do.*

B.—*Composition.*

172. I. Compound words are formed by the union or composition of two or more words into one, as οἰκοδόμος, *a house-builder,* from οἶκος (stem οἰκο) and δέμω.

(1.) The first member of a compound generally presents the pure stem, as in οἰκο-δόμος; but with stems which end in a consonant, and some others, a connecting vowel is often employed, or the final letters of the stem are altered for the sake of euphony.

(*a.*) With connecting vowel—

　　Stem, ἀνδριαντ,　　ἀνδριαντ-ο-ποιός, *statuary.*

　　　,,　φυσι,　　　　φυσι-ο-λόγος,　*physiologist.*

(*b.*) With alteration—

　　Stem, τειχες,　　τειχο-μαχία, *wall-fight.*

　　　,,　ξιφες,　　ξιφο-κτόνος, *slaying with sword.*

Obs. As ο is the vowel in which a large number of stems end, it came to be regarded as the normal ending of the first half of a compound.

(2) Sometimes we find in the case of a noun the first part of a compound, *e.g.* :—

Gen. οὐδενός-ωρος, *of no value.*

Dat. ὀρεσσι-βάτης, *wandering on mountains.*

Loc. χαμαι-πετής, *fallen on the ground.*

(3.) Many compounds alter the termination of the *second* part of the compounded word, *e.g.*—

  Stem **πραγματ**,   πολυ-πράγμων, *busy.*

    ,, **σθενες** (Nom. -os), Δημο-σθένης, *Demosthenes.*

Obs. In compounds of which the second part is derived from verbs, such an alteration is of course necessary, *e.g.*—

  Stem **βλαβ** (βλάπτω), ἀ-βλαβής, *unharmed.*

   ,, **σφαλ** (σφάλλω), ἀ-σφαλής, *safe.*

II. *Compound Verbs and Abstract Substantives.*

173. (1.) Verbs can be immediately compounded with prepositions only, *e.g.* φέρειν, ἐκ-φέρειν, ἀπο-φέρειν. If any further composition is required, a noun of agency must be formed from the verb, and the compound formed with this. The new verb is then derived from the compound noun. Thus, to unite δυς and φέρω we must form a noun δύσ-φορος, *hard to bear*; and from this derive the verb δυσ-φορέ-ω, *I am impatient.* So εὐ-ἀγγέλλω, εὐ-άγγελος, εὐαγγελέω, *I bring good news.* (Similarly, in English, we do not say *to house-build*, but *to be a house-builder*.)

(2.) In the same manner, compound substantives of abstract meaning, unless the first part is a preposition, must be derived from nouns of agency, *e.g.* συμ-φορά, *calamity;* ἐκ-φορά, *burial;* προ-βουλή,—but λαμπαδ-η-φορ-ία, *torch-carrying*, from λαμπαδη-φόρος; λιθοβολία, *stone-throwing*, from λιθοβόλος.

III. *Meaning of Compounds.*

174. Compound words may be divided according to their meaning into (*a.*) Definitive; and (*b.*) Objective compounds.

(*a.*) *Definitive.* In these the first part of the compound defines the second, as ἡ ἀκρό-πολις, *the citadel,*=ἡ ἄκρα πόλις. When the compound so formed is an adjective, and attributed to a substantive, it may be called an *attributive* compound, (= *having* —); *e.g.* λευκώλενος, *having white arms*, of Hera, πολύτροπος, *having many devices*, of Odysseus.

(*b.*) In *Objective* compounds one part of the word stands to the other in the relation expressed by an oblique case, *e.g.* πλήξιππος, *horse-smiting*; οἰκο-γενής, *born in the house.*

Obs. The meaning of some objective compounds differs according to the accent, thus—

πατροκτόνος = *slaying a father.*
πατρόκτονος = *slain by a father*

APPENDIX IV.*

175. Homeric Forms.

THE language of the Homeric poems, Old Ionic, or Epic, as it is called to distinguish it from the New Ionic, is not a dialect in the strict sense of the word. It was not, in all probability, *spoken* at any time; it is rather an artificial product, adapted by a succession of minstrels to the requirements of Epic poems. We find the most various forms existing side by side, *e.g.* ἐμέο, ἐμεῖο, ἐμεῦ, ἐμέθεν, ἐν, εἰν, ἐνί, εἰνί, which is only conceivable when we regard them as different forms, belonging to different periods or places, but retained in the traditional language of poetry because suitable to metre, and at the same time giving an air of antiquity to the style. The greater part of these Homeric forms are Ionic ; but Aeolisms also occur.

176. Vowels.

The Homeric poems have η where Attic has α, χώρη for χώρα, σοφίη for σοφία, νηῦς for ναῦς.

Considerable variation is found in the quantity of vowels : ἠΰς and ἐΰς (Attic εὖ), κονίη and κονίη, ἴομεν and ἴομεν (subj. from εἶμι), δύο and δύω, ἕνεκα and εἵνεκα, πολύς and πουλύς, etc.

Consonants.

Traces of the *digamma* (F) are found in many words, of which the most common are ἄναξ, ἄστυ, ἔαρ (ver), ἕκαστος, εἴκοσι (viginti), ἔπος, ἔργον (*work*), ἕσπερος (vesper), ἰδεῖν (videre), ἔοικα, ἴσος (for Attic ἴσος), οἶκος (vicus), οἶνος (vinum).

177. First or A-Declension.

(1.) η is common for α in the singular of feminines ; cp. also Dat. plur.

* Cf. Monro, *Iliad*, i. p. xxxix. ff.

(2.) For *nom. sing.* of masc. nouns we find -a beside -ης, *e.g.* ἱππότα, ἱππηλάτα. With these we may compare the Latin scriba. But observe that the words in which this form is found are 'titular epithets.'

(3.) For the *gen. sing.* of masc. nouns we find -ᾱο, -εω, and, after a vowel, -ω for ου, *e.g.* Ἀτρεΐδᾱο, Ἀτρεΐδεω, Βορέω. The *gen. plur.* ends regularly in -αων, -εων. The contracted (Attic) form is only found after vowels, *e.g.* Μαλειῶν, παρειῶν.

(4.) The *dative plural* ends in -ης before vowels, and -ῃσι.

178.   Second or O-Declension.

(1.) The forms of the *nom.* of the "Attic Declension" are found even in Homer beside forms in -αος; in *proper names*, *e.g.* Ἀγέλεως, Ἀγέλᾱος, Βριάρεως; but only λαός, νηός, ἴλαος.

(2.) *Gen. sing.*—Beside the forms in -ου we find also a longer form in -οιο,—μεγάλου, μεγάλοιο, and probably a form in -οο (Ἰλίοο, *Il.* xv. 66; ἀγρίοο, *Il.* xxii. 313, etc.).

(3.) The *gen. and dat. dual* ends in -οιιν, *e.g.* ὤμοιιν, ὀφθαλμοῖιν.

(4.) The *dat. plur.* ends in -οις and -οισι.

(5.) Contraction is seldom found.

179.   Third Declension.

(1.) *Voc. sing.* — Κάλχαν, Θόαν, but always Πουλυδάμα, Λαοδάμα. The *voc.* of ἄναξ is regularly ἄναξ, except in prayers, when it is ἄνα.

(2.) *Acc. sing.*—Barytones (28) in -ις and -υς (from stems in dentals) have sometimes ν, sometimes α,—ἔριν, ἔριδα, φύλοπιν, φυλόπιδα, κόρυν, κόρυθα (44).

(3.) For the *gen.* of πόλις we find πόλι-ος and πόληος. Similarly we find Πηλέος and Πηλῆος, from Πηλεύς. The gen. sing. of ς stems (49) contracts into -ευς instead of -ους, *e.g.* ἐρέβευς, θάρσευς, θέρευς. This is a peculiarity of the Ionic dialect.

(4.) For the *dative sing.* words in -ις have sometimes ει, sometimes ῑ, *e.g.* κόνῑ, μήτῑ, Θέτῑ.

(5.) The *Dual* ends in -οιιν, but the only forms are πόδοιιν, Σειρήνοιιν.

(6.) *Acc. plur.*—Stems in ι and υ have two forms, *e.g.* σῦς and σύας, ἰχθῦς and ἰχθύας; so also πόλις and πόλιας, etc. βοῦς also has βόας and βοῦς. We need not regard the shorter forms as contracted from the longer; they may be formed differently, so that σῦς is for συν-s, but σύας for συϜ-ας, βοῦς for βουν-s, βόας for βοϜ-ας.

(7.) In the *dative plural* we have a variety of forms. Thus from χείρ, χείρεσσι, χείρεσι, χερσί; from πούς, πόδεσσι, ποσσί, ποσί; from ἔπος, ἐπέεσσι, ἔπεσσι, ἔπεσι; from βοῦς, βόεσσι, βουσί.

(8.) Contraction as a rule is not found in nouns from stems in ς, with *nom.* in -ης and -ος. But words in -ως and -ω are always contracted, *e.g.* Καλύψους, Λητοῖ, Λητώ, αἰδῶ, ἠῶ. Neuters in -ας are partly contracted, partly not so, κρέα, δέπα, κέρα, κρείων, τέραα, γήραος, γήραϊ, δεπάων, etc. Words in -υς always contract the dat. sing., πληθυῖ, ἰχθυῖ.

180. In addition to the usual case-terminations, Epic poets use certain suffixes to express the relation of case, or preposition (56).

(1.) φι(ν) for gen. and dative : βίηφι(ν), παλάμηφι(ν), κεφαλῆφι(ν), ἐσχαρόφιν, δακρυόφιν, θεόφιν, ὄχεσφιν, στήθεσφιν, κράτεσφιν, ναῦφι(ν), ἐτέρηφι, φαινομένηφι, αὐτόφιν, δεξιόφιν, ἀριστερόφιν.

(2.) θε(ν) to express the relation *Whence?* and for the genitive : Ἴδηθεν, κλισίηθεν, Τροίηθεν, ἀγορῆθεν, οὐρανόθεν, etc. When attached to a noun θεν never loses the termination ν.

(3.) θι to express the relation *Where?*—οἴκοθι, κηρόθι, Ἰλιόθι, οὐρανόθι, ἠῶθι, ἄλλοθι, αὐτόθι, ὑψόθι, τόθι, ὅθι, πόθι.

(4.) δε, σε, ζε to express the relation *Whither?*—Ἰθάκηνδε, Τροίηνδε, ἀγορήνδε, Οὐλυμπόνδε, οἰκόνδε, πεδίονδε, ἄλαδε, ἄστυδε, φόωσδε, τέλοσδε, οἴκαδε, φύγαδε, ὄνδε δόμονδε, κυκλόσε, ὑψόσε, πάντοσε, τηλόσε, πόσε, ἔραζε. θύραζε, χάμαζε, etc.

181.   Irregular Forms.

'Αΐδης 'Αΐδαο, 'Αΐδεο "Αϊδος "Αϊδι, Αἰδωνεύς.

γόνυ, γουνός γοῦνα, γούνων, γούνεσσι (*i.e.* the stem **γονατ** is rejected and **γουν** is used), γούνατα, γούνασι; the υ of γόνυ is transferred to the preceding syllable by the figure called *Epenthesis.*

δόρυ, δουρί, δοῦρε, δούρεσσι (as if from **δουρ**), δούρατι, δούρατα.

Ζεύς, besides the forms Διός, Διΐ, Δία, has Ζηνός, Ζηνί, Ζῆνα as if from a stem **Ζην** (54).

κάρη has various forms. κάρητος, κάρητι, as if from **καρητ**; καρήατος, καρήατι, καρήατα, as if from **καρηατ**; κράατος, κράατι, κράατα, with metathesis of ρ; κρατός, κρατί, κρᾶτα, κράτων, κρασίν, with metathesis and contraction; κάρ, acc. sing.; κρῆθεν.

νηῦς = ναῦς has forms in η and ε. νηός, νεός, νῆα, νηυσί, νέες, νέεσι (νήεσσι), νεῶν (52).

υἱός has a shorter form in addition to those given (52), υἷος, υἷι, υἷα, υἷε, υἷες, υἱάσι, υἷας.

The forms in -τηρ retain or omit the ε—μητρί μητέρι, θύγατρα θυγάτερα, θύγατρες θυγάτερες, etc. (47).

182.   Adjectives.

(1.) In Homer adjectives of *three* terminations are often used as having only *two, e.g.* ἰφθίμους ψυχάς, ἄγριος ἄτη, ὀλοώτατος ὀδμή, ὑλήεντι Ζακύνθῳ, etc.

(2.) On the other hand, *compound adjectives have often a fem. form,* ἀθανάτη, ἀσβέστη, ἀβρότη, ἀριγνώτη, ἀμφιρύτη, etc.

(3.) πολύς besides the usual forms (66) has also πολέος, πολέες πολεῖς, πολέσι πολέεσσι, πολέας, and πολλός πολλόν.

183.   Comparison of Adjectives.

From μέσος μέσσος we have μέσσατος, from νεός, νέατος and νείατος. For χείρων we find χερείων, χειρότερος, χερειότερος. For ῥάων ῥᾷστος, ῥηίτερος ῥηίτατος and ῥήιστος, from ῥηίδιος, the Ionic η taking the place of α, and ι being written after instead of under the long vowel.

184. Numerals.

For μία (88) we find ἴα ; for τέσσαρες, πίσυρες, an Aeolic form.

185. Pronouns.

(1.) *Personal* :—ἐγώ, ἐγών, ἐμέο ἐμεῖο ἐμεῦ. ἐμέθεν (formed by the addition of θεν, 186 (2)). ἡμεῖς ἄμμες—ἡμέων ἡμείων —ἡμῖν ἄμμι(ν) (an Aeolic form), ἡμέας ἡμᾶς ἄμμε (an Aeolic form).

σύ τύνη—σέο σεῦ σεῖο. σέθεν, τεοῖο perhaps like *tui*, the gen. of the possessive used for the personal pronoun. σοί τοί (cp. Lat. *tu*), τεΐν. ὑμεῖς ὕμμες (an Aeolic form) ; ὑμέων ὑμείων —ὑμῖν ὕμμι(ν) (Aeolic) ; ὑμέας ὕμμε (Aeolic).

ἑό εἷο εὗ, ἕθεν, οἷ ἑοῖ, ἕ ἕέ, μιν, σφέων σφείων σφίσι(ν) σφι(ν), σφέας σφάς σφέ.

(2.) *Possessive* :—τεός=σός, ἑός=ὅς ; ἁμός, ὑμός, σφός, for ἡμέτερος, ὑμέτερος, σφέτερος.

(3.) *Demonstrative* :—ὁ, ἡ, τό is regularly used as a pronoun. ὅδε in *dat. plur.* sometimes makes τοίσδεσι τοίσδεσσι, *i.e.* the termination -σσι is added to the form τοῖσδε, though this is already complete in itself.

(4.) *Relative* :—the demonstr. ὅ is often used for the relative. For οὗ we find a form ὅου (*Il.* ii. 325; *Od.* i. 70) which is explained as wrongly written for ὅο. ὅς τις and ὅτις, ὅτευ ὅττεο, ὅτεῳ, ὅτινα, ὅτεων, ὁτέοισι, ὅτινας, neut. ἄσσα, sing. ὅτι and ὅττι.

186. Prepositions (cp. 101).

εἰς ἐς—ἐν εἰν ἐνί εἰνί—in these forms we see the influence of epenthesis (cp. 187).   From ἐνί arose εἰνί, and this by abbreviation becomes εἰν. πρός προτί ποτί ; προτί is no doubt the original form, and προς=προτ, since τ cannot remain at the end of a word (24). σύν ξύν—ὑπό ὑπαί—παρά παραί—κατά καταί (once only) ; the forms with ι are no doubt the older, and represent locative cases of stems ὑπα, παρα, κατα.

The prepositions also undergo *apocope*. Thus πάρ for παρά ; ἄν for ἄνα, ἄμ πεδίον—κάτ for κατά, κάββαλεν = κατέβαλεν, κὰγ γόνυ = κατὰ γόνυ, κὰδ δέ = κατὰ δέ, κὰμ μέσσον = κατὰ μέσσον, etc.

187.   The Verb.—Augment, Reduplication.

(1.) *The Augment*, syllabic and temporal, is retained or dropped as the verse requires, *e.g.* ἔθηκεν, *Il.* i. 3, τεῦχε 4, ἐτελείετο 5, διαστήτην 6, ὦρσε and ὀλέκοντο 10, λίσσετο 15, etc. Words which had the digamma can have a syllabic augment, *e.g.* ἔειπον, ἐέλπετο, ἐήνδανε, ἐάγην, ἐείσατο (123).

(2.) *The liquids and σ are doubled*, if the verse requires it, after the augment—ἔλλαβε, ἐλλιτάνευε, ἔμμαθε, ἔμμορε, ἔρρεον, ἐρρίγησε, ἔρριψε, etc., ἔσσευε ἔσσυτο.   On the other hand, the single ρ is sometimes found, *e.g.* ἔρεζον, ἔρεζα, ἐρύσατο.

(3.) *Reduplication* is found in many *aorists*, λέλαθον, λελαβέσθαι, κεχάροιτο, κεκύθωσι, πεφιδέσθαι, etc.

188.   The Verb.—Terminations.

(1.) -μι is found in 1 S. Conj. of some -ω verbs, *e.g.* ἐθέλωμι, τύχωμι, ἴδωμι, etc.

(2.) The 2 S. of Conj. and Optat. sometimes ends in -σθα, *e.g.* ἐθέλῃσθα, εἴπῃσθα, βάλοισθα, κλαίοισθα, etc.

(3.) The 3d conj. S. sometimes ends in -σι : ἐθέλῃσι, λάβῃσι, etc. ; cp. the verbs in -μι, 3d sing. Indic.

(4.) In 2d pers. pl. middle we find, as a rule, εαι in Indic., ηαι in Conj., *e.g.* βούλεαι, γένηαι ; βούλεαι = βουλε-σαι βούλε-αι.

(5.) For -μεθα in 1 pl. mid. we find sometimes a longer form, -μεσθα, cp. σθα (2).

(6.) The 3d plur. of Ind., Perf., and Pluper. middle, and Optat. mid. ends in -αται and -ατο for -νται -ντο, *e.g.* εἰρύαται βεβλήαται, κέαται, εἴατο, γενοίατο, πυθοίατο. The form in -ατο is the only one found in Homer after ι.

(7.) The 3d plur. of the *Passive aorists* ends in -εν, for -ησαν— κοίμηθεν, φόβηθεν, φάανθεν, etc.

(8.) After ῠ and ῐ the iota of the *Optative* is sometimes allowed to drop, *e.g.* ἐκδῦμεν, δαινῦτο, λελῦτο.

(9.) The forms of the *Infinitive* are various.

a. Verbs in -ω—ἀμύνειν, ἀμύνεμεν, ἀμυνέμεναι.
εἰπεῖν, εἰπέμεν, εἰπέμεναι.
ἀρήξειν, ἀρήξεμεν, ἀρηξέμεναι.

b. Verbs in -μι end in -ναι, -μεναι—στῆναι, στήμεναι.
So also Passive aorist stems, μιγῆναι, μιγήμεναι,
and Perfect, ἐστάμεναι, τεθνάμεναι.

It is noticeable that all the longest forms of the Infinitive end in -αι. Compare the termination of the prepositions. It is probable that the infinitive is the case of a noun-stem (Locative or Dative), *e.g.* στήμεναι is a case of a stem στημενα, and means strictly " in standing," " for standing."

189. The Verb.—Contracted Verbs.

(1.) Verbs in -άω seldom remain uncontracted (ναιετάω is an exception), *but they undergo a peculiar kind of extension, the long vowel arising from contraction taking the shorter form of the vowel before it.* Thus,—ὁρόω, ὁράᾳς, ὁράᾳ, ὁρόωμεν ὁράαν, and even with two long vowels, ἡβώωσα, δρώωσι.

(2.) Verbs in -έω generally remain uncontracted ; when contraction of εο takes place it is into ευ, not into ου—καλεῦντο, πωλεύμην.

(3.) The verbs in -όω are for the most part contracted, and in some instances they also, like the verbs in -άω, are extended, *e.g.* ἀρόωσιν, and also ἱδρώοντα.

190. The Verb.—The Future.

(1.) Futures without σ (133) are treated like contracted verbs in -έω.

(2.) The Future without σ is found in some verbs with stems not ending in a liquid, *e.g.* τελέω, ἀντιόω, δαμάᾳ, and δαμᾷ, κρεμόω, etc.

191. The Verb.—The Aorist.

(1.) There are Aorists with α but without σ, *e.g.* ἤνεικα, ἔκηα (καίω) ἔχεα (χέω), ἔσσευα (σεύω), ἠλεύατο (ἀλεύομαι).

(2.) There are also Aorists with σ but without α—ἐβήσετο, ἐδύσετο, ἷξον, βήσεο, ὄρσεο, ἄξετε, etc.

(3.) Several verbs have both strong and weak Aorists passive —ἐμίγην ἐμίχθην, ἐφάνην ἐφαάνθην, ἐπάγην ἐπήχθην, ἐτάρπην ἐτάρφθην ἐτέρφθην. There are also many instances of Aorists middle and passive from the same verb with the same meaning, *e.g.* κοιμήσαντο ἐκοιμήθην, and of Aorists active and middle, *e.g.* ἔβη ἐβήσετο, ἔδυ ἐδύσετο.

(4.) Syncopated Aorists are not uncommon, *e.g.* ἔβλητο βλῆσθαι βλήμενος, λύτο λύντο λύμην, κτάσθαι κτάμενος, ἐφθίμην φθίσθαι φθίμενος, χύτο χύντο χύμενος, ἐδέγμην ἔδεκτο δέχθαι δέγμενος, ἔγρετο ἐγρόμενος, etc.

(5.) Many weak Aorists in Homer have a double sigma, *e.g.* ἔλασσα, ἐτέλεσσα, νάσσα.

192.   The Verb.—Perfect and Pluperfect.

(1.) The *Perfects* ἔστηκα βέβηκα, τέθνηκα. τέτληκα, μέμονα, γέγονα, πέφυκα, δείδια, are syncopated, ἔστατε, βεβάασι, τεθνάμεν, γεγάασι, τέτλαθι, δείδιμεν, μέματον, τεθναίην, πεφύασι. So too the Participles κεκμηώς, κεχαρηώς, πεπτηώς, τετιηώς, βεβαρηώς, κεκοτηώς.

(2.) Some forms of the Perfect have δ inserted—ἐρηρέδαται, ἐρράδαται, ἀκηχέδαται, ἐληλέδατο.

(3.) The 1st Sing. of the *Pluperfect* sometimes ends in -εα— ἐτεθήπεα, πεποίθεα, ἠνώγεα, ᾔδεα.

(4.) In some forms the termination is united directly with the stem without any connecting vowel—ἐγρήγορθε (ἐγείρω), πέποσθε (πάσχω), ἤϊκτο (ἔοικα), ἐπέπιθμεν (πείθω).

(5.) There are remnants of an older formation of the Pluperfect, in which terminations like those of the Imperfect are added to the reduplicated stem, *e.g.* ἐ-πέπληγ-ο-ν, cp. ἔ-τυπτ-ο-ν. But others regard these forms as reduplicated strong aorists.

193.   Verbs in -μι.

(1.) These are sometimes treated as contracted verbs, *e.g.* τιθεῖ, μεθιεῖς, μεθιεῖ, ἀνιεῖς, διδοῖς, διδοῖ, ἐδίδου, ἐτίθει, etc.

(2.) The Conjunctive is rarely contracted. The usual forms are, *e.g.* ἀφέῃ, βέῃς, ἔῃς, στέωμεν, θέωμεν. The ε often becomes ει, θείω, βείω, or η, θήῃς θήῃ, στήῃς, στήῃ. The same change occurs in the passive aorists δαμείω, δαμήῃς, etc. The ο or η of the Conjunctive is often shortened, *e.g.* ἴομεν, κιχείομεν, θείομεν, στήομεν, στήετε.

(3.) In the 3d pl. of the Past tenses the termination is formed like the passive aorists, *e.g.* ξύνιεν, μέθιεν, πρότιθεν, ἔσταν, ἔβαν, ἔφαν.

(4.) Forms of εἰμί; 2d pers. sing. ἐσσί and εἶς both enclitic; so also εἰσί, but not ἔᾱσι. Conj. ἔω, ἔῃς, Infin. εἶναι, ἔμμεναι (=ἐσμεναι), ἔμμεν (=ἐσ-μεν), ἔμεναι, ἔμεν. Part. ἐών, ἐοῦσα (=ἐσων, ἐσοντια). Imperat. mid. ἔσσ-ο. Imperf. ἦα (=ἦσα, *eram*, with augt.) ἔα (=ἔσα without augment), ἔον (=ἔσον, as if from an ω-verb). 3d pl. ἔσαν and ἦσαν. Fut. ἔσσομαι ἔσομαι, ἔσσεται ἔσεται ἔσται.

(5.) εἶμι, mostly with future signification; but there is also a Future form, εἴσομαι, and aorist, εἴσατο, ἐείσατο. Imperf. ἤια ἤα ἤιον (as from an ω-verb). 3d S., sometimes ἴε. Inf. ἴμεναι and ἴμεν.

(6.) φημί, 2d pers. φής and φῆσθα. Imperf. φῆς, φῆσθα, ἔφησθα. 3d pers. pl. ἔφᾰν, φάν. Future, φήσω. Middle aor. (or imperfect), ἐφάμην, ἔφατο, φάτο. Imperat. φάο, φάσθω. Infin. φάσθαι. Part. φάμενος.

(7.) οἶδα, 1st pers. pl. ἴδμεν. 2d pers. sing. οἶσθα οἶδας (only once). Inf. ἴδμεναι, ἴδμεν. Part. εἰδώς, εἰδυῖα, ἰδυῖα. Imperf. ᾔδεα, ᾔδησθα, ᾔείδεις. 3d. pers. ἠείδη, ᾔδη. 3d pl. ἴσαν (without augment). Fut. εἴσομαι.

VOCABULARY.

Substantives.*

FIRST DECLENSION.

A *Stems.*

MASCULINES.

Like νεανίᾱς—

Βορέας,	Boreas (N.N.E. wind).
Λοξίας,	Loxias (Apollo).
ταμίας,	steward.
Ἀρχίας,	Archias.

Like κριτής—

αὐλητής,	flute-player.
γεω-μέτρης,	land-measurer.
δικαστής,	juror.
ἐπιβάτης,	marine.
εὐεργέτης,	benefactor.
ἱκέτης,	suppliant.
λῃστής,	robber.
ναύτης,	sailor.
νομο-θέτης,	lawgiver.
ὁπλίτης,	heavy-armed soldier.
:τελταστής,	targeteer.
Πέρσης,	Persian.
ποιητής,	maker, poet.
πολῑτης,	citizen.
σαλπιγκτής,	trumpeter.
Σκύθης,	Scythian.
στρατιώτης,	soldier.
συκοφάντης,	informer.
τεχνῑτης,	artificer.
τοξότης,	bowman.

ὑβριστής,	insulter.
ὑποκριτής,	actor.

FEMININES.

Like χώρᾱ—

ἀγορά	market.
αἰτία,	cause.
ἀλήθειᾰ,	truth.
ἀνδρεία,	manliness.
βασιλεία,	kingdom.
βασίλειᾰ,	queen.
βίᾰ,	force.
διαφορά,	difference.
ἐκκλησία,	assembly.
ἐπιθυμία,	zeal, desire.
ἑσπέρα,	evening.
ἡμέρα,	day.
θύρα,	door.
λεία,	spoil.
μαντεία,	oracle.
μοῖρᾰ,	fate.
ναυμαχία,	sea-fight.
οἰκία,	dwelling.
πεῖρᾰ,	attempt.
σοφία,	wisdom.
στρατιά,	army.
συμφορά,	misfortune.
ὑποψία,	suspicion.
φιλία,	friendship.
ὥρα,	season.

---

* The number of examples given is in some proportion to the number of existing words of the particular class.

A *Nouns.*

Like τῑμή—

αἰχμή,	spear-point.
ἀνάγκη,	necessity.
ἀρετή,	virtue.
ἀρχή,	beginning.
βοή,	shout.
βουλή,	counsel.
γῆ,	earth.
γνώμη,	opinion.
δίκη,	justice.
εἰρήνη,	peace.
ἑορτή,	festival.
εὐχή,	prayer
ἡδονή,	pleasure.
κεφαλή,	head.
λύπη,	grief.
μάχη,	battle.
νίκη,	victory.
ὀργή,	anger.
πηγή,	spring, well.

πύλή,	gate.
ῥώμη,	might.
σελήνη,	moon.
σῑγή,	silence.
σκηνή,	tent.
τύχη,	chance.
φύγή,	flight.
φωνή,	sound.
ψῡχή,	breath, soul.

Like μοῦσᾰ—

γλῶσσα,	tongue.
δέσποινα,	mistress.
δίαιτα,	way of living.
δίψα,	thirst.
δόξα,	opinion.
ἧσσα,	worsting, defeat.
θάλασσα,	sea.
ῥίζα,	root.
τόλμα,	daring.
τράπεζα,	table.

SECOND DECLENSION.

O *Nouns*

Like λόγος, mostly masculine—

ἄγγελος,	messenger.
ἀδελφός,	brother.
ἄνεμος,	wind.
βίος,	life.
βωμός,	altar.
δῆμος,	people.
δόλος,	fraud.
δοῦλος,	slave.
ἥλιος,	sun.
θάνατος,	death.
θησαυρός,	treasure.
θυμός,	courage, spirit.
ἵππος,	horse.
καιρός,	opportunity.
κίνδῡνος,	danger.
κύριος,	lord.
λίθος,	stone.
μισθός,	pay.
μῦθος,	fable.
νόμος,	law.
ξένος,	host, guest.
οἶνος,	wine.

ὅρος,	boundary.
ὀφθαλμός,	eye.
ὄχλος,	crowd.
πλοῦτος,	wealth.
πόλεμος,	war.
πόνος,	toil.
ποταμός,	river.
σίδηρος,	iron.
σῖτος (τὰ σῖτα),	corn, food.
στρατηγός,	general.
σύμμαχος,	ally.
ταῦρος,	bull.
ὕπνος,	sleep.
φόβος,	fear.
χαλκός,	copper, bronze.
χρόνος,	time.
χρυσός,	gold.

Like ζυγόν, neuter—

ἄριστον,	breakfast.
δεῖπνον,	dinner.
δένδρον,	tree.
δῶρον,	gift.
ἐπιτήδεια, pl.,	necessaries.
ἔργον,	work.

ζῷον,	living thing.	Ἀλκάθους (for oo-s),	Alcathous.
ἱμάτιον,	garment.	θροῦς (for oo-s),	noise.
κέντρον,	goad, spur.	πλοῦ* (for oo-s),	voyage.
μέτρον,	measure.	ῥοῦς (ιor oo-s),	stream.
ὅπλον,	armour (of defence).	χνοῦς (for oo-s),	down, foam.
πεδίον,	plain.		
πρόσωπον,	face.		
σημεῖον,	sign.	Like λεώς, masc. or fem.—	
στρατόπεδον,	camp.		
τόξον,	bow.	ἅλως, ἡ,	threshing-floor.
τροπαῖον,	trophy.	Ἄθως,	Mount Athos.
χωρίον,	place, spot.	λαγώς, ὁ,	hare.
		Μίνως, ὁ,	Minos.
Like νοῦς (for νόος), masc.—		Μενέλεως,	Menelaus.
ἀδελφιδοῦς (for εο-s), nephew.		νεώς, ὁ,	temple.

THIRD DECLENSION.

Soft-Vowel Stems.

Like πόλις, mostly feminine—

αἴσθησις, ἡ,	perception.
ἀνάβασις, ἡ,	going-up.
δύναμις, ἡ,	power.
ἕξις, ἡ,	habit.
κρίσις, ἡ,	judgment, decision.
λύσις, ἡ,	release.
μάθησις, ἡ,	learning.
μάντις, ὁ,	soothsayer.
ὄφις, ὁ,	snake.
ὄψις, ἡ,	sight, vision.
πίστις, ἡ,	trust, assurance.
πρᾶξις, ἡ,	doing, action.
πρόφᾰσις, ἡ,	excuse.
στάσις, ἡ,	position, faction.
τάξις, ἡ,	arrangement.
τέρψις, ἡ,	delight.
φῦσις, ἡ,	nature.

Like σῦς, masc. or fem.—

ἄρκυς, ἡ,	net.
βότρυς, ὁ,	grape-cluster.
γένυς, ἡ,	cheek.
δρῦς, ἡ,	oak.
ἰσχύς, ἡ,	strength.
μῦς, ὁ,	mouse.
ὀφρύς, ἡ,	eyebrow.
πίτυς, ἡ,	pine-tree.
στάχυς, ὁ,	ear of corn.

Like πῆχυς, only three—

ἔγχελυς, ὁ,	eel.
πέλεκυς, ὁ,	axe.
πρέσβυς, ὁ,	old man.

Like βασιλεύς, all masculine—

ἁλιεύς,	fisherman.
γονεύς,	parent.
γραμματεύς,	clerk.
γραφεύς,	painter.
ἑρμηνεύς,	interpreter.
ἱερεύς,	priest.
ἱππεύς,	horseman.
κεραμεύς,	potter.
νομεύς,	shepherd.
συγγραφεύς,	historian.
φονεύς,	murderer.

Consonant-Stems.

Stems in gutturals.　No Neuters.

αἴξ (γ), ὁ, ἡ,	goat.
διῶρυξ (ὔχ), ἡ,	trench.
θώραξ (ᾱκ), ὁ,	breastplate.
κόραξ (ᾰκ), ὁ,	raven.
πτέρυξ (ὔγ), ἡ,	wing.
σάλπιγξ (ιγγ), ἡ,	war-trumpet.
σάρξ (κ), ἡ,	flesh.
σφήξ (κ), ὁ,	wasp.
Σφίγξ (ιγγ), ἡ,	Sphinx.
φάλαγξ (αγγ), ἡ,	phalanx.
φλόξ (γ), ἡ,	flame.
φοῖνιξ (ῑκ), ὁ,	palm-tree.

Stems in dentals τ, δ, θ. M. or F.

Ἄρτεμις (ῐδ),	Artemis.
ἀσπίς (ῐδ), ἡ,	shield.
γυμνής (ητ), ὁ,	light-armed soldier.
Ἑλλάς (ᾰδ), ἡ,	Hellas.
ἐλπίς (ῐδ), ἡ,	hope.
ἐσθής (ητ), ἡ,	clothing.
ἱδρώς (ωτ), ὁ,	sweat.
λαμπρότης (ητ), ἡ,	splendour.
μυριάς (ᾰδ), ἡ,	myriad (10,000).
νεότης (ητ), ἡ,	newness, youth.
ὁλκάς (ᾰδ), ἡ,	merchantman.
πατρίς (ῐδ), ἡ,	fatherland.
φροντίς (ῐδ), ἡ,	thought, care.

Stems in dentals. Neuters.

Like σῶμα—

ἄγαλμα,	delight, honour.
αἷμα,	blood.
ἅρμα,	chariot.
ἔγκλημα,	accusation.
κτῆμα,	possession.
μέλι (ῐτ)	honey.
ὄμμα,	eye.
ὄνομα,	name.
πνεῦμα,	wind, air.
σῆμα,	sign.
σπέρμα,	seed.
στόμα,	mouth.
τέρμα,	boundary.
τραῦμα,	wound.
χεῖμα,	winter.
χρῆμα,	thing.
ψήφισμα,	measure passed (by vote).

Like κέρας—

γέρας,*	reward.
γῆρας,*	old age.
κρέας,*	flesh.
πέρας,†	end.
σέλας,*	flash.
φῶς (ωτ),†	light.

* These have the contracted form only.
† These never drop τ.

Stems in dentals ντ. **All Masc.**

Like γίγας—

Αἴας,	Ajax,
ἐλέφας,	ivory.
ἱμάς,	thong.

Like λέων—

δράκων (οντ),	serpent.
θεράπων (οντ),	attendant.
Ξενοφῶν (ωντ),	Xenophon.

Stems in labials π, β, (φ). **No Neuters.**

λαῖλαψ (ᾰπ), ἡ,	storm.
μύωψ (ωπ), ὁ,	goad, gadfly.
χέρνιψ (ῐβ), ἡ,	holy water.

Stems in liquids (λ), ρ.

Like θήρ or ῥήτωρ. **All Masc.**

ἀγήτωρ (ορ),	leader.
ἀήρ (ερ),	atmosphere.
αἰθήρ (ερ),	upper air.
κρατήρ (ηρ),	mixing bowl.
μνηστήρ (ηρ),	suitor.
μυκτήρ (ηρ),	nose, trunk.
ὀπτήρ (ηρ),	spy, eyewitness.
πεντηκοντήρ,	captain of fifty.

Stems in liquids. **Neuter.**

ἔαρ (ᾰρ),	spring.
ἦτορ (ορ),	heart.
νέκτᾰρ (ᾰρ),	nectar.
πῦρ (ῠρ),	fire.

Stems in nasals. **No Neuters.**

ἀηδών (ον), ἡ,	nightingale.
ἀνδρών (ων), ὁ,	men's apartment.
ἄξων (ον), ὁ,	axle.
αὐχήν (εν), ὁ,	neck.
Βαβυλών (ων), ἡ,	Babylon.
ἱππών (ων), ὁ,	stable.
κανών (ον), ὁ,	rule, rod.
λιμήν (εν), ὁ,	harbour.

παιάν (ᾱν), ὁ,	paean (war-song).
τέκτων (ον), ὁ,	craftsman.
χειμών (ων), ὁ,	storm, winter.
χιτών (ων), ὁ,	tunic.
χιών (ον), ἡ,	snow.

Like δελφίς.

θίς (ῑν), ἡ,	heap.
ἴς (ῑν), ἡ,	force.
ῥηγμίς (ῑν), ὁ,	surf.
ὠδίς (ῑν), ἡ,	pang.

Stems in spirants, s, F.

Like Δημοσθένης.   All Masc.

Ἀριστοτέλης,	Aristotle.
Δημοκράτης,	Democrates.
Ἑρμογένης,	Hermogenes.
Ἡρακλῆς (173 e),	Heracles.
Θεμιστοκλῆς,	Themistocles.
Θηραμένης,	Theramenes.
Περικλῆς (173 e),	Pericles.
Σοφοκλῆς (173 e),	Sophocles.

Like γένος.   All neuter.

ἄλγος,	grief.
ἄνθος,	flower.
βέλος,	missile.
ἔπος,	word.
ἔτος,	year.
ἦθος,	character.
θέρος,	summer.
κάλλος,	beauty.
κέρδος,	gain.
κλέος,	glory.
λέχος,	bed.
μένος,	force, spirit.
μέρος,	part.
ὄρος,	mountain.
πάθος,	suffering.
πλῆθος,	throng.
σθένος,	strength.
σκεῦος,	implement, pl. gear.
τεῖχος,	city-wall.
τέλος,	end.

Like πειθώ.   All feminine.

Γοργώ,	Gorgon.
Ἰώ,	Io.
Λητώ,	Latona.

ADJECTIVES OF THREE TERMINATIONS.

Vowel Stems of Declensions II. and I.

Like σοφός, σοφή, σοφόν—

δῆλος,	evident.
ἕκαστος,	each (*quisque*).
ἐσθλός,	noble.
θνητός,	mortal.
ἱκανός,	sufficient.
καινός,	new.
κενός,	empty.
κοινός,	common.
κοῦφος,	light.
λίθινος,	of stone.
λοιπός,	remaining.
μόνος,	alone.
ὅλος,	whole.
ὀρθός,	straight.
πιστός,	trusty.
σεμνός,	revered, proud.
στενός,	narrow.
χαλεπός,	difficult.
χρηστός,	useful, good.

Like φίλιος, φιλίᾱ, φίλιον—

ἀθρόος (uncontr.),	crowded.
ἀμφότερος,	both.
ἄξιος,	worthy.
ἀριστερός,	on the left.
δεξιός,	on the right.
δίκαιος,	just.
ἑκάτερος,	each (*uterque*).
ἐλεύθερος,	free.
ἕτερος,	the other.
ἐχθρός,	hostile.

ἴδιος,	own.
ἰσχῡρός,	strong.
καθαρός,	pure.
μακρός,	long.
νέος,	new.
ὅμοιος,	like.
παλαιός,	ancient.
πικρός,	keen, bitter.
πολέμιος,	hostile.
πρότερος,	former.
φανερός,	open, manifest.

Like χρύσεος, χρυσέᾱ, χρύσεον—

χάλκεος,	of bronze.
λίνεος,	of flax.

Like ἀργύρεος, -ρέᾱ, -ρεον—

πορφῠ́ρεος,	dark-gleaming.
σιδήρεος,	of iron.

Like ἁπλόος, ἁπλόη, ἁπλόον—

διπλόος,	two-fold.

Soft Vowel Stems, Decl. III.

Like ἡδύς, ἡδεῖα, ἡδύ—

βαθύς,	deep.
βαρύς,	heavy.
βραχύς,	short.
γλυκύς,	sweet.
εὐρύς,	wide.
ἥμισυς,	half.
θρασύς,	bold.
ὀξύς,	sharp.
παχύς,	thick.
ταχύς,	swift.
τρᾱχύς,	rough.

ADJECTIVES OF TWO TERMINATIONS.

Vowel Stems of Declension II.

Like ἀθάνατος, ἀθάνατον—

ἄδικος,	unjust.
ἄπειρος,	untried.
ἄπιστος,	untrustworthy.
ἄπρακτος,	᾿nsuccessful.
ἄφθονος,	ungrudging.
βόρβαρος,	foreign.
βέβαιος,	firm.
ἔνδοξος,	held in repute.
ἔρημος,	desolate.
ἕτοιμος,	ready.
ῥάδιος,	easy.
ὑπήκοος,	subject.

Like εὔνους, εὔνουν—

ἀπόπλους,	sailing off.
δύσνους,	disaffected.
κακόνους,	malicious.
πρόπλους,	sailing before.
σύμπλους,	sailing with.

Like ἵλεως, ἵλεων—

ἀξιόχρεως,	trustworthy.
ἔκπλεως,	full.

Consonant Stems, Decl. III.

Like εὔφρων, εὔφρον—

ἐπιστήμων,	skilled in.
ἄρρην (εν),	male.
εὐδαίμων,	happy.
εὐσχήμων,	graceful.
ὁμογνώμων,	like-minded.
πέπων,	ripe.
συγγνώμων,	indulgent.
σώφρων,	prudent.
τλήμων,	wretched.

Like εὐγενής, εὐγενές.

ἀκρᾱτής,	incontinent.
ἀκρῑβής,	accurate.
ἀληθής,	true.

ἀναιδής,	shameless.	εὐσεβής.	reverent.
ἀσθενής,	feeble.	εὐτὔχής,	fortunate.
ἀσφαλής,	safe.	πλήρης,	full.
δυσμενής,	hostile.	σαφής,	clear.
ἐγκρᾰτής,	self-controlled.	συγγενής,	akin.
ἐμφανής,	manifest.	ψευδής,	false.

Regular Verbs.*

Imperfects, A. and M.—

αἰτιάομαι,	accuse.
ἀγνοέω,	am ignorant.
αὐλίζομαι,	camp out.
δι-άγω,	lead across.
δια-τελέω,	bring to an end.
εἴργω,	keep off.
ἐκ-βαίνω,	go out.
ἐν-οικέω,	inhabit.
ἐπ-αινέω,	praise.
ἐρωτάω,	ask (question).
ἡγέομαι,	lead.
οἴομαι,	think.
οἴχομαι,	am gone.
ὁμολογέω,	confess.
περι-αιρέω,	take away all round.
ῥέω,	flow.
συγ-καλέω,	call together.
ὑπ-οπτεύω,	suspect.
ὠθέω,	push.

Futures, A. and M.—

ἀγαπάω,	love.
ἀπ-αντάομαι,	go to meet.
ἀπο-στρέφω,	turn away.
ἄρχω,	rule.
βλάπτω,	hurt.

βουλεύομαι,	deliberate.
δέχομαι,	receive.
δια-τρίβω,	waste, consume.
ἐλ-λείπω,	fail.
ἐπι-βοηθέω,	reinforce.
ἐπι-τρέπω,	allow.
ἐργάζομαι,	work.
κατ-ανύτω,	accomplish.
κλέπτω,	steal.
λέγω,	say.
ὀρθόω,	set straight.
σπεύδω,	hasten.
τάσσω,	arrange.
φράζω,	tell.

τρέφω (26),	nourish.
θεάομαι (132 *Obs.*),	view.
περάω (132 *Obs.*),	pass through.

Futures, A. and M. Liquid, Nasal, and Attic.

ἀγωνίζομαι,	struggle.
ἀγγέλλω,	announce.
ἀμύνομαι,	requite.
ἀφανίζω,	conceal.
δια-βιβάζω,	send across.

* The Verbs in these lists are chosen with the view of giving the beginner practice in the Rules for the change of consonants, and for Augment and Reduplication. Present-stems in σσ may be taken as belonging to the Guttural class, those in ζ to the Dental, and those in ππ to the Labial. In the case of exceptions the character of the Verb-stem is given in brackets.

ἐθίζω,	accustom.
ἐκ-πορίζω,	provide, furnish.
ἐπ-αγγέλλομαι,	promise.
καθαίρω,	purify.
κερδαίνω,	get gain.
μένω,	remain.
μετα-βάλλω,	change.
νομίζω,	think.
οἰκίζομαι,	colonise.
ὀργίζομαι,	am angry.
σημαίνω,	shew (by sign).
τεκμαίρομαι,	infer, conclude.
ὑπερ-άλλομαι,	leap over.
φαίνομαι,	appear.
φθείρω,	destroy.
χαρίζομαι,	gratify.

Weak Aorists, A. and M.

ἀκολουθέω,	follow.
ἀνα-βλέπω,	look up.
ἀνα-βοάω,	raise a shout.
ἅπτομαι,	grasp.
ἁρμόζω,	fit.
βρέχω,	wet.
δι-ορύσσω,	dig through.
ἐγ-γράφω,	inscribe.
ἐκ-λάμπω,	shine forth.
ἐν-νοέω,	reflect.
ἐπ-εύχομαι,	pray to.
ἐπι-διώκω,	pursue after.
ἡβάω,	am in prime of life.
κατα-δακρύω,	weep.
κατ-ηγορέω,	accuse.
κουφίζω,	lighten.
περι-βλέπω,	look around.
περι-πτύσσω,	enfold.
πορίζω,	furnish.
προσ-αιτέω,	ask in addition.
σείω,	shake, move.
στενάζω(χ),	groan.
συγ-καθ-είργω,	shut up with.
συν-άπτω,	fit-together.
συ-στρατεύομαι,	join in expedition.
τελευτάω,	finish.
ὑπάρχω,	begin.
ὑπ-οπτεύω,	suspect.
ὑπο-πτήσσω,	cower.
ψεύδομαι,	lie, speak falsely.

θηράω (132 *Obs.*)	hunt.
ἰάομαι (132 *Obs.*)	heal.
κατα-θεάομαι (132 *Obs.*),	view below.

Weak Aorists, A. and M.
Liquid and Nasal.

αἴρω,	ἀρ,	raise.
ἀπο-στέλλω,	στελ,	send away.
ἀπο-φαίνομαι,	φαν,	show forth.
δια-τείνομαι,	τεν,	stretch (intr.)
δια-φθείρω,	φθερ,	destroy.
ἐγ-κλίνω,	κλιν,	incline (trans.)
εἰσ-άλλομαι,	ἀλ,	leap into.
ἐκ-δέρω,	δερ,	flay.
ἐν-τέλλομαι,	τελ,	enjoin.
ἐπι-μαρτύρομαι,	μαρτυρ,	testify.
εὐφραίνω,	εὔφραν,	gladden.
καθαίρω,	καθαρ,	purify.
κατα-κτείνω,	κτεν,	slay.
μένω,	μεν,	remain.
παρ-οξύνω,	ὀξυν,	urge, provoke.
σημαίνω,	σημαν,	show (by sign).
σφάλλω,	σφαλ,	make to fall.
ὑγιαίνω,	ὑγιαν,	am healthy.
χαλεπαίνω,	χαλεπαν,	am angry.

Perfects Act. Strong and Weak.

[Strong Perfects must be formed from Guttural and Labial Stems, and Weak Perfects from the rest.]

ἀνα-κύπτω (asp.),		pop up.
ἀνα-φαίνω,	φαν,	display.
ἀπορέω,		am at a loss.
ἀπο-στερέω,		deprive.
ἀπο-χωρέω,		retreat.
ἁρπάζω,		snatch.
ἀσκέω,		exercise.
γαμέω,		marry (a wife).
δια-σώζω,		preserve.
ἐκ-κόπτω (asp.),		cut out.
ζηλόω,		vie with, emulate.
θάπτω,	ταφ,	bury.
θαυμάζω,		wonder at.
κατα-νοέω,		understand.
κατα-πράσσω,		perform.
κομίζω,		convey.
παρα-χωρέω,		go aside.
πονέω,		toil.
προσ-κομίζω,		convey to.

σπευδάζω,　　am zealous.
συγ-γράφω,　　compose.
φροντίζω,　　consider.

Perfects and Pluperfects, M. and P.

ἀγγέλλω,　　announce.
αἱματόω,　　stain with blood.
ἀνα-παύομαι,　　cease.
ἀνα-πτύσσω,　　unfold.
ἀνα-σκευάζω,　　pack up baggage.
ἀνα-τειχίζω,　　rebuild (walls).
ἀπο-κηρύσσω,　　forbid by herald.
ἀπο-κόπτω,　　cut off.
ἀπο-σχίζω,　　split off.
ἀριστοποιέομαι,　　breakfast.
ἁρπάζω,　　seize.
ἀφ-αιρέω,　　carry off, rob.
βουλεύομαι,　　take counsel.
δια-θρύπτω,　　break asunder.
δι-αιρέω,　　divide.
δια-φθείρω,　φθαρ, destroy.
ἐγ-καλύπτω,　　cover.
ἐκ-καθαίρω,　　cleanse out.
ἐκ-λέγω,　　choose out.
ἐκ-πλήσσω,　　scare.
ἡσσάομαι,　　am worsted.
θύω,　　sacrifice.
κατα-στρέφω,　στραφ, overthrow.
κατα-τρίβω,　　wear down.
κατα-ψηφίζω,　　condemn by vote.
οἰκοδομέω,　　build (house).
ὁπλίζω,　　arm.
ὁρμάομαι,　　start.

παρα-σκευάζω,　　prepare.
σφάλλομαι,　　stumble, fail.
σώζω,　　save.
φοβέομαι,　　fear.
φράσσω,　　fence.
φυλάσσω,　　guard.
χωρίζω,　　separate.
ψεύδω,　　cheat, deceive.
ψιλόω,　　strip.

Weak Aorists, Pass.

ἀθροίζω,　　collect.
αἰτιάομαι,　　am accused.
αἰσχύνομαι,　　am ashamed.
ἀδικέω,　　wrong.
ἀν-άγω,　　lead up.
ἀναγκάζω,　　compel.
ἀν-αρπάζω,　　snatch up.
ἀξιόω,　　deem worthy.
αὐλίζομαι,　　camp out.
βιάζω,　　constrain, overpower.
βρέχω,　　wet.
δια-λέγομαι,　　converse.
εἰκάζω,　　conjecture.
ἐλέγχω,　　convince.
ἐξ-απατάω,　　deceive thoroughly
ἐξ-αίρω, ἀρ,　　raise.
ζημιόω,　　punish by **fine**.
ζωγρέω,　　take alive.
κηρύσσω,　　proclaim.
κοιμάομαι,　　go to sleep.
κολάζω,　　punish.
μετα-πέμπω,　　send after.
προσ-τάσσω,　　order, enjoin.

END OF ACCIDENCE

SYNTAX

PREFACE.

THE following outline of the chief Rules of Greek Syntax, which is intended as a sequel to the " Primer of Greek Accidence," lays no claim to originality of treatment. The Editor has freely consulted the usual authorities, especially the well-known "Greek Moods and Tenses," and the later "Elementary Greek Grammar," of Professor W. W. Goodwin, and has only aimed at stating Rules simply and concisely, and so grouping them as to indicate general principles and prepare the beginner for the use of a fuller treatise. He is largely indebted in the first part of the Syntax to material kindly placed at his disposal by Mr. Evelyn Abbott, which, however, has for teaching purposes been thrown into a shape for which the Editor alone is responsible. His best thanks are due to many friends who have kindly read the proofs and aided him with valuable criticism and advice.

GREEK SYNTAX.

PART I.

THE PARTS OF SPEECH.

Agreement.

1. The general rules for Agreement are the same in Greek as in Latin, but the following points must be noticed :—

2. A neuter plural Subject is usually followed by a singular Verb :

> θαυμαστὰ ταῦτα φαίνεται.
> *These things appear wonderful.*

Obs. Neuter Plurals which signify living things, as τὰ ἀνδρά-ποδα, *the slaves,* τὰ τέκνα, *the children,* often take a plural verb.

3. The Accusative of a Relative is often attracted into the Case of its Antecedent, when that is a Genitive or Dative :

> χρῶμαι βιβλίοις οἷς ἔχω (for ἃ ἔχω).
> *I use the books which I have.*

> ψεῦδος οὐδὲν ὧν λέγω (for τούτων ἅ).
> *Nought of what I say is false.*

The Cases.

4. The Nominative is the case of the Subject of the Finite Verb.

Obs. For the use of the Nominative as Subject of an Infinitive, see **157** (*a*).

5. The Vocative is the case of the person addressed, as ὦ παῖ, *O boy ;* but the Nominative is often used.

The Accusative Case.

6. The Accusative Case implies—I. Motion to; II. Motion along or Extension over.

I. THE ACCUSATIVE OF MOTION TO.

7. Transitive Verbs take an Accusative of the Nearer Object :

> ἐπάταξε τὴν θύραν.
> *He tapped the door.*

8. Some Transitive Verbs, such as *ask, teach, remind, put on,* can take two Accusatives, one of the Person, the other of the Thing :

> Θηβαίους χρήματα ᾔτησαν.
> *They asked the Thebans for money.*
> οἱ παῖδες τὴν μουσικὴν διδάσκονται.
> *The boys are taught music.*

9. An Accusative of the Complement in agreement with the Object is added to complete the sense of Factitive Verbs, that is, Verbs of *making, calling, thinking,* and the like :

> Ὁ Κῦρος τὸν Γωβρύαν ἀπέδειξε στρατηγόν.
> *Cyrus appointed Gobryas general.*

II. THE ACCUSATIVE OF EXTENT.

10. Extent of Space is put in the Accusative in answering the question " How far ?" :

> ἀπέχει ἡ Πλάταια τῶν Θηβῶν σταδίους ἑβδομήκοντα.
> *Plataea is seventy stades from Thebes.*

11. Extent of Time is put in the Accusative in answering the question " How long ?" :

> τρεῖς ἡμέρας ἀπῆν.
> *He was away three days.*

12. Extent of Action or Predication is expressed by the Accusative of Respect, limiting a Verb or Adjective :

> ἀλγῶ τὸν πόδα.
> *I have a pain in my foot.*
> θαυμαστός ἐστι τὸ κάλλος.
> *He is marvellous in his beauty.*
> Λυδὸς ἦν τὸ γένος.
> *He was a Lydian by birth.*

Obs. Under this head may be classed what are called Adverbial Accusatives, as οὐδέν, *not at all;* τἆλλα, *as to the rest;* and also the so-called *Accusative Absolute* of certain Participles from Impersonal Verbs, as ἐξόν, δέον (106).

13. An Accusative of kindred meaning is used with Intransitive Verbs to define the action more closely :

> κίνδυνον κινδυνεύει.
> *He runs a risk.*
> νίκην καλλίστην νικήσομεν.
> *We shall win a glorious victory.*

The Genitive Case.

14. The Genitive Case represents the Noun (1) as a point of Aim, or (2) as a standard of Reference, or (3) as a point of Departure. Its various uses may therefore be classed as follows :—

I. THE GENITIVE OF AIM.

15. A Genitive of the Object aimed at follows Substantives and Adjectives (and some Verbs) that imply a direction of energy :

> τοξεύειν σκοποῦ.
> *To shoot at a mark.*
> τῶν ἡδέων ἐφίενται.
> *They aim at pleasure.*
> ἐπιθυμία χρημάτων.
> *Desire for wealth.*
> ἀκούει τοῦ Σωκράτους.
> *He listens to Socrates.*

II. THE GENITIVE OF RELATION.

16. The Genitive of Reference is found :

(*a.*) With many Substantives and Adjectives :

ἐπιστήμονες τοῦ ναυτικοῦ.
Skilled in (with respect to) *naval matters.*

πόνου μνήμων.
Mindful of toil.

(*b.*) After Verbs of *accusing, condemning, acquitting,* and the like :

διώκει αὐτοὺς φόνου.
He prosecutes them for murder.

(*c.*) After Verbs* that express *emotion* :

ζηλῶ σε τοῦ νοῦ, τῆς δὲ δειλίας στυγῶ.
I envy you for your prudence, but for your cowardice I detest you.

Obs. Hence a Genitive is found in exclamations :

φεῦ, τῆς ἀνοίας.   τοῦ σχήματος.
Alas ! for the folly.   *What a figure !*

17. The Genitive of the Possessor or Author :

τοῦτο τὸ πεδίον ἦν ποτε Χωρασμίων.
This plain belonged once to the Chorasmians.

στρατηλάτου χρηστοῦ τὰ κρείσσω λέγειν.
It is the part of a good general to talk of success.

18. The Genitive with Partitive words :

τρία μέρη τῆς ἡμέρας.
Three parts of the day.

ἄριστος Ἀχαιῶν.
Best of the Achaeans.

(*a.*) A similar Genitive expresses that within which a point is taken, as

ἐγένετο τῆς νυκτός.
It happened in the night.

πόλις τῆς Βοιωτίας.
A city in Boeotia.

---

* Such Verbs are ἄγαμαι, ἐπιθυμῶ, ζηλῶ, θαυμάζω, μέλει, στυγῶ, χαλεπαίνω.

19. The Genitive Absolute may stand for an Adverbial clause introduced by *when, if, because,* or *although* (**105**) :

> θεῶν διδόντων οὔτις ἐκφεύγει κακά.
> *If the gods send them, no one escapes miseries.*

20. The Genitive of Quality is limited in Greek to expressions of magnitude and value :

> ὁδὸς τριῶν ἡμερῶν.
> *A journey of three days.*
> οὐσία τεττάρων καὶ δέκα ταλάντων.
> *A property of fourteen talents.*

III. THE GENITIVE IMPLYING POINT OF
DEPARTURE (ABLATIVE).

21. The Genitive of Separation :

> τῆς οἰκίας ἐξῄει.
> *He went out of the house.*
> ἀποστερεῖ αὐτὸν τῶν χρημάτων.
> *He deprives him of his money.*
> κενὸς φρονήσεως.
> *Void of sense.*
> παύομαι τοῦ πόνου.
> *I cease from toil.*

22. The Genitive of Origin :

> πατρὸς λέγεται ὁ Κῦρος γενέσθαι Καμβύσου.
> *Cyrus is said to have been the son of Cambyses.*

23. The Genitive of Comparison follows Adjectives and Adverbs of the Comparative degree, and a few Verbs that imply a comparison :

> μείζων ἐκείνου.
> *Greater than he.*
> πολλῷ διήνεγκε τῶν ἄλλων.
> *He far surpassed the rest.*

24. The Agent is expressed by the Genitive with ὑπό, *from under* (**52**).

25. The Genitive of Material :

οἴνου πίμπλησι τὸν κρατῆρα.
He fills the bowl with wine.
λίθων μεγάλων ᾠκοδομήθη.
It was built of great stones.

26. The Genitive of Price :

μεγάλης ἐπρίατο τιμῆς.
He purchased it at a great price.
πολλοῦ ἄξιόν ἐστι.
It is worth much.

The Dative Case.

27. The Dative is the case of the thing touched. Its uses may be classified thus :— I. The Dative of Contact; II. The Dative of the Recipient.

I. THE DATIVE OF CONTACT.

28. A Dative of Actual Contact is found, but is generally expressed by a Preposition in Attic Greek :

ἕπεσθαι τῷ στρατῷ.
To follow the army.

29. The Dative defines a point in Time or Space :

εὑρεῖ πόντῳ.
On the broad sea.

τρίτῃ ἡμέρᾳ.
On the third day.

τρισὶν ἡμέραις ὕστερον.
Three days afterwards.

Obs. A Preposition is very commonly used to express a point in space, as ἐν τῇ πόλει, *in the city.*

30. The Dative of Resemblance and its opposite :

τούτῳ οὐδὲν ἔοικεν.
He is not at all like this man.

So after ισος, ὁ αὐτός, ὅμοιος.

31. The Dative, like the Latin Ablative, is used to denote Instrument, Cause, Manner, Measure :

Instrument, as—ξίφει αὐτὴν ἀπέκτεινεν.
               He slew her with a sword.

Cause,   as—ἀγνοίᾳ ἥμαρτεν.
               He erred through ignorance.

Manner. with Epithet,
          as—πολλῷ θορύβῳ ἐπεξῆλθον.
               They came on with a great tumult.

Measure,   as—πολλῷ μείζων.
               Much greater.

II. THE DATIVE OF THE RECIPIENT.

32. The Dative is the case of the Person or Thing for whose advantage or disadvantage anything exists or is done :

    ἔδωκε τήνδε τὴν δωρεὰν ἐμοί.
    He gave me this gift.

    ὁ Σόλων Ἀθηναίοις νόμους ἔθηκεν.
    Solon made laws for the Athenians.

    πολλαὶ ἡμῖν νῆές εἰσιν.
    We have many ships.

    οὐδὲν μέλει μοι.
    It is no matter to me.

Obs. 1. Hence a Dative of the Agent is often found with the Perfects and Pluperfects of Passive Verbs, and generally with Verbals in -τέος :

    τοῦτ᾽ ἐμοὶ πέπρακται, *This has been done by me.*

Obs. 2. Hence also the *Ethic Dative,* expressive of interest in a thing said or done :

    τί μοι λέγει; *What is he saying, I should like to know?*
    χαῖρέ μοι. *I wish you good day.*

Prepositions.

33. The Prepositions were originally cases, chiefly of Pronominal Stems.

In the first instance they were probably used only with the Verb as adverbs, and from the Verb were afterwards transferred to the cases of Nouns. Prepositions do not strictly govern cases; they merely serve to modify or to bring out more clearly the meaning of the cases with which they stand.

A. Prepositions with one Case only.

I. *Prepositions with the Accusative only—*ἀνά, εἰς, ὡς.

34. ἀνά, *up-along*, with Accusative of Extent.*

ἀνὰ ποταμόν, *up the river;* ἀνὰ πᾶσαν τὴν ἡμέραν, *all the day.*

IDIOMS.—ἀνὰ στόμα ἔχων, (*having in the mouth*) *speaking of;* ἀνα κράτος, *with all one's might.*

Obs. ἀνά in most of its uses is exactly the opposite of κατα; see 44.

35. εἰς (or ἐς), *into*, with Accusative of Motion-to (=Latin *in* with Acc.).

εἰς τὴν Αττικήν, *into Attica;* εἰς ἑσπέραν, *towards evening.*

Metaphor. εἰς καιρόν, *opportunely;* εἰς τετρακοσίους, *to the number of four hundred;* εἰς κέρδος, *with a view to gain.*

Obs. ὡς is used for εἰς in speaking of persons, as ὡς βασιλέα, *to the king.*

II. *Prepositions with the Genitive only—*ἀντί, ἀπο, ἐκ (or ἐξ), πρό.

36. ἀντί, *opposite to* (compare ἐν-αντί-ος).
Metaphor. *in place of, in exchange for.* ἀντ' ἐμοῦ, *in place of me.*

---

* ἀνά with Dative, *up-on*, is found in Poetry, ἀνὰ σκάπτῳ, *upon a sceptre.*

37. ἀπό, *from* (= Lat. *ab*), with Genitive of Separation.

ἀπ᾽ Ἀθηνῶν, *from Athens;* ἀπὸ δείπνου, *after supper;* ἀπὸ παίδων, *from childhood.*

Metaphor. οἱ ἀπὸ τῶν Ἀθηναίων Ἴωνες, *the Ionians descended from the Athenians;* αὐτόνομος ἀπὸ τῆς εἰρήνης, *independent in consequence of the peace;* ἀπο χρημάτων, *with money.*

IDIOMS.—αφ᾽ ἵππου μάχεσθαι, *to fight on horseback;* ἀπὸ τοῦ ἀδοκήτου, *unexpectedly;* ἀπὸ στόματος, *by rote.*

38. ἐκ (or ἐξ), (= Lat. *e, ex*), *out of*, with Genitive of Separation.

ἀπέδρα ἐκ Σαρδέων, *he ran away from (out of) Sardis;* ἐκ τούτων, *after this.*

IDIOMS.—ἐξ ἴσου, *equally;* ἐκ τῶν ἐνόντων, *as well as the circumstances admit;* ἐξ ἀπροσδοκήτου, *suddenly;* ἐξ ἀριστερᾶς, *on the left.*

39. πρό, *before* (= Lat. *pro*).

πρὸ θυρῶν, *before the door;* τὰ πρὸ τῶν Μηδικῶν, *affairs before the Persian war.*

Metaphor. πρὸ τῶνδε φωνεῖν, *to speak on behalf of these.*

40. The following *improper* Prepositions are also used with the Genitive only :— ἄνευ, ἄτερ, *without;* ἄχρι, μέχρι, *until;* μεταξύ, *between;* ἕνεκα, *on account of;* πλήν, *except.*

III. *Prepositions with the Dative only—*ἐν, σύν.

41. ἐν, *within* (= Lat. *in* with Ablative).

ἐν πόλει, *in the city;* ἐν τούτῳ, *meanwhile;* ἐν τῷ παρόντι, *at present;* ἐν σπονδαῖς, *in a time of truce.*

Metaphor. ἐν ὑμῖν, *in your place,* or *in your hands.*

IDIOMS.—ἐν χρῷ, *near* or *close;* ἐν Διονύσου, *in (the temple) of Dionysus.*

42. σύν, *together-with* (= Lat. *cum*).

σὺν πρέσβεσι, *in company with the ambassadors;* σὺν Θεῷ, *with (the aid of) God.*

Obs. σύν is rarely used of the instrument, and then only because it is regarded as an accompaniment.

B. Prepositions used with Two Cases.

διά, κατά, ὑπέρ.

An Accusative or Genitive is found with διά, κατά, ὑπέρ.

43. διά, *through* (originally *between*, akin to δύο).

With Accusative—usually *on account of* (= Lat. *propter*). διὰ τοῦτον οὐκ ἀπέβη, *owing to this person he did not go away.*

With Genitive—usually *through* (= Lat. *per*). διὰ χιόνος ἐπορεύοντο, *they were marching through snow.*

Metaphor. δι' ἀγγέλων, *by means of messengers.*

Idioms.—δι' ὀλίγου, *after a short interval;* διὰ χειρῶν ἔχειν, *to hold in one's hands;* διὰ δίκης ἰέναι, *to go to law with any one.*

44. κατά, *down.*

With Accusative—of Extent, *down-along* (the opposite of ἀνά). κατὰ τὸν ποταμόν, *down the river;* κατὰ γῆν, *by land;* κατὰ θάλατταν, *by sea.*

Metaphor. κατὰ τὸν νόμον, *according to the law.*

With Genitive—(a.) of Separation, *down-from.* ἄλλεσθαι κατὰ τῆς πέτρας, *to spring down from the rock;* κατ' ἄκρας, *utterly,* lit. from top (to bottom).

(b.) of Aim, *down-upon.* μύρον κατὰ τῆς κεφαλῆς καταχεῖν, *to pour myrrh-oil upon the head.*

Metaphor. of denunciation, πολλὰ κατ' αὐτοῦ ἔλενεν, *he said a good deal against him.*

45. ὑπέρ, *over* (= Lat. *super*).

With Accusative—*to-beyond.* ὑπὲρ Αἴγυπτον ἰόντι, *to one going beyond Egypt;* ὑπὲρ δύναμιν, *beyond one's power.*

With Genitive—*above* (and away from). ἔστι δὲ λιμήν, καὶ πόλις ὑπὲρ αὐτοῦ, *there is a harbour, and above it a city.*

Metaphor. *on behalf of.* ὑπὲρ τούτων λέγειν, *to speak on behalf of these men.*

C. Prepositions used with Three Cases.

ἀμφί, ἐπί, μετά, παρά, περί, πρός, ὑπό.

46. ἀμφί, *about, on both sides* (akin to ἄμφω).

With Accusative—*about.* ἀμφὶ Δωδώνην, *near Dodona;* ἀμφὶ Πλειάδων δύσιν, *about the setting of the Pleiades;* ἀμφὶ δέκα ἔτη, *about ten years.*

Idioms.—οἱ ἀμφὶ Πλάτωνα, *the followers   Plato;* ἔχειν ἀμφί τι, *to be engaged in a thing.*

With Genitive—(poetical) *about.* ἀμφὶ πόλεως, *round the city;* ἀμφὶ γυναικὸς μάχεσθαι, *to fight about a woman.*

With Dative—(poetical) *at or near* (of Place); also to express the Cause, ἀμφὶ φόβῳ, *from fear.*

47. ἐπί, *upon.*

With Accusative—(*a.*) of Motion *on to.* ἀναβαίνειν ἐφ' ἵππον, *to mount a horse;* ἐπὶ τοὺς πολεμίους, *against the enemy.*

(*b.*) of Extent *over.* ἐπὶ πόντον, *over the sea;* ἐπὶ δέκα ἔτη, *during ten years.*

Idiom.—ἐπὶ τὸ πολύ, *for the most part.*

With Genitive—(*a.*) of Point (18. *a*). ἐπὶ γῆς, *on land;* ἐφ' ἑσπέρας, *at evening;* ἐπὶ Κέκροπος, *in the time of Cecrops;* ἐπὶ πολλῶν προτέρων ἀγώνων, *in many former trials;* ἐπὶ μειζόνων, *in greater matters;* ἐφ' ἵππου, *on horseback.*
(*b.*) of Aim. ἐπ' οἴκου, *homewards.*

Idioms.—ἐπὶ τεττάρων, *four deep* (military); ἐφ' ἑαυτοῦ, *by oneself.*

With Dative—of Contact. ἐπὶ τῇ θαλάττῃ, *on the sea;* χαίρειν ἐπ' αἰσχραῖς ἡδόναις, *to delight in base pleasures;* ἐπὶ τῷ ἐξιέναι, *on condition of going out.*

Idiom.—ἐφ' ᾧ, or ἐφ' ᾧ τε, *on condition that.*   (190.)

48. μετά (originally *amid*).

With Accusative—(*a.*) of Motion *to the midst,* generally *after.* μετὰ ταῦτα, *after this;* μετὰ χαλκόν, *in quest of (to fetch) bronze.*

(*b.*) of Extension *over the midst.* μεθ' ἡμέραν, *in the day.*

With Genitive—generally *with.* μετὰ τούτων, *along with these.*

With Dative—*among*, only found in the older poetry. μετὰ Κυκλώπεσσιν ἄνασσεν, *he reigned among the Cyclops.*

49. παρά, *beside.*

With Accusative—(*a.*) of Motion *to the side of.* ἀφίκοντο παρὰ Κροῖσον, *they came to Croesus' court.*

(*b.*) of Extension *alongside of.* παρὰ τὸν ποταμόν, *along the river;* παρὰ ὅλον τὸν βίον, *during my whole life.*

Metaphor. παρὰ ταῦτα, *besides this.*

Idioms.—παρὰ τὸ ἀδίκημα, *at the time of the offence;* παρὰ νύκτα ἐγένετο αὐτῷ ἑλεῖν τὴν πόλιν, *he was within a night (aside of a night) of taking the city;* παρὰ τὴν ἀσέλγειαν ἐχθαίρεται, *he is hated because of (along of) his outrageous behaviour;* παρὰ νόμον, *contrary to (beside) the law.*

With Genitive—of Departure *from the side of.* αὐτομολεῖν παρὰ βασιλέως, *to desert from the king;* αἱ παρὰ σοῦ ἐλπίδες, *the hopes that come from thee;* παρ' ἄλλου δέχεσθαι, *to receive from another.*

With Dative—*at the side of.* ἦν παρὰ τῷ βασιλεῖ, *he was by the king;* παρὰ τούτῳ κεῖται, *it lies with him.*

50. περί, *around, on all sides.*

With Accusative—of Motion or Extension *around* (very like ἀμφί). ἰέναι περὶ τὴν πόλιν, *to go round the city;* ᾤκουν οἱ Φοίνικες περὶ πᾶσαν τὴν Σικελίαν, *the Phoenicians used to live all over (about) Sicily.*

Metaphor. (of Number and Time). νῆες περὶ ἑβδομήκοντα, *about seventy ships;* περὶ πλήθουσαν ἀγοράν, *about the time when the market is fullest.*

Idiom.—οἱ περὶ Ἀρχίαν πολέμαρχοι, *Archias and his colleagues.*

With Genitive—*concerning* (= Lat. *de*). περὶ τοῦ ἀγαθοῦ διαλέγεσθαι, *to discourse about the good;* πυθέσθαι περὶ τοῦ ἀνθρώπου, *to inquire about the man.*

Idioms.—περὶ πολλοῦ (ὀλίγου, οὐδενὸς) ποιεῖσθαι, *to reckon of great (small, no) importance.*

With Dative—of Contact, *about* (rare). οἱ Θρᾷκες χίτωνας φοροῦσιν καὶ περὶ τοῖς μηροῖς, *the Thracians wear tunics even round their thighs.* Generally with verbs expressing *care*: δεῖσαι περὶ τῷ χωρίῳ, *to be alarmed about the place.*

51. πρός (akin to πρό), *fronting.*

With Accusative—of Motion *to the face of.* πρὸς τὴν πόλιν, *towards the city ;* ἰέναι πρὸς τὸ ἔργον, *to advance to the work.*

Metaphor. πρὸς χάριν, *with a view to pleasing ;* πρὸς τὸ συμφέρον, *with a view to advantage*

Idioms.—πρὸς βίαν, *forcibly ;* πρὸς ὀργήν, *angrily ;* πρὸς ὕβριν, *insultingly ;* πρὸς ταῦτα, *therefore (in view of, looking to).*

With Genitive—(*a.*) of Point of Departure. ἀκούειν πρός τινος, *to hear from some one.* Sometimes even of the Agent: πρὸς ἁπάντων θεραπεύεσθαι, *to be courted by all.*

(*b.*) of Aim, *facing towards.* τὸ πρὸς ἑσπέρας τεῖχος, *the wall facing the west.*

Metaphor. πρὸς πατρός, *on the father's side ;* πρὸς τῶν πολεμίων ἦν τὸ χωρίον, *the ground was in favour of the enemy ;* πρὸς σώφρονός ἐστι, *it belongs to a prudent man.* So in adjuration: πρὸς θεῶν, *by (in presence of) the gods, in heaven's name.*

With Dative—of Contact, *at the face of.* πρὸς τῇ θύρᾳ, *at the door.*

Metaphor. *in addition to.* πρὸς τούτοις, *in addition to this.*

52. ὑπό, *under* (= Lat. *sub*).

With Accusative—of Motion *to, under.* ἰέναι ὑπὸ τὴν γῆν, *to go under the earth ;* ὑπὸ τὸ τεῖχος, *under the wall ;* ὑπὸ νύκτα (*sub noctem*), *towards night ;* ὑπὸ τὸν σεισμόν, *immediately after the earthquake.*

With Genitive— of Departure, *from under ;* ὑπὸ πτερῶν σπάσας, *dragging from under the wings.* Often with a notion of dependence : ὑπὸ κήρυκος, *at the bidding of a herald ;* ὑπὸ σάλπιγγος, *at the sound of a trumpet.*

So of the Agent: ὑπὸ τούτου ἐπράχθη, *it was done by this man ;* πάσχειν κακὰ ὑπό τινος, *to suffer evil at a man's hands.* Also of the Cause : ὑπὸ δειλίας, *through cowardice.*

With Dative—of Contact. ὑπ' αὐτῇ τῇ πόλει, *close to (under) the city itself,* ὑπὸ νόμοις εἶναι, *to be under law.*

The Article.

53. The Article, ὁ, ἡ, τό, was originally a Personal Pronoun (*he, she, it*), and traces of this old usage are found in the phrases ὁ μέν, *the one;* ὁ δέ, *the other.* ὁ δέ is also used at the beginning of a sentence with reference to a person previously mentioned, and marks a change in the subject of the Verb:

ἐκέλευεν αὐτὸν παρελθεῖν, ὁ δὲ παρῆλθεν ταχέως.
He bade him come forward, and he came forward at once.

Obs. So τὰ καὶ τά, *such and such things;* πρὸ τοῦ, *aforetime.*

54. The Article is used to point out a definite person or thing, generally known or previously spoken of :

ὁ κριτής, *the judge* (of whom we were speaking); ὁ παρὼν χρόνος, *the present time;* οἱ ἔνδον, *those within;* τὸ ἐρᾶν, *love.*

So with Proper names : ὁ Σωκράτης, *Socrates* (whom all men know); ὁ Κῦρος, *Cyrus* (previously mentioned).

Obs. 1. The Article often stands for an unemphatic Possessive Pronoun, as παρῆλθε σὺν τοῖς φίλοις, *he came forward with his friends.*

Obs. 2. The Article also precedes the Possessive Pronouns, as ὁ σὸς δοῦλος, *your slave;* ἡ ἐμὴ γυνή, *my wife.*

55. The Article is also used with words denoting a class, or an individual who represents a class :

οἱ πλούσιοι, *rich men;* οἱ κριταί, *judges;* ὁ βοῦς, *the ox* (that is, oxen generally).

So with Participles, the Article specifies some individual or group, as ὁ πέμπων, *he who sends;* οἱ δυνάμενοι, *those who are able.*

56. The Article often distinguishes the Subject of a sentence from the Complement :

βασιλεὺς ἐγένετο ὁ πτωχός.   *The beggar became a king.*

57. (*a.*) Hence, if the Article is used at all, it stands before all qualifying words :

ἡ καλὴ γυνή
ἡ γυνὴ ἡ καλή   } = *the beautiful woman.*

So ὁ νῦν χρόνος, *the present time;* ἡ ἐν Μαραθῶνι μάχη, *the battle of Marathon;* ἡ τῶν Περσῶν ἀρχή, *the Persian kingdom.*

Obs. ὁ Εὐφράτης ποταμός, *the river Euphrates;* ἡ Μένδη πόλις, *the city of Mende.*

58. (*b.*) Hence also, if the Substantive have the Article, the Adjective that stands without one must be a Predicate :

$$\left.\begin{array}{l} ἡ \ γυνὴ \ καλή \\ καλὴ \ ἡ \ γυνή \end{array}\right\} = the \ woman \ (is) \ beautiful.$$

Obs. Note in the following the use of the Article and the predicative force of the Adjective :

ὁ κύων μακρὰν ἔχει τὴν οὐράν.
The dog has a long tail (a tail that is long).

πιστὸν φιλῶ τὸν κύνα. *Faithful is the dog that I love.*

59. The following Pronouns and Adjectives take the position of a Predicate when the Article is used :

The Demonstratives—οὗτος, ὅδε, ἐκεῖνος.
The Pronominals—ἑκάτερος, ἀμφότερος, ἄμφω.
The Adjectives—ἄκρος, πᾶς, ἔσχατος, μέσος, ἥμισυς, ὅλος.

οὗτος ὁ ἀνήρ,	*this man.*
ἥδε ἡ πόλις,	*this city.*
ἑκάτερον τὸ κέρας,	*each wing* (of an army).
ἀμφότερα τὰ στρατόπεδα,	*both the camps.*
ἐν ἄκρῳ τῷ δένδρῳ,	*on the top of the tree.*
πάντες οἱ στρατηγοί,	*all the generals.*
ἐν ἐσχάτῃ τῇ νήσῳ,	*at the end of the island.*
ἐν μέσῃ τῇ ὕλῃ,	*in the midst of the wood.*

In each case the Pronoun or Adjective might stand last, but would then receive more emphasis.

Obs. The meaning of an Adjective sometimes varies with its position :—

αὐτὸς ὁ βασιλεύς.	ὁ αὐτὸς βασιλεύς.
the king himself.	*the same king.*
μόνος ὁ παῖς ἦλθε.	ὁ μόνος παῖς ἦλθε.
the boy alone came.	*the only son came.*
διὰ μέσης τῆς πόλεως.	ἡ μέση πόλις.
through the midst of the city.	*the middle city* (e.g. of three).

Pronouns.

60. PERSONAL.—The nominative of the Personal Pronoun is not expressed except for the sake of emphasis or distinction :

σὺ γράφεις τάδ᾽ εἶναι στρατιωτικά ; μὰ Δί᾽, οὐκ ἔγωγε.

*Do you propose that this should be a fund for the army?
By Zeus ! not I.*

61. POSSESSIVE.—I. Where emphasis is not required :

(*a.*) The Article only is used if the meaning is quite clear :

ἔπεμψα τὴν θυγατέρα, *I sent my daughter.*

(*b.*) If the meaning is not quite clear, or a slight opposition is intended, the Genitive of the Personal Pronoun is used :

ἐγὼ καὶ ὁ πατήρ μου, *I and my father.*

POSSESSIVE.—II. Where emphasis is required, either the Possessive or the Genitive of the Reflexive is used in the 1st and 2d Persons : in the 3d Person the Genitive of a Demonstrative or of the Reflexive, according to the sense :

ὁ ἐμὸς φίλος, ὁ σὸς φίλος, ὁ ἐκείνου φίλος, etc., or τὸν ἐμαυτοῦ
φίλον, τὸν σαυτοῦ, τὸν ἑαυτοῦ φίλον.

62. DEFINITIVE.—The regular Definitive is αὐτός, *self,* placed as a Predicate ; preceded by the Article it means *same.*

αὐτὸς ὁ βασιλεύς ⎱
ὁ βασιλεὺς αὐτός ⎰ *the king himself,* or *in person.*

ὁ αὐτὸς βασιλεύς ⎱
βασιλεύς ὁ αὐτός ⎰ *the same king.*

Obs. The Nom. αὐτός, like the Latin *ipse,* is used in a dependent clause to repeat the subject of the principal sentence, and in Indirect statement ; this is the case even with the infinitive, as οὐκ ἔφη αὐτὸς στρατηγεῖν (**157** *a*).

63. REFLEXIVE.—The emphatic Reflexive of the 3d Person is ἑαυτόν, plural σφᾶς αὐτούς, but the cases οἷ σφῶν, σφισί, from ἕ, are not uncommonly used as Reflexives :

προηγόρευε ὅτι ʼΑρχίδαμός οἱ ξένος εἴη.
He (Pericles) announced that Archidamus was his friend.

δείσας μὴ σφῶν κυκλωθείη τὸ εὐώνυμον.
Being afraid that their left would be turned.

Obs. In turning direct speech into indirect in the third person, the speaker is either omitted or represented by αὐτός or ἑαυτόν, the person addressed becomes αὐτόν, and the person spoken of is ἐκεῖνον.

64. DEMONSTRATIVE.—οὗτος and τοιοῦτος generally refer to something that has gone before; ὅδε and τοιόσδε to something that is to follow :

ταῦτʼ ἀκούσας ἔλεξε τάδε.
On hearing this he spoke as follows.

Obs. The oblique cases of αὐτός, when standing as Substantives, are merely Personal, *him, her, it,* etc.

65. INTERROGATIVE.—There are two forms of the Interrogative Pronoun (*Accidence* **99**) :

(1.) Direct, τίς ; *who ?* πότερος ; *which of two ?*

as τίς τοῦτʼ ἐποίησε ;
Who made this?

(2.) Indirect, ὅστις, *who* ; ὁπότερος, *which of two,*

as ἤρετο ὅστις τοῦτʼ ποιῆσαι (or ἐποίησε).
He asked who made this.

But the Direct form is often used in Indirect speech.

The Tenses.

66. The Tenses are employed to denote distinctions of Time. Time can be divided into Present, Past, and Future; and an action in Present, Past, or Future Time can be regarded as—(*a.*) Momentary; (*b.*) Continuous; (*c.*) Complete.

67. Hence we get nine possible Tenses :—

	(*a.*) **Momentary.**	(*b.*) **Continuous.**	(*c.*) **Complete.**
I. PRESENT,	*I write* scribo γράφω	*I am writing* scribo γράφω	*I have (now) written* scripsi γέγραφα
II. PAST,	*I wrote* scripsi ἔγραψα	*I was writing* scribebam ἔγραφον	*I had written* scripseram ἐγεγράφη
III. FUTURE,	*I shall write* scribam γράψω	*I shall be writing* none none	*I shall have written* scripsero none in Act.

68. The scheme of Greek Tenses may be supplemented as follows :—

The Momentary Present (I. *a*) is sometimes expressed in Greek by an Aorist, as ἐδεξάμην τὸ ῥηθέν, *I welcome your words (what is said)*; ἐπήνεσ' ἔργον, *I commend your deed.*

The Continuous Future (III. *b*) is fully expressed by a paraphrase of the Present Participle with ἔσομαι, as ποιῶν ἔσει, *you will be doing;* but the simple Future is often used.

The Complete Future (III. *c*) is expressed by the Future Perfect, or paraphrased by a Participle with ἔσομαι, as πεποιηκὼς ἔσομαι (*I-shall-be having-done*), *I shall have done.*

Notes on the Tenses.

69. PRESENT AND IMPERFECT.—These Tenses denote continued or customary action in Present and Past Time respectively, without reference to the beginning or end. Hence

Pres. Indic., γράφω, *I am writing*, or *I write* (habitually).
Imperfect, ἔγραφον, *I was writing*, or *I used to write*.

70. In other Moods than the Indicative the idea of Present time disappears, and the Present simply denotes continued action, except in Indirect Speech.

Obs. 1. The continued action of the Present and Imperfect is often extended by the addition of an Adverb or phrase of duration into time which is past, as πάλαι σοὶ ταῦτα λέγω, *I am telling you this (and have been telling you) a long time;* τρία ἔτη φεύγει, *he has been three years in exile.*

Obs. 2. The Present and Imperfect are sometimes limited to attempted action, as δίδωμι (I try to give), *I offer;* ἔπειθον (I tried to persuade), *I urged;* ἃ ἐπράσσετο οὐκ ἐγένετο, *what was attempted did not take place.*

Obs. 3. In a few Verbs the Present has a Perfect meaning, that is, expresses completion, as ἥκω, *I am come;* οἴχομαι, *I am gone;* φεύγω, *I am in banishment;* ἁλίσκομαι, *I am captured.* The Imperfect of these Verbs has a Pluperfect meaning.

Obs. 4. The *Historic Present* is often used for the Aorist to narrate facts with vividness.

71. PERFECT AND PLUPERFECT.—The Perfect represents an action as complete at the present time; the Pluperfect as finished at some point in past time. This idea of completion accompanies the Perfect, so far as possible, in all the Moods:

ταῦτα εἰρήσθω.
Let this be said (and no more).

Obs. 1. The Perfect Conjunctive is often expressed in the Active Voice, as it is always in the Passive, by the Participle with the Conjunctive of εἰμί. Thus πεποιηκὼς ὦ, εἴην as λελυμένος ὦ, εἴην.

Obs. 2. Some Perfects are best translated by simple Presents :—

οἶδα (I have seen), *I know.*
δέδοικα (fear has come upon me), *I fear.*
κέκτημαι (I have gained), *I possess.*

72. AORIST.—The Aorist Indicative expresses a single (momentary) action in past time, as ἔπραξα, *I did.* In the other Moods it contains no idea of past time, except in Indirect Speech, and merely expresses a single momentary act. Thus

λαβέ, *take.*	λάμβανε, *keep taking.*
ἐὰν κλέψῃς, *if you steal (this).*	ἐὰν κλέπτῃς, *if you go on stealing.*
βούλεται πέμψαι, *he wishes to send.*	βούλεται πέμπειν, *he wishes to keep sending.*

But in Indirect Speech :—

ἔφη { πέμψαι. / πέμπειν. }　*He said* { *that he sent (or had sent).* / *that he was sending.* }

So with the Participles :—

ταῦτα λέγων ἀπῆλθεν, *while saying this he went away.*
ταῦτα εἰπὼν ἀπῆλθεν, *after saying this he went away.*

Obs. 1. The Augment is the true sign of past time, and unaugmented tenses cannot really express time *actually* past, though they may be used of time *relatively* past.

Obs. 2. The Aorist often expresses some moment, the first or the last, of the continued state expressed by the Present. Thus νοσῶ, *I am ill*; ἐνόσησα, *I fell ill* (*ingressive aorist*).

Similarly ἄρξαι, *to begin to rule*; πρᾶξαι, *to complete an action*; δακρῦσαι, *to burst into tears*; γελάσαι, *to burst into a laugh.*

Obs. 3. When the Verb is one which denotes a state or condition, its Aorist is used to refer to the condition merely as a fact, as ἐβασίλευε δέκα ἔτη, *he was king for ten years*; ἐβασίλευσε δέκα ἔτη, *he had a reign of ten years*; συνεστράτευον, *they joined in the campaign*; συνεστράτευσαν, *they were their allies.*

Obs. 4. The Aorist is also used in general statements, where there is no note of time (*gnomic aorist*) :

πολλὰ παρὰ γνώμην ἔπεσεν.
Many things happen contrary to experience.

73. FUTURE AND FUTURE PERFECT.—The Future gener-ally denotes a single (momentary) act,* while the Future Perfect expresses a state.   Thus

κληθήσεται.
He shall be called (name shall be given).

κεκλήσεται.
He shall be called (name shall be).

74. There is no Future in the Imperative and Primary Conjunctive Moods.   The second person of the Future Indicative is sometimes used with the force of an Impera-tive :

πάντως δὲ τοῦτο δράσεις.
And by all means do this.

75. The only use of the Historic Conjunctive of the Future is to represent in Indirect Speech the Future Indicative of the Direct :

εἶπεν ὅτι ἀποστήσοιντο αἱ πόλεις.
He said that the cities would revolt.
(Direct—ἀποστήσονται, *they will revolt.*)

Obs. A paraphrase of μέλλω with the Present or Future In-finitive is commonly used to express an *intention*, or an *immediate Future*, as τοῦτο μέλλει ποιήσειν, *he is about to do this.*

The Moods.

76. A Verb is said to be in a Mood when it shows by its form whether the action is regarded as existing in-dependently or as conceived (more or less distinctly) in

---

* In the Passive the Futures are formed directly from the Aorists, and in the Active and Middle the stems of Aorists and Futures are closely connected.

the mind. Strictly speaking, therefore, there are two Moods only, the Indicative and Conjunctive, for the Imperative is only an adaptation of the Indicative.

77. The INDICATIVE is the Mood for the simple statement of facts, and the IMPERATIVE is used only in direct commands.

78. The CONJUNCTIVE has two forms, (1.) the Near or Primary Conjunctive (sometimes called Subjunctive), which is used to express conceptions nearer and more distinct to the speaker's mind, as ἐὰν ἔλθῃ, *if he comes;* (2.) the Remote or Historic Conjunctive (sometimes called Optative), which expresses conceptions further removed and less clear and distinct, as εἰ ἔλθοι, *if he were to come.*

79. In the Compound Sentence the subordination of these two forms of Conjunctive to the Principal Verb is called *Sequence,* and is a Sequence of Mood rather than, as in Latin, a Sequence of Tense.

RULES FOR SEQUENCE.

80. I. Primary Tenses { Present / Future / Perfect } are followed by the Primary Conjunctive.

II. Historic Tenses { Imperf. / Aorist / Pluperf. } are followed by the Historic Conjunctive.

Primary, ἔρχεται ἵνα ἴδῃ, *he is coming that he may see.*
Historic, ἦλθεν ἵνα ἴδοι, *he came that he might see.*

81. Observe that it is the Mood, not the Tense, of the Dependent Clause which is affected by the Primary or Historic Time of the Principal Verb. The Tense might be Present or Aorist, according as the 'seeing' was a continued or a momentary (single) act.

82. In Indirect Speech, however, Primary Tenses are always followed by the Indicative if a Finite Verb is used at all.

λέγει ὅτι τοῦτο ἀληθὲς ἐστίν.
He says that this is true.
ἐρωτᾷ τί (or ὅ τι) ἔγραψαν.
He asks what they wrote.

83. The Greeks very often used the Primary Sequence after a Historic Verb, from a desire to put very clearly the point of view of the person whose thought or speech they represented. This is called *Vivid Sequence.* Thus we may write—

ἦλθεν ἵνα ἴδοι (or ἴδῃ), *he came that he might* (or *may*) *see.*
His thought was '*that I may see.*'
εἶπεν ὅτι γράφοιεν (or γράφουσι), *he said that they were* (or *are*) *writing.*
His words were '*they are writing.*'

84. The Verb Infinite contains

Infinitives (Substantives).
Participles
Verbal Adjectives } (Adjectives).

THE INFINITIVE.

85. The INFINITIVE, like the Prepositions, is a case of a Verbal Substantive, which was used as an Adverb and afterwards came to be considered as a part of the Verb. It has, in fact, almost all the functions of the Verb; it can govern a case, express time, have a subject, and be qualified by an Adverb. It cannot express Person, and hence is called the Unlimited Verb. Its various uses may be classified as—I. SUBSTANTIVAL; II. ADVERBIAL. [Negative always μή.]

I. *The Infinitive as a Substantive.*

86. The Infinitive in the Nominative Case is used as Subject with or without the Article ; as Complement, without the Article :

> τὸ γνῶναι ἐπιστήμην λαβεῖν ἐστίν.
> *Learning is acquiring knowledge.*
> ἀδύνατόν ἐστι τοῦτο ποιῆσαι.
> *Doing this is impossible.*

87. The Infinitive as an Accusative Case is used

(*a.*) With the Article as an ordinary Abstract Substantive :

> αὐτὸ τὸ ἀποθνήσκειν οὐδεὶς φοβεῖται.
> *Death itself no one fears.*
> διὰ τὸ ξένον εἶναι τὸν ἄνδρα.
> *On account of the man being a stranger.*

(*b.*) Prolatively, without the Article, to extend or limit the meaning of a Verb or Adjective :

δύναται ἀπελθεῖν.	δεινὸς λέγειν.
He can go away.	*Skilled in speaking.*
δυνατὸς ποιεῖν.	
Able to do.	

88. The Infinitive as a Genitive or Dative always has the Article :

> νέοις τὸ σιγᾶν κρεῖττόν ἐστι τοῦ λαλεῖν.
> *For the young silence is better than talking.*
> πρὸς τῷ μηδὲν λαβεῖν.
> *In addition to receiving nothing.*

II. *The Infinitive as an Adverb.*

89. The Infinitive, like the Latin Supine in -*u*, is used with Adjectives :

> αἰσχρὸν ὁρᾶν.
> *Disgraceful to see* (foedum visu).
> χαλεπὸν ποιεῖν.
> *Hard to do* (difficile factu).

90. The Infinitive, either with or without ὡς, is often inserted as a parenthesis in an adverbial relation to the whole sentence, as

ὡς εἰπεῖν, *so to speak;* ὡς συνελόντι εἰπεῖν, *in a word;* (ὡς) ἐμοὶ δοκεῖν, *in my opinion.*

Obs. The following adverbial expressions may be noticed :—
ἑκὼν εἶναι, *willingly at least* (always with a negative); τὸ νῦν εἶναι, *at present;* τὸ ἐπ᾽ ἐκείνοις εἶναι, *as far as depends on them;* as

ἑκὼν γὰρ εἶναι οὐδὲν ψεύσομαι.
Willingly at any rate I will tell no lie.

91. The Infinitive is used *explanatorily,* especially after Verbs of *choosing* and *assigning* :

τὴν ἄκραν φυλάττειν αὐτοῖς παρέδωκαν.
They gave up the citadel to them to guard.

92. In addition to the above uses, the Infinitive also stands with an Accusative for its subject in the Indirect Statement (157); after πρίν Temporal (174); after ὥστε Consecutive (170).

The Participle.

93. In addition to its use as a simple attribute, the PARTICIPLE (1) represents Dependent Clauses of several kinds, and (2) has some special idiomatic uses.

(I.) *Dependent Clauses represented by Participles.*

94. SUBSTANTIVAL.—Indirect statement after certain Verbs of Perception :

οἶδα { σε θνητὸν ὄντα.
{ θνητὸς ὤν.
I know { *that you are mortal.*
{ *that I am mortal.*

95. ADJECTIVAL.—The Participle with the Article corresponds to the English Relative clause with a Pronominal antecedent :

ὁ ταῦτα λέγων, *he who is saying* (or *was saying*) *this.*

Obs. The Negative is οὐ if the clause is Definite, μή if it is Indefinite (164) :

οἱ οὐ βουλόμενοι, *those* (particular persons) *who do not wish.*
οἱ μὴ βουλόμενοι, *whoever do not wish.*

96. ADVERBIAL.—[Negative always οὐ except in Conditional clauses.]

97. I. *Final.*—The Future Participle is used to express a purpose :

ἦλθε τὴν θυγατέρα λυσόμενος.
He came to ransom his daughter.

98. II. *Temporal :*

ταῦτα εἰπὼν ἀπῄει.
When he had said this he went away.

ταῦτα πράξει στρατηγῶν.
This he will do when he is general.

99. III. *Conditional.*—(Negative always μή.)

μὴ λέγων =
$$\begin{cases} εἰ μὴ λέγεις, \textit{unless you are saying.} \\ εἰ μὴ ἔλεγες, \textit{if you had not been saying.} \\ ἐὰν μὴ λέγῃς, \textit{unless you say} \text{ (future).} \\ εἰ μὴ λέγοις, \textit{unless you were to say.} \end{cases}$$

100. IV. *Concessive.*—The Participle stands either alone or with a particle, as καίπερ, and the principal Verb is often strengthened by ὅμως (*nevertheless*) :

πείθου γυναιξί, καίπερ οὐ στέργων, ὅμως.
Give way to women, though you love them not.

101. V. *Causal :*

ἀπείχοντο κερδῶν, αἰσχρὰ νομίζοντες εἶναι.
They abstained from money-making because they thought it disgraceful.

102. VI. *Comparative.*—With ὥσπερ :

ὥσπερ ἤδη σαφῶς εἰδότες οὐκ ἐθέλετ' ἀκούειν.
You are unwilling to hear as if you already knew it well.

103. The use of ὡς with the Participle in a Final
or Causal sense represents the end or reason as existing
in the mind of the prominent agent, but not necessarily
accepted and indorsed by the speaker :

Συλλαμβάνει Κῦρον ὡς ἀποκτενῶν.
He seizes Cyrus with the intention of putting him to death.

τὸν Περικλέα ἐν αἰτίᾳ εἶχον ὡς πείσαντα σφᾶς πολεμεῖν.
*They were blaming Pericles on the ground that he had persuaded
them to engage in the war.*

104. The use of ἅτε or οἷον (*inasmuch as*) with a Causal
Participle assigns the reason solely on the authority of the
speaker :

Ὁ Κῦρος, ἅτε παῖς ὤν, ἥδετο τῇ στολῇ.
Cyrus, inasmuch as he was a child, was pleased with the dress.

105. In all these Adverbial relations the Participle
may agree with its Substantive in the Genitive Absolute,
if the Substantive stands apart from the Sentence. **(19.)**

ταῦτ' ἐπράχθη Κόνωνος στρατηγοῦντος.
These things were done when Conon was general.

106. The Participles of Impersonal Verbs, or of Verbs
used impersonally, stand absolutely in the Neuter Accusa
tive Singular :

ἐξόν, *it being permitted;* δέον, *it being a duty;* δόξαν, *it being
resolved;* εἰρημένον, *it having been stated;* ἀδύνατον ὄν, *it being
impossible.*

ἁπλᾶς δὲ λύπας ἐξὸν (sc. φέρειν) οὐκ οἴσω διπλᾶς.
Since I may have a single grief I will not bear a double.

II. *Special Idioms of the Participle.*

107. A Participle is used, like the Prolate Infinitive, to carry on the meaning of certain Verbs : *

οὐκ ἀνέξομαι ζῶσα.
I shall not endure to live.

108. Sometimes the Participle contains the leading idea of the predicate, especially with the Verbs λανθάνω, τυγχάνω, φθάνω, φαίνομαι, and the phrases δῆλός εἰμι, φανερός εἰμι :

ἔτυχον ὁπλῖται ἐν τῇ ἀγορᾷ καθεύδοντες.
It so chanced that some hoplites were sleeping in the market.

δῆλος εἶ καταφρονῶν μου.
You evidently despise me.

109. With some Verbs the Infinitive and Participle have different meanings :

{ αἰσχύνομαι λέγειν, *I am ashamed to say* (and do not).
{ αἰσχύνομαι λέγων, *I say with shame.*
{ φαίνεται ποιεῖν, *he appears to be doing it* (videtur).
{ φαίνεται ποιῶν, *he evidently is doing it* (apparet).

110. The Participle is often used as a simple Adverb :

ἀρχόμενος ἔλεγεν.
He used to say at first.

τελευτῶν εἶπε.
At last he said.

λαθὼν ἐποίησε.
He did it secretly.

ἀνύσας ἄνοιγε.
Open quickly.

φθάσας ἀφίκετο.
He arrived first.

Obs. ἔχων, ἄγων, φέρων, are often best translated '*with.*'
ὤφθη ξίφος ἔχων, *he was seen with a sword.*

---

* Such Verbs are αἰσχύνομαι. ἄρχομαι, παύομαι, παύω, ἀνέχομαι, περιορῶ.

The Verbal Adjective.

111. The VERBAL in -τέος is the Greek Gerundive
implying necessity, and, as in Latin, it is constructed
either Attributively or Impersonally. The Agent is
generally put in the Dative Case.

112. I. The Attributive construction, where the Verbal
is a simple attribute in agreement with its substantive,
is used, as in Latin, only with Transitive Verbs :

> ἡ πόλις σοι ὠφελητέᾱ ἐστιν.
> *The state must be assisted by you.*

113. II. The Impersonal construction is used both with
Transitive and Intransitive Verbs :

> ὠφελητέον ἡμῖν ἐστι τὴν πόλιν.
> *We must assist the state.*
> ἀρκτέον.
> *Rule must be maintained.*

Obs. The Neuter Plural is often found in the Impersonal
Construction : πολεμητέᾱ ἦν, *we had to fight;* οὐ παραδοτέα
ἐστὶ τοὺς συμμάχους, *we must not betray our allies.*

The Negatives Οὐ and μή.

114. Οὐ is the Negative of facts, μή of conceptions.
Hence οὐ is used with

> Statements, Direct or Indirect.
> Questions which seem to expect the answer 'Yes.'
> Relative clauses with Definite Antecedent.
> Definite Temporal clauses.
> Consecutive clauses (of *actual* consequence).
> Causal clauses.
> All Participles, except those used in a Conditional sense,
>   or standing for a Relative clause with Indefinite
>   Antecedent.

115. And μή is used with

Commands, Direct or Indirect.
Questions which seem to expect the answer 'No.'
Relative clauses with Indefinite Antecedent.
Indefinite Temporal clauses.
Final clauses.
Consecutive clauses (with Infin. of *natural* consequence).
Conditional clauses (Protasis only).
Expressions of a Wish.
Infinitives (all adverbial uses).
Participles in Conditional sense, or standing for a Relative clause with Indefinite Antecedent.

116. A number of Negatives in the same sentence only strengthen the negation :

> ἀκούει δ' οὐδὲν οὐδεὶς οὐδενός.
> *No one obeys any one in anything.*

Obs. But when a simple negative (οὐ or μή) follows another negative applied to the same word, the two form an affirmative ; thus οὐχ ὁρᾷ οὐδείς, *no one sees;* but οὐδεὶς οὐχ ὁρᾷ, *no one does not see,* i.e. *every one sees.*

117. In Indirect Speech the Negative of the clause is with certain verbs placed before the principal Verb :

> οὔ φημι δρᾶσαι.
> *I say that I did not do it.*

So οὐκ ἐῶ, *I forbid ;* οὐ νομίζω, *I think that it is not ;* οὐκ ἀξιῶ, *I advise you not.*

μή and μὴ οὐ.

118. After Verbs of Hindering, Denying, Forbidding, and Verbs generally which contain a Negative idea, μή is often inserted before the Infinitive, repeating the Negative idea of the Verb :

> εἴργει σε μὴ τοῦτο ποιεῖν.
> *He hinders you from doing this.*
> ἀρνεῖται ἀληθὲς τοῦτο μὴ εἶναι.
> *He denies that this is true.*

119. If a Negative (expressed or implied) precedes the principal Verb, this also is repeated with the Infinitive :

> οὐκ εἴργει σε μὴ οὐ τοῦτο ποιεῖν.
> *He does not prevent you from doing this.*
> τίς ἀρνεῖται μὴ οὐκ ἀληθὲς εἶναι ;
> *Who denies (i.e. no one denies) that this is true ?*

οὐ μή.

120. οὐ μή is used with the Primary Conjunctive in vehement denials :

> οὐ μὴ πίθηται.
> *He will certainly not obey you.*

121. οὐ μή with the Second Person of the Future Indicative is used interrogatively as a strong prohibition :

> οὐ μὴ ληρήσεις.
> *Don't talk nonsense.*

Obs. 1. Sometimes the οὐ has to be supplied from a preceding question, as οὐ σῖγ' ἀνέξει μηδὲ δειλίαν ἀρεῖς, *be still, nor suffer coward fears to rise.*

Obs. 2. οὐ μή, with other persons of the Future, is used in strong negatious, as οὔ σοι μὴ μεθέψομαί ποτε, *with thee I certainly will never go.*

Conjunctions and Particles.

122. In addition to the Conjunctions used in introducing the dependent moods which are treated of under Adverbial sentences (**167-185**), there are in Greek a number of words used partly to combine sentences, and called Conjunctions, partly to give emphasis to particular expressions, and called Particles. The same word may indeed be a Conjunction and a Particle (cp. δή, μέν). The abundance and variety of these words is one of the most striking characteristics of Greek.

Conjunctions.

123. Copulative—

καί, *and, also:* καλὸς καὶ ἀγαθός, *fair and good;* καὶ τοῦτ' ἑώρακα, *this also I have seen.*

καί is sometimes repeated: καὶ εἶδον καὶ ἔφυγον, *I both saw and I escaped.*

τε, *and.* τε is not commonly used *by itself* as the copula in Attic (except in older writers). The most frequent use is τε . . . καί, as εἶδόν τε καὶ ἔφυγον, *I both saw and escaped* (*I saw and* (*therefore*) *I escaped*). τε . . . τε is also found, especially in enumerations.

124. Disjunctive—

ἤ, *or.*

ἤ   . . . ἤ,   *either* . . . *or.*

εἴτε   . . . εἴτε,   *whether* . . . *or* (hypothetically).

οὔτε   . . . οὔτε,   *neither* . . . *nor* ⎫
                              ⎬ See **114.**
μήτε   . . . μήτε,   *neither* . . . *nor* ⎭

οὐδέ, μηδέ, *not even.*

οὔτε καλὸς οὔτε ἀγαθός, *neither handsome nor good.*
οὐ καλὸς οὐδὲ ἀγαθός, *not handsome nor even good.*

125. Adversative—

ἀλλά, *but.*

μέντοι, *however.*

καίτοι, *and yet.*

καίπερ, *although,* with participles.

δέ, *but;* ὅμως, *nevertheless;* αὖ, *on the other hand.*

(1.) δέ is the commonest conjunction for connecting sentences; it indicates that what is said in the new sentence is a new fact, but yet standing in connection with what goes before.

(2.) δέ is often preceded by μέν when the clauses are to be brought into close relation. The two clauses are then regarded as being as it were in equilibrium; the clause with μέν precedes and expects the response of the clause with δέ, as καλὸς μὲν πονηρὸς δέ. Compare the use of τε . . . καί, and the words *protasis* and *apodosis.* μέν is sometimes used, with implied antithesis, to emphasize a single word such as ἐγώ, δοκῶ, οἶμαι.

126. Comparative—

 ὡς, *as ;* ὥσπερ, *just as,* in comparisons and similes.
 ἤ, *than,* after comparatives (*quam*).

127. Inferential—

 δή, *therefore ;* τοίνυν, *therefore, in consequence ;* οὖν, *then ;* ἄρα, *accordingly ;* (τοιγάρ, *therefore.*)

τοίνυν and οὖν express a more logical inference than δή and ἄρα, τοίνυν is more used in narration of the development of the various stages of a story, οὖν resumes and sums up a train of thought. (δή may often be paraphrased by *you know,* ἄρα by *as I find.*)

128. Causal—

 γάρ, *for ;* τοῦτο γὰρ εἶδον, *for this I saw.*

129. Of these Conjunctions, τε, μέν, δέ, αὖ, μέντοι, ἄρα, δὴ, οὖν, τοίνυν, and γάρ, cannot stand first in the sentence, and τε is an enclitic.

Particles.

130. ἆρα, ἆρ' οὐ, ἆρα μή, μῶν, ἤ, πότερον, εἰ, are the chief Interrogative particles. For uses see **149, 150.**

131. οὐ and μή are the chief Negatives. For uses see **114.**

In oaths νή is used in assertions, νὴ Δία, *yes ! by Zeus.* μά in negations, μὰ Δία, *no ! by Zeus.*

132. ἄν is without an equivalent in English. It is used

(1.) With the Historic Conjunctive and Historic Indicative in the Apodosis of conditional sentences (**179**), as οὐκ ἂν λέγοιμι, *I would not say ;* οὐκ ἂν ἐποίει, *he would not have been doing it ;* οὐκ ἂν ἐποίησε, *he would not have done it.*

(2.) With the Infinitive and Participles, when an Apodosis with ἄν is stated Indirectly (192-194), οὐκ ἄν φασιν εἰσελθεῖν, *they say that they would not come in* (or *have come in*); ὄμνυμί σοι μήδ᾽ ἀποδιδόντος δέξασθαι ἄν, *I swear to thee that I would not take it back* (or *have taken*), *even if he offered it.* (In this use the Infinitive Present represents the Imperfect Indicative.)

(3.) Indefinitely, like the English *-ever*, in combination with Relatives and Temporal Conjunctions: ὃς ἄν, *whoever;* ὅταν, *whenever.* In this sense it is found in *Primary Sequence only* (166, 173): ὃς ἄν ἔλθῃ, *whoever comes;* ὅταν ἔλθῃς, *whenever you come.*

(4.) Sometimes with ὅπως and ὡς Final followed by Subjunctive (167, *Obs.* 4), ὅπως ἄν ἐκμάθῃς, *in order that you may learn.* The difference of meaning whether ἄν is added or omitted is very slight.

Obs. 1. ἄν is not unfrequently added to the Imperfect or Aorist Indicative to express a repeated act: ἔλεγεν ἄν, *he would say, he kept saying* (as opportunity offered).

Obs. 2. ἀν is never used with the Indicative Present, or Perfect; and never in Attic Greek with the Indicative Future.

133. δή, *indeed.* δή is sometimes used to introduce a sentence (127) as a conjunction, but it is more commonly employed to give force to words or other Particles, as

ὅτι μὲν δὴ δεῖ βοηθεῖν, πάντες ἐγνώκαμεν, *that we ought indeed to send help, we are all agreed;* καὶ δὴ πέπαυμαι, *indeed I have ceased;* καὶ τότε δή, *then and then indeed, then at last;* πλήν γε δή, *except of course.*

134. δήπου, *no doubt.*

ταῦτα δήπου πάντες ἴσασιν, *these things no doubt* (*I suppose*) *all know.*

135. γε, *at least,* adds emphasis to what precedes.

ταῦτά γε, *these things* (*if nothing else*), *these things* (*of all*). φησίν γε, *he says* (*whatever his statement may be worth*).

Hence γε often in dialogue assents to a previous state-ment, and may be translated by the English ' *yes.*'

136. δῆτα is generally used in questions and answers, as τί δῆτα, *what then?* πῶς ταῦτ' ἂν εἴη ἀληθῆ ; *how could this be true?* πῶς δῆτα ; *how indeed?* so οὐ δῆτα, *no, indeed !*

137. ἢ, *verily,* or interrogative.

ἢ δεινόν, *truly it is strange ;* ἢ μενεῖς ; *will you remain ?*

In both senses ἢ is often assisted by other Particles, as ἢ που, ἢ δή, ἢ γάρ. In asseverations ἢ μήν is used.

138. μέν οὖν sometimes has, especially in dialogue, the sense of the Latin *imo, nay rather,* correcting a previous statement.

139. μήν strengthens an assertion, but it is commonly joined to other Particles, *e.g.* ἢ μὴν in asseverations ; καὶ μήν, *and verily,* calling attention to a new matter, and especially to the entrance of a new actor in a play ; ἀλλὰ μὴν, *but verily.*

140. τοι, *in truth.* τοι often introduces a general statement, or apophthegm, and in this case it may be combined with ἢ and written ἢτοι. More rarely τοι merely strengthens the preceding word : ὑφ' ἡδονῆς τοι, *by delight.* τοι is often combined with other Particles and Con-junctions : τοιγάρ, *therefore ;* τοιγάρτοι, τοιγαροῦν.

141. As regards position in the sentence, γε and τοι are enclitic. δή, δήπου, δῆτα, μέν, μήν are placed after the word to which they refer, and can never stand at the beginning of a sentence.

PART II.

THE SIMPLE AND COMPOUND SENTENCE.

The Simple Sentence.

142. A Simple Sentence is the expression of single thought, and contains one Finite Verb.

143. The Three Forms of Simple Sentence are Direct Statement, Direct Command (or wish), and Direct Question.

DIRECT STATEMENT.

144. Direct Statements are usually expressed by the Indicative.

DIRECT COMMAND.

145. I. In Positive Commands the Imperative is used if the Person is Second or Third :

> Ζεῦ, Ζεῦ, θεωρὸς τῶνδε πραγμάτων γενοῦ.
> *Zeus, Zeus, be thou a spectator of these deeds.*
> Ὁ δ' οὖν ἴτω.
> *Let him then go.*

146. II. In Negative Commands in the Second or Third Person the Present Imperative is used for a *general* Prohibition, and the Aorist Primary Conjunctive for a *special* Prohibition, the Negative being always μή :

μὴ κλέπτε.   μὴ κλέψῃς.
Do not go on stealing (general).   *Do not steal* (*this*), (special).

147. III. The Primary Conjunctive is used *hortatively* in the First Person, often introduced by ἄγε or φέρε :

ἴωμεν.   μὴ μέλλωμεν.
Let us go.   *Let us not delay.*

φέρε δὴ τὰς μαρτυρίας ὑμῖν ἀναγνῶ.
Come, let me read you the depositions.

EXPRESSION OF A WISH.

148. Wishes referring to Future Time are regularly expressed by the Optative.   [Negative μή.]

μὴ γένοιτο.
God forbid ! (*may it not be so.*)

Obs. A wish can also be expressed—

(1.) By εἰ or εἴθε with Optative when referring to the Future, with Indicative when referring to the Present or Past, and therefore implying non-fulfilment (a Conditional Protasis).

εἴθε ἔλθοι, *O if he would come !* εἰ γὰρ παρῆν, *O if he now had been here !* εἴθε μὴ ἐγένετο, *would that it had not happened !*

(2.) By πῶς ἄν with the Optative, which asks a question that implies the wish (a Conditional Apodosis).

πῶς ἂν ὀλοίμην; (*how could* (*can*) *I possibly perish?*), *might I but perish !*

(3.) By ὤφελον (Aorist of ὀφείλω) with Present or Aorist Infinitive.

ὤφελον ἀκούειν, *would that I heard !*
μὴ ὤφελεν ἐλθεῖν, *would that he had not come !*

DIRECT QUESTION.

149. I. Questions that can be answered by Yes or No may be thus expressed (ἆρα being often omitted) :

ἆρα (Lat. -*ně*), expecting either answer.
ἆρ' οὐ (Lat. *nonne*), expecting the answer *Yes.*
ἆρα μή (Lat. *num*), expecting the answer *No.*
μῶν (= μὴ οὖν) is a stronger phrase for this last.

ἆρά γε μὴ ἐμοῦ προμηθεῖ;
You are not anxious on my account, are you?

150. II. In Alternative Questions the forms are

πότερον (πότερα) . . .	ἤ,	Direct or Indirect.
. . . .	ἤ,	Direct or Indirect.
εἰ	ἤ,	Indirect only.
εἴτε	εἴτε,	Indirect only.

πότερον ἄκων ἢ ἑκὼν δέδρακεν ;
Has he done it unwillingly or willingly ?

151. III. Deliberative Questions are expressed, as in Latin, by the Primary Conjunctive.   [Negative μή.]

τί φῶ ;   πότερον ἑλώμεθα ;
What am I to say?   Which of the two are we to choose?

The Compound Sentence.

152. A *Compound Sentence* consists of a Simple Sentence with the addition of one or more dependent clauses.

153. *Dependent Clauses* are classified as Substantival. Adjectival, or Adverbial.

154. *Substantival Clauses* are of three kinds :—Indirect Statement, Indirect Command, and Indirect Question. All these are included in the term Indirect Speech (or *Oratio Obliqua*).   A Substantival Clause may stand either as the Subject of an Impersonal Verb, or as the Object of a Transitive Verb.

155. *Adjectival Clauses* include all those which are introduced by Relative Pronouns.

156. *Adverbial Clauses* include all Clauses introduced by Conjunctions which attach to the Principal Verb any Adverbial notion.   These are classified as (1) Final, (2) Consecutive, (3) Temporal, (4) Conditional, (5) Concessive, (6) Causal.

Substantival Clauses.

INDIRECT STATEMENT.

157. I. The Accusative with the Infinitive is used in reporting Statements, whether thought or spoken, after any Verb which can fitly introduce a Statement. The *Tense* of the Direct Statement is retained in the Indirect:

ἔφη Νικίαν στρατηγεῖν, *he said that Nicias was general.*

His words were $\begin{cases} \text{Νικίας στρατηγεῖ.} \\ \text{\textit{Nicias is general.}} \end{cases}$

(*a.*) The Subject of the Infinitive, if it is the same as that of the principal Verb, is placed in the Nominative:

οὐκ ἔφη αὐτὸς ἀλλὰ Νικίαν στρατηγεῖν.
He said that he was not in command, but Nicias.

This Nominative is omitted unless it is emphatic:

ἔφη ἕψεσθαι.
He said that he would follow.

158. II. After Verbs of *feeling* or *knowing* * the Participle is more frequently used, agreeing in case with the word, whether Subject or Object, to which it refers:

ἑώρων οἱ στρατηγοὶ οὐ κατορθοῦντες καὶ τοὺς στρατιώτας ἀχθομένους.
The generals saw that they (themselves) were not succeeding, and that the soldiers were becoming annoyed.

159. III. The Indirect Statement is also very commonly constructed with the Conjunction ὅτι or ὡς followed by an Indicative after a Primary Tense, or a Historic Conjunctive after a Historic Tense:

(Prim.) ἐρεῖ ὡς οὐκ ἔστιν ἀληθὲς τοῦτο.
He will say that this is not true.

---

* Such Verbs are αἰσθάνομαι, ἀκούω, γιγνώσκω, μέμνημαι, οἶδα, ὁρῶ, etc. The same construction is often found with ἀγγέλλω and δείκνυμι.

(Hist.) Περικλῆς προηγόρευε ὅτι Ἀρχίδαμός οἱ ξένος εἴη.
             Pericles announced that Archidamus was his friend.

His words were { Ἀρχίδαμός μοι ξένος ἐστιν.
                    { *Archidamus is my friend.*

160. In Primary Time the Tense and Mood of the Direct Statement are retained (with alteration of Person if necessary). Very frequently too, even in Historic time, the Indicative used in the speaker's actual words is preferred to the Historic Conjunctive, for the sake of *vivid representation* in narrative. Thus :—

DIRECT.

γράφω,	γράψω,	ἔγραψα,	γέγραφα,
I write,	*shall write,*	*wrote,*	*have written.*

INDIRECT.

Prim. λέγει ὅτι γράφει,   γράψει,   ἔγραψε,   γέγραφε.
      He says that he writes, shall write, wrote, has written.

Hist. εἶπεν ὅτι γράφοι,   γράψοι,   γράψειε,   γεγραφὼς εἴη.
      „   „   γράφει,   γράψει,   ἔγραψε,   γέγραφε.
      He said that he was writing, would write, had written.

INDIRECT COMMAND.

161. A Simple Infinitive, or an Infinitive with Accusative of the Subject, is commonly used in reporting a command or request. A less usual construction is with ὅπως followed by a Fut. Indic. [Negative always μή.]

    οἱ Ἕλληνες ἐβόων ἀλλήλοις μὴ θεῖν δρόμῳ.
    The Greeks kept shouting to one another not to double.

INDIRECT QUESTION.

162. An Indirect Question is introduced by any Verb of Asking, Doubting, Explaining, or the like. The Interrogative Pronoun or Particle is followed in Primary time by the Tense and Mood of the Direct Question, in

Historic time by the Historic Conjunctive, or by the more vivid Indicative :

οὐκ οἶδα ὅστις ἐστι.
I know not who he is.
ἐπυνθάνετο εἰ οἰκοῖτο ἡ χώρα (or οἰκεῖται).
He was asking whether the country was inhabited.

163. Deliberative Questions (151) retain the Primary Conjunctive in Indirect speech after a Primary Tense, and pass into the Historic Conjunctive after an Historic Tense :

ἀπορεῖ ὅποι τράπηται.
He is at a loss which way to turn.
οὐκ ἔχω τί φῶ.
I know not what to say.
ἠπόρει ὅποι τράποιτο.
He was at a loss which way to turn.

(His words were :—Ποῖ ράπωμαι ; *whither am I to turn ?*)

Here also the Mood of the Direct may be used in *Vivid Sequence*

Adjectival Clauses.

164. Adjectival Clauses are of two kinds :—

I. *Definite*, where the Antecedent of the Relative is some particular Person, Place, or Thing, expressed or understood.

II. *Indefinite*, where the Antecedent is not a particular Person, Place, or Thing, but a class of Persons, Places, or Things, expressed or understood, and the Relative has the force of the English *whoever, whatever, wherever*, etc.

Obs. The same distinction between Definite and Indefinite holds good with Temporal Conjunctions, most of which are, strictly speaking, Relative Particles referring to an Antecedent, usually understood.

165. I. The Relative with a Definite Antecedent takes the Indicative in Direct Speech.   [Negative οὐ.]

ἄνδρα ἄγω, ὃν εἶρξαι δεῖ.
I bring a man whom it is necessary to lock up.

166. II. With an Indefinite Antecedent the Relative in Primary time has ἄν, and its Verb is in the Primary Conjunctive.   In Historic time the Relative stands without ἄν, and the Verb is in the Historic Conjunctive.   [Negative μή.]   The Primary construction may also be used *vividly* in Historic time :

Primary $\begin{cases} \text{ὁποῖον ἂν συμβῇ τλήσομαι.} \\ \textit{I will bear whatever happens.} \end{cases}$

Historic $\begin{cases} \text{εἵποντο ὅποι τις ἡγοῖτο.} \\ \textit{They would follow wherever any one might lead.} \end{cases}$

Adverbial Clauses.

(1.) FINAL CLAUSES.

167. The Final Conjunctions ἵνα, ὡς, ὅπως, *in order that* [negatively ἵνα μή, ὡς μή, ὅπως μή], are used with Primary Conjunctive after a Primary Tense, Historic Conjunctive after an Historic Tense :

διανοεῖται τὴν γεφύραν λῦσαι, ὡς μὴ διαβῆτε.
He intends to break down the bridge that you may not cross.
ἐπεθύμει τιμᾶσθαι, ἵνα πλείω κερδαίνοι.
He was anxious to be honoured, that he might be getting more gain.

Obs. 1. To express more vividly the actual thought of the person who conceives the purpose, the Primary Conjunctive is often used after an Historic Tense, *e.g.* ἦλθεν ἵνα ἴδῃ, *he came that he might see.*   His thought was, 'that I may see.'

Obs. 2. A Past Tense of the Indicative is sometimes used after these Conjunctions, implying that the purpose was not attained, as ἐχρῆν σε Πηγάσου ζεῦξαι πτερόν, ὅπως ἐφαίνου τοῖς θεοῖς τραγικώτερος, *you ought to have put on Pegasus' wing, that you might appear to the gods more tragic.*

Obs. 3. A Purpose may also be expressed by a Relative Clause (187), or by a Participle (97).

Obs. 4. ὅπως and ὡς (not ἵνα) sometimes take ἄν. τοῦτ᾽ αὐτὸ νῦν δίδασκ᾽ ὅπως ἂν ἐκμάθω, *explain now this very thing that I may learn it thoroughly.*

168. Verbs of *Effort* and *Precaution** are usually followed by ὅπως, ὅπως μή with a Future Indicative both in Primary and Historic Time. The regular sequence of the Final Sentence is also found :

> σκόπει ὅπως μὴ ἔξαρνος ἔσει ἃ νῦν λέγεις.
> *See that you don't deny what you are now asserting.*
> ἔπρασσον ὅπως τις βοήθεια ἥξει.
> *They were negotiating for some aid to be sent them.*

Obs. If the Clause is in the Second Person the principal Verb is usually omitted :

> ὅπως οὖν ἔσεσθε ἄνδρες ἄξιοι τῆς ἐλευθερίας.
> *Prove yourselves then men worthy of freedom* (scil. σκοπεῖτε).
> ὅπως μὴ σαυτὸν οἰκτιεῖς ποτε.
> *See that you have not to pity yourself some day.*

169. Verbs of *fearing* are usually followed by μή (*ne*), or negatively μὴ οὐ (*ut* or *ne non*), with Primary or Historic Conjunctive in regular sequence :

> φοβοῦμαι μὴ γένηται.
> *I fear that it may happen.*
> ἐφοβούμην μὴ οὐ γένοιτο.
> *I feared that it might not happen.*

Obs. 1. Here also the Primary Conjunctive may be used in Vivid Sequence after an Historic Tense :

> οἱ θεώμενοι ἐφοβοῦντο μή τι πάθῃ.
> *The spectators were afraid that he would take some hurt.*

Obs. 2. A Present or Past Indicative is used to express a fear that something is happening or has happened :

> νῦν δὲ φοβούμεθα μὴ ἀμφοτέρων ἡμαρτήκαμεν.
> *But now we are afraid that we have missed both.*

---

* Such Verbs are βουλεύω, ἐπιμελοῦμαι, μηχανῶμαι, ὀρῶ, παρασκευάζομαι, πράττω, προθυμοῦμαι, πρόνοιαν ἔχω, σκοπῶ, σπουδάζω, φυλάττω.

(2.) Consecutive Clauses.

170. To express a consequence, ὥστε (*so as, so that*) is used either (1) with the Infinitive [Negative μή], or (2) with the Indicative, if narrative stress is laid on the fact that the consequence actually took place.   [Negative οὐ.]

(1.) πᾶν ποιοῦσιν ὥστε δίκην μὴ διδόναι.
   They manage everything so as not to be punished.

(2.) νῦν δ᾽ οὕτως ἡ πόλις διάκειται, ὥστε οὐκέτι ὧν οὗτοι κλέπτουσιν ὀργίζεσθε.
   But such is the present temper of the city that you are no longer angry at the thefts of these rascals.

For the use of Relatives in a Consecutive sense see **187, 188.**

(3.) Temporal Clauses.

171. The Temporal Conjunctions, including some purely Relative expressions, may be classed as follows :—

(1.) Of *Time Before* the Principal Verb.
   ἐπεί, ἐπειδή, ὡς, *when, after that;* ἐξ οὗ, ἀφ᾽ οὗ, *since.*

(2.) Of *Same Time* as Principal Verb.
   ὅτε, ὁπότε, ὡς, *when, at the time that.*
   ἕως, ἐν ᾧ, ἐν ὅσῳ, *whilst, as long as.*

(3.) Of *Time After* the Principal Verb.
   ἕως, ἔστε, μέχρι οὗ, *until.*
   πρίν, *before that, until.*

Two general rules may be given for the use of all these, except πρίν, which is peculiar.

172. I. *Definite.*   If the Temporal Clause expresses a fixed, known, and definite time, the Verb is in the Indicative.   [Negative οὐ.]

(1.) ἐπειδὴ καλῶς αὐτῷ εἶχεν, ἀπιὼν ᾤχετο.
   When he was satisfied he went away.

(2.) οὐ θαυμαστὸν δ᾽ εἰ τότε τὰς μορίας ἐξέκοπτον, ἐν ᾧ οὐδὲ
τὰ ἡμέτερ᾽ αὐτῶν φυλάττειν ἠδυνάμεθα.
*It is not surprising that they were felling the sacred olives
at a time when we could not protect even our own.*

ἕως ἐτιμᾶτο, πιστὸν ἑαυτὸν παρεῖχεν.
As long as he was held in honour he proved himself loyal.

(3.) οὐ πρότερον εἴασε τὴν ἐκκλησίαν γενέσθαι, ἕως ὁ λεγό-
μενος καιρὸς ἐτηρήθη.
*He did not permit the assembly to be held until the fixed
period had been observed.*

173. II. *Indefinite.* If the Conjunction refers to a number
of occasions (Engl. when-*ever*), or to some time which is
not fixed or known, the usual Indefinite construction is
used. Thus in Primary time the Conjunction with ἄν is
followed by the Primary Conjunctive. In Historic time
the Conjunction without ἄν is followed by the Historic
Conjunctive. [Negative μή.]

(1.) ἐπειδὰν δὲ ἡ ἐκφορὰ ᾖ, λάρνακας κυπαρισσίνας ἄγουσιν
ἅμαξαι.
*Whenever there is a funeral procession, cars bring coffins
of cypress.*

παρήγγειλεν ἐπειδὴ δειπνήσειαν πάντας ἀναπαύεσθαι.
He gave orders that all should rest when they had dined.

(2.) οὐκοῦν, ὅταν δὴ μὴ σθένω, πεπαύσομαι.
*Therefore, when I shall have no more strength, I will be at
rest.*

ὅτε ἔξω τοῦ δεινοῦ γένοιντο, πολλοὶ αὐτὸν ἀπέλειπον.
When they were out of danger, many used to desert him.

(3.) ἐπίσχες ἔστ᾽ ἂν καὶ τὰ λοιπὰ προσμάθῃς.
Wait until you learn the rest also.

περιεμένομεν ἑκάστοτε ἕως ἀνοιχθείη τὸ δεσμωτήριον.
We used to wait each time until the prison should be opened.

Obs. 1. With ἐπεί, ἐπειδή, ὅτε, ὁπότε, ἄν coalesces, forming ἐπάν
(or ἐπήν), ἐπειδάν, ὅταν, ὁπόταν.

Obs. 2. The Conjunctions of *Time After* (= *until*) do not
require ἄν, being by their nature indefinite.

Uses of πρίν.

174. If the Principal Sentence is Affirmative, πρίν (*before that*) takes the Infinitive :

λέξαι θέλω σοι πρὶν θανεῖν ἃ βούλομαι.
I wish to tell you before I die what I desire.

175 If the Principal Sentence is Negative, πρίν (*until*) takes the Indicative when the main verb is past, and the usual Indefinite construction when the main verb is future :

οὐ πρόσθεν ἐξενεγκεῖν ἐτόλμησαν πρὸς ἡμᾶς πόλεμον πρὶν τοὺς στρατηγοὺς ἡμῶν συνέλαβον.
They dared not make war on us till they had seized our generals.

οὐχὶ παύσομαι
πρὶν ἄν σε τῶν σῶν κύριον στήσω τέκνων.
I will not leave off until I make you master of your children.

(4.) CONDITIONAL CLAUSES.

176. The Conditional Conjunction εἰ is used with the Indicative or Historic Conjunctive, or, in the form of ἐάν, ἄν, or ἤν (for εἰ ἄν), with the Primary Conjunctive. [Negative μή.]

The conditional or *if* clause is called the *Protasis*, and the principal sentence, which draws the conclusion, is called the *Apodosis*.

177. Conditional Clauses are of four kinds. The first two (*a*) deal with conditions in Present or Past Time which either are or are not now fulfilled, but from their nature are no longer open. These require the Indicative.

The last two (*b*) deal with conditions in Future Time, which are still open. These take the Conjunctive, Primary or Historic.

(a.) *Conditions in Present or Past Time.*

178. I. *Fulfilled Condition.*—Here the speaker *assumes* the fulfilment of the condition, though the words imply no knowledge about it. Protasis, εἰ with Indicative, Apodosis also Indicative :

> ἀδικοῦσιν, εἰ περὶ τούτου μάχονται.
> *They are in the wrong, if they are fighting about this.*

Obs. When a Future Tense is used in this Protasis, it always implies a *present intention*, and is equivalent to μέλλω with Infinitive, as ἀδικεῖ εἰ περὶ τούτου μαχεῖται, *he is in the wrong, if he is going to fight about this* (for μέλλει μάχεσθαι).

179. II. *Unfulfilled Condition.*—Here the speaker implies that the condition is not (or was not) fulfilled, and states what would be (or would have been) the result in the case of its fulfilment. Protasis εἰ with Past Indicative : Apodosis, Past Indicative with ἄν :

> (*Impf.*) εἰ τοῦτο ἐποίουν, βέλτιον ἂν ἦν.
> *If they were doing this, it would* (now) *be better.*
>
> (*Aor.*) εἰ τοῦτο ἔπραξεν, ἐσώθη ἄν.
> *If he had done this, he would have been saved.*

(b.) *Conditions in Future Time.*

180. III. *Distinct Future Condition.*—When the Future Condition is *distinctly and vividly* pictured in the speaker's mind, as in speaking of a thing near and practical, and he states what *will be* the result, if something *happens* or *shall happen*, the Protasis has ἐάν (ἄν or ἤν) with Primary Conjunctive, the Apodosis Future Indicative :

> ἢν ἐς Ποτίδαιαν ἴωσιν Ἀθηναῖοι, ἐς τὴν Ἀττικὴν ἐσβαλοῦμεν.
> *If the Athenians go to Potidaea, we shall invade Attica.*

Obs. This condition is often stated still more vividly by εἰ with a Future Indicative in Protasis, as εἰ μὴ καθέξεις γλῶσσαν, ἔσται σοι κακά, *if you do not restrain your tongue, you will have trouble.*

181. IV. *Indistinct Future Condition.*—When the Future Condition, being something remote and unpractical, is *less distinct and vivid* to the speaker's mind, and he states what *would be* the result, if something *should happen* or *were to happen*, the Protasis has εἰ with Historic Conjunctive ; the Apodosis, Historic Conjunctive with ἄν :

εἰ ταῦτα δρῴην, ἄξιος ἂν εἴην θανάτου.
If I were to do this, I should be worthy of death.

General Conditions.

182. *General Conditions* are those in which the *if* clause refers to no definite act or time, and the speaker states the result as true in a number of instances, or as a general rule. The usual Indefinite construction is then used in the Protasis, namely :

In Primary Time—ἐάν with Primary Conjunctive.
In Historic Time—εἰ with Historic Conjunctive.

The Apodosis has the Present or Imperfect Indicative :

ἅπας λόγος, ἐὰν ἀπῇ τὰ πράγματα, μάταιόν τι φαίνεται καὶ κενόν.   (Primary.)
If deeds are wanting, all words appear mere vanity and emptiness.

ἀλλ' εἴ τι μὴ φέροιμεν, ὤτρυνεν φέρειν.
But if (ever) we failed to bring anything, he would urge us to bring it.   (Historic.)

For the treatment of Conditionals in Indirect Speech, see **195**.

(5.) CONCESSIVE CLAUSES.

183. Concessive Clauses are expressed in Greek by one of the regular forms of the Conditional Protasis after εἰ καί, καὶ εἰ, or ἐάν.   [Negative μή.]

εἰ καὶ μὴ βλέπεις, φρονεῖς δ' ὅμως.
Even though you do not see, you have sense.

A commoner use is καίπερ with a Participle ; see **100**.

(6.) CAUSAL CLAUSES.

184. The Causal Conjunctions ὅτι, διότι, *because*, ὡς, ἐπεί, ἐπειδή, *as*, *since*, are used with an Indicative [Negative οὐ], when the reason given is a definite fact :

εὐδαίμων μοι Σωκράτης ἐφαίνετο ὡς ἀδεῶς ἐτελεύτα.
Socrates appeared to me happy because he died without fear.

185. If, however, the reason is given as existing in the mind of another person (not the speaker), the clause is *virtually Indirect.* This does not alter the construction in Primary Time, but in Historic Time the Historic Conjunctive is used :

τὸν Περικλέα ἐκάκιζον, ὅτι οὐκ ἐπεξάγοι.
They were abusing Pericles because he did not lead them out.

(The Indicative ἐπεξῆγεν would have given the reason on the authority of the historian alone.)

Obs. For other ways of expressing Cause, see **43, 103, 104, 191.**

Adjectival Clauses with Adverbial Force.

186. Adjectival Clauses sometimes convey an Adverbial meaning. *These do not, as in Latin, require the Conjunctive,* but the antecedent may be Indefinite or the Mood may be influenced by Indirect Speech.

187. In a Final sense the Relative takes a Future Indicative.   [Negative μή.]

καὶ πόλει πέμψον τίν' ὅστις σημανεῖ.
And send some one to give the city warning.

188. In a Consecutive sense the Relative ὅς stands with an Indicative, if the Principal Sentence is negative :

οὐκ ἔστιν οὕτω μῶρος ὃς θανεῖν ἐρᾷ.
There is no man so foolish that he wishes to die.

189. In a Consecutive sense the Relatives οἷος, *such* (qualis), ὅσος, *so great* (quantus), are followed by the Infinitive :

ἔφθασε τοσοῦτον ὅσον Πάχητα ἀνεγνωκέναι τὸ ψήφισμα.
(The ship) was so much beforehand that Paches had only just read the decree.

190. Ἐφ᾽ ᾧ or ἐφ᾽ ᾧτε, *on condition that*, takes an Infinitive, or a Future Indicative.   [Negative μή.]

ἀφίεμέν σε, ἐπὶ τούτῳ μέντοι, ἐφ᾽ ᾧτε μηκέτι φιλοσοφεῖν.
We let you go, on this condition however, that you never again talk philosophy.

σπονδὰς ἐποιήσαντο ἐφ᾽ ᾧ τοὺς ἄνδρας κομιοῦνται.
They made a treaty providing for the recovery of the men.

191. A Relative clause is sometimes used to express the cause. The Indicative is used, and the Negative is οὐ :

θαυμαστὸν ποιεῖς ὃς ἡμῖν οὐδὲν δίδως.
You do a strange thing in giving us nothing.

Further Rules for Indirect Speech.

192. A Principal Sentence sometimes, as in the Apodosis of Conditional Sentences, takes the form of an Indicative or Optative with ἄν. In turning these forms into Indirect Speech two rules must be observed.

193. I. If an Indirect Statement with ὅτι or ὡς, or an Indirect Question. is to be formed, the Indicative with ἄν, or Optative with ἄν, remains unaltered both in Primary and Historic Time :

λέγει ὅτι (or ἤρετο εἰ) οὗτος ἐσώθη ἄν.

He says that (or he asked whether) this man would have been saved.

λέγει ὅτι (or ἤρετο εἰ) ἄξιος ἂν εἴη θανάτου.

He says that (or he asked whether) he should be worthy of death (if he were to do this).

194. II. If the Infinitive form of Indirect Statement is to be used, the Indicative or Optative is turned into the same tense of the Infinitive, ἄν being retained :

φησὶ τοῦτον σωθῆναι ἄν.

He says that this man would have been saved.

ἔφη ἄξιος ἂν εἶναι θανάτου.

He said that he should be worthy of death (if he were to do so).

(*a.*) The same Rule applies to the Participial Construction :

οἶδα τοῦτον σωθέντα ἄν.

I know that this man would have been saved.

ᾔδει ἄξιος ἂν ὢν θανάτου.

He knew that he should be worthy of death.

Dependent Clauses in Indirect Speech.

195. Adjectival and Adverbial Clauses qualifying words in Indirect Speech are subject to the following rules :—

196. I. If the Principal Verb is Primary, dependent clauses keep the Tense and Mood of Direct Speech.

φησὶν ἄνδρα ἄγειν ὃν εἶρξαι δεῖ.

He says that he is bringing a man, whom it is necessary to lock up.

(For Direct Form see **165.**)

λέγει ἄξιος ἂν εἶναι θανάτου, εἰ ταῦτα δρῴη.
He says he should be worthy of death, if he were to do this.

(For Direct Form see **181**.)

197. II. If the Principal Verb is Historic, either—(a) all *Primary* Indicatives and Primary Conjunctives are turned in strict sequence into Historic Conjunctive, or (b) the Tense and Mood of Direct Speech are retained. This is always the case with Imperfects, Aorists, and Pluperfects Indicative :

(a.) εἶπεν ὅτι ἄνδρα ἄγοι ὃν εἶρξαι δέοι.
      He said that he was bringing a man whom it was necessary to lock up.

      ἔφη αὐτοὺς ἀδικεῖν, εἰ περὶ τούτου μάχοιντο.
      He said that they were in the wrong, if they were fighting about this.

      (For Direct Form see **178**.)

(a.) ὑπέσχοντο, εἰ ἐς Ποτίδαιαν ἴοιεν Ἀθηναῖοι, ἐς τὴν Ἀττικὴν ἐσβαλεῖν.
      They promised to invade Attica, if the Athenians went to Potidaea.

      (For Direct Form see **180**.)

(b.) $\begin{cases} εἶπον \ ὅτι \ ἐσώθη \ ἄν, \\ ἔφασαν \ αὐτὸν \ σωθῆναι \ ἄν, \end{cases}$ εἰ μὴ τοῦτο ἔπραξεν.
      They said he would have been saved, if he had not done this
      (For Direct Form see **179**.)

THE END